The
Concise Book
of
Lying

The Concise Book of Lying

Evelin Sullivan

Picador USA

Farrar, Straus and Giroux

New York

www.picadorusa.com

Picador® is a U.S. registered trademark and is used by Farrar, Straus and Giroux under license from Pan Books Limited.

For information on Picador USA Reading Group Guides, as well as ordering, please contact the Trade Marketing department at
St. Martin's Press.
Phone: 1-800-221-7945 extension 763
Fax: 212-677-7456
E-mail: trademarketing@stmartins.com

Grateful acknowledgment is made to Universal Press Syndicate for permission to reprint the Bizarro cartoon. Bizarro © 1998 by Dan Piraro. All rights reserved.

Library of Congress Cataloging-in-Publication Data

Sullivan, Evelin E., 1947–
    The concise book of lying / Evelin Sullivan.—1st Picador USA ed.
        p. cm.
    Originally published: New York : Farrar, Straus and Giroux, 2001.
    Includes bibliographical references and index.
    ISBN 0-312-42047-1
    1. Deception. 2. Truthfulness and falsehood. 3. Deception—Social aspects. 4. Truthfulness and falsehood—Social aspects. I. Title.

BF637.D42 S85 2002
177'.3—dc21   2002025154

First published in the United States by Farrar, Straus and Giroux

First Picador USA Edition: August 2002

10 9 8 7 6 5 4 3 2 1

FOR MIKE
who listened
and
FOR MY MOTHER
without whom none of it would have been possible

Are you not, in fact, a chronic and habitual liar?

Witness for the Prosecution, United Artists, 1957

Contents

x   Contents

Prologue

The first version of this prologue began with a visit to Athens in the fourth century B.C. Diogenes was striding through the streets, conducting his legendary search for an honest man—in broad daylight and with a lighted lantern. The archetypal cynic, he was driving home the point that honesty is a thing so difficult to find that extraordinary means are needed if the one looking is to have any hope of locating it. My own point was that, when it comes to a despairing view of human dishonesty, we have not improved upon the Greeks. Yes, we could fill a volume with a collection of complaints—culled from books and newspapers of the last decade alone—about lies being rampant and infecting all areas of public and private life, but no amount of moaning can pack the metaphorical punch of this lone figure with his lighted lamp in the middle of the day seeking and not finding.

The second version put Diogenes at the end and began instead with two safe claims: the number of people who have never once in their lives told a lie is nil, and even those of us furnished with so spectacularly bad a memory, or such hyperactive faculties of repression, that they do not recall any instance in which they themselves have lied will not deny that on occasion others have lied to them.

And on it went to a general overview of the book in terms of what deception has meant at different times and under different circumstances for folk as varied as generals and slaves, the authors of the Bible, lie-detector operators and Jesuits, gods and bishops, advice columnists, and so forth.

Then, some three years into the project, it occurred to me that readers about to go on a lengthy journey through the Land of Lying may want to know something about their guide's credentials before taking the first step. Ideally, a résumé would spell out how familiar the author is with the lay of the land, how knowledgeable about its dangers and charms, how good at picking a path that won't leave the reader sweaty, scratched and itching from the sting of exotic bugs. Unfortunately, I cannot provide such a résumé, and, as has often been the case for explorers gearing up at the last outpost before they plunge into the green wall of the jungle, a first impression (of, say, an honest face or air of competence) will have to do. What may help that first impression is my (honest) description of the first lie I remember telling and of its repercussions.

I was three and a half years old and in kindergarten. Judging by my behavior on that day, I was not the world's most delightful little girl. I remember being outside on the playground in the midst of a fight with a boy my age. We traded insults, I was furious, and finally I vented my rage by shoving him to the ground. There he lay, possibly hurt, certainly crying, which meant that adults were about to descend on us. Bad news for me, since what I knew to be the case—I had been the more belligerent—had to be obvious to anyone who saw me standing and him lying on the ground. At which point, I had what was possibly the first dazzling insight of my life, and I grabbed my upper arm and began to cry. My insight was that adults seeing two crying children would do the lazy thing. They'd assume that both were to blame for whatever hurts had been inflicted, would dry our tears, tell us to behave, and leave it at that. I remember the boy's expression of pure rage when he realized what I was doing and the impossibility of justice being served—the powers that be would never know that he had not struck me but I had shoved him. Case closed.

And that was how it went. I blubbered that he'd hit me, he protested that I was lying. I remember some unease at what I was doing, some sense of its being wrong, but a greater concern with pulling it off. We were scolded for misbehaving, and that was that. Except it wasn't. I don't recollect the gathering clouds, but my memory returns at the moment, some days later, when the same boy picked up a stone and hurled it at me. It struck the bony ridge over my right eye and the result was a startlingly large amount of blood gushing from the cut in my eyebrow. Clearly, he was the aggressor this time (although, for all I know, I may have provoked him by calling him names), and he got detention while I was patched up and lay on a cot feeling tremendously important and telling everyone that I was "wounded." I remember little else but the remark the boy's mother made when she came to pick him up that, thank God, the stone had missed my eye. My own mother was shocked at this cavalier attitude, but I thought nothing of the close call—the fact that I might have lost an eye didn't sink in, which probably simply means I hadn't yet acquired the imaginative ability to shudder at life's what-ifs.

That losing an eye would have been a larger-than-biblical retribution—an eye for a lie—did not occur to me until I was far into the writing of this book, at which time something else occurred to me: the lie and the incidents surrounding it form my first coherent and sustained memory. Odd but probably not all that unusual. The insight that by lying we can extricate ourselves from a sticky situation is the kind of discovery that is guaranteed to register in anyone's brain. Anything that adds to our arsenal for self-preservation tends to be earmarked for future use. That I bear to this day a scar attributable to my first lie may or may not be meaningfully connected with a lifelong fascination with deception that finally crystallized as this book.

Consciously or subconsciously, I learned several lessons from the experience. For one, that a lie is a cousin of make-believe—it can be the substitution of an event that only *might* have happened for one that *did* happen. For another, that the liar's intention is to make others believe what the liar knows to be untrue, and that the motive is to gain something by doing so. I also learned that fear and hostility invite lies, that a bad conscience may attend them, and that, if they are unjust accusations, they injure those lied about. Finally, I learned that they can enrage their victims. As the germ of my fascination with deception, my experience in kindergarten was no doubt useful. I hope the victim of my slander profited from it in the long run as much as I did. I also hope that if he ever recalled the event, he did so in a charitable frame of mind and concluded that my precociousness at lying notwithstanding, I did not necessarily turn into an inveterate liar.

A note on the material: The specific areas and things I've chosen to investigate are those that have caught my fancy in the years of writing this book. No one alive will not rapidly come up with scores of other areas I might have rooted through and recollect anecdotes and examples I might have cited. Clearly, deception, like love, has its private attractions as well as its universal dimension, and here, for better or worse, is my own take on a universal phenomenon.

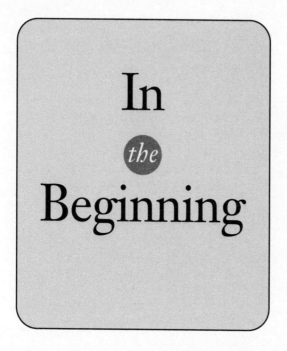

In *the* Beginning

The Bible: A Casebook

> *By telling a lie to save a life, one is not touched by sin.*
> *Mahābhārata*

The story so far: God has created the heaven and the earth, and night and day. He has separated the water from the dry land and has made the earth bring forth grass, herbs, and fruit-bearing trees. He has made the sun, moon, and stars, and sea animals, birds, and land animals. Finally, he has made beings in his own image, male and female, to rule the world and has told them to be fruitful and multiply, replenish the earth, subdue it, and have dominion over all the animals. And he has seen that everything he has made is very good.

Now the narrative doubles back to the world as yet uncontaminated by life. A mist rises up from the earth and waters the land, and God creates a man (*adam* in the story's original language) out of the dust of the ground and breathes into his nostrils the breath of life. A garden full of trees pleasant to the sight and good for food is next on the agenda. Two special trees, the tree of life and the tree of the knowledge of good and evil, are in the midst of the garden. God instructs the man that he may freely eat the fruit of every tree,

> But of the tree of the knowledge of good and evil, thou shalt not eat: for in the day that thou eatest thereof thou shalt surely die.

Deciding that it is not good for the man to be alone, God makes all the animals and shows them to Adam so he can give them names and find himself "an help meet" from among them. As it turns out, none of the animals will do, and God makes Adam fall into a deep sleep, takes one of his ribs, and fashions from it a woman.

The two versions of this part of the story of Genesis have been attributed by scholars to two of the three "strands of tradition" or "sources" that run through the Old Testament, Christianity's name for the Hebrew Bible, and they were written down centuries apart. These sources are known as "J" (Yahwist, from the German *Jahweh*), "E" (Elohist), according to the name by which God is called in the various passages, and "P" (Priestly, for the priests who are conjectured to have taught the P traditions). The first version, assigned to P and customarily dated after 539 B.C., offers a benign, uncomplicated creation myth. The physical universe comes into being in a series of stands-to-reason steps: the earth has to be separated from the water before plants can grow; the world is populated with animals; man and woman are created simultaneously, both in God's image, endowed with the ability to procreate and rule the earth.

The second version, attributed to the author who looms large in the J source, is dated earlier (ca. 950 B.C.) and is a great deal more elaborate and complex. It is tied to the mythologies of Assyro-Babylonian and other Middle East cultures: we have a golden age akin to that of Greek tradition in which men, unlike the gods, were mortal but death was neither painful nor fearful; presto, a magical talking beast appears—a serpent tempting mortals to hubris. A little later sons of God intermarry with mortal women and generate a race of heroes in another variation on a Greek theme.

But J is also explaining the roots of his own people. He traces back to first events the structure, workings, preoccupations, and so forth of the tribal society of which he is a member, and he accounts for the ever-present reality of death. The result is a far more interesting narrative. We now have a tree of life and a tree of knowledge of good and evil, an injunction against eating from the latter uttered by God (who somehow fails to mention the former), the threat of death, and a first woman, who in the very act of and reason for her creation is second and inferior to the first man.

The tale gets even more intriguing in a hurry: The serpent, "more subtil than any beast of the field which the LORD God had made," asks the woman: "Yea, hath God said, Ye shall not eat of every tree of the garden?" She answers,

> We may eat of the fruit of the trees of the garden: But of the fruit of the tree which *is* in the midst of the garden, God hath said, Ye shall not eat of it, neither shall ye touch it, lest ye die.

The serpent begs to differ:

> Ye shall surely not die: For God doth know that in the day ye eat thereof, then your eyes shall be opened, and ye shall be as gods, knowing good and evil.

Liking what she is hearing, the woman eats from the tree, and so does her husband.

God finds out soon enough that his creatures have disobeyed him when he discovers Adam worried about being naked. Asked by God whether he ate from the forbidden tree, Adam snitches on his wife—she was the one who gave him fruit from the tree. God asks the woman, "What is it that thou hast done?" She answers, "The serpent beguiled me, and I did eat."

The rest, one might say, is history.

In Judeo-Christian tradition, the serpent in the Garden of Eden stands for evil, and its talk with Eve is seen as the first instance of deception in the history of the world. In *Paradise Lost*, Milton has the animal's body invaded by Satan, and it is Satan, masquerading as the serpent, who tempts the as yet unnamed Eve to eat the fruit. He does so by telling her the lie that he acquired the powers of intellect and speech by eating fruit from a particular tree in the garden and suggesting that if he, formerly a mere brute, so profited from eating fruit from that tree, the woman and her husband will certainly become godlike once they eat from it. When Eve eagerly follows the serpent to this tree of miracles, it turns out to be the forbidden tree of the knowledge of good and evil. The serpent is undaunted. By feigning "zeal and love / To man, and indignation at his wrong" (Book IX, ll. 665–66) and repeating to Eve that she and Adam will be as gods, he gets her to eat.

This interpretation of the serpent as the devil who beguiled Eve ("tricked" in the New Revised Standard Version) was, by the time of Milton, a cast-iron element of Christian theology. According to it, the serpent and Eve represent the prototypical instance of something repeated over and over throughout the ages—the devil deceiving and tempting mankind in the hope of triumphing over all creation—and it is part of the West's cultural baggage. Genesis, however, says otherwise. Eve may believe the serpent tricked her, and certainly this subtlest of all beasts was deceptive when it feigned ignorance about something it obviously knew—that God had forbidden the man and woman to eat from the tree of the knowledge of good and evil. But according to the text, this is as far as it goes. Divested of a mythological gloss given it much later, the serpent is unrecognizable as the Satan of Christianity, and no supernatural entity that is the archenemy of God and man appears in the story of creation or other early texts of the Hebrew Bible. Not until the third century B.C. and the apocryphal writings appearing even closer in time to the birth of Jesus does a character fitting the description begin to emerge in Judaism. An entity called "Satan" does appear in Job 1–2 and Zechariah 3:1–7 but he functions as an adversary or accuser of man, a servant of God whose intention is to expose the weaknesses of men esteemed by God. Job's Satan bears little, if any, resemblance to the creature the Pharisees call "Beelzebub [Hebrew *Baal-zebub*, literally Lord of Flies] the prince of the devils" in Matthew 12:24, or to Lucifer, the fallen angel of Luke 10:18, or to the Satan of Revelation 12:9, "which deceiveth the whole world."

The absence of an archenemy of God in the Old Testament and the presence of such an entity in the New Testament is emblematic of the differences between the worldviews embedded in the two books and, in particular, of a fundamental change in the relationship between God and his creatures. As we'll see, the two books' radically different approaches to deception bring this difference into sharp relief.

The two books of the Bible are worlds apart. The Old Testament is the work of a tribal culture whose earliest authors drew on history and legends told in song and poetry. Its various sections were written many centuries apart by authors approaching the task from a variety of political and religious perspectives and with a large variety of agendas. The historical and legendary events they described spanned millennia, and the genres they wrote in range from genealogy and legal code to lyrical poetry. By comparison, the New Testament, although also by several, largely unknown, authors, is a study in simplicity. The most important events it describes occupy one year in the "synoptic" ("seen together")* gospels of Matthew, Mark, and Luke, and a time span covering three Passovers in the "odd book out," the Gospel According to St. John. Acts of the Apostles and the Epistles deal with a larger time frame, and Revelation is cosmic in scope, but the stage of the New Testament is minuscule compared to that of the Old. In terms of genre, Revelation is the only jaw-dropping departure.

The New Testament's most celebrated books, the four gospels, were shaped by unknown hands fifty or more years after the death of Jesus in accordance with the writer's particular theological interests. To create written records of the teachings and "works" of Jesus and the major events of his life was one of their aims. Another was to address specific needs of the early Church and to deal with issues such as the tension between Jewish and Gentile converts to the new faith and the political situation of conflict and persecution coming out of the recent past, two of whose cataclysmic events were the destruction of Jerusalem by the Romans in A.D. 70 and the expulsion of Jewish Christians from the synagogues around A.D. 85–90.

Given the vast differences in concerns and religious climate, it is not surprising that there is a difference between how deception

---

*So called because of their close similarities, which allow their side-by-side comparison.

is treated in the Old and the New Testament. What is surprising is how vast that difference is and how closely connected to a fundamental change in how the world is seen. It is worthwhile to return to the beginning of Genesis for a first glimpse of the Old Testament approach to deception.

The serpent is indeed subtle, all the more so because what it says is laced with truth. It tricks Eve, yes, but what it tells is not a lie. It claims God knows that when the woman and the man eat the tree's fruit they will be "as gods, knowing good and evil." 'Od's truth! None other than the LORD God himself says so when he discovers his creatures' disobedience: "Behold, the man is become as one of us, to know good and evil." Also, the serpent's claim that if they eat the tree's fruit they will not die is correct. One of the Bible's interpreters guardedly concedes the point: the serpent "in a sense speaks truly." Which raises the question of whether God "in a sense" lied somewhere along the line. The serpent does in fact insinuate more than a measure of deception from those quarters. God has kept from you the true result of eating the forbidden fruit, it suggests. But more incriminating is the question of Adam and Eve surely dying on the day they eat the fruit. Not only do they not die but God hastily expels them from the garden, lest the man—who "is become as one of us . . . put forth his hand, and take also of the tree of life, and eat, and live for ever."

Clearly, eternal life was not one of the attributes possessed by Adam and Eve in the Garden of Eden. Ergo, the tempting interpretation that God's threat—if you eat of the tree of the knowledge of good and evil, you'll die today—is meant metaphorically and distinguishes eternal life in Eden from mortal life in the world does not wash. Adam and Eve and their descendants die because the serpent either did not know, or did not get around to telling, or did not care to tell, Eve about the tree of life.

The blunt fact is that the first character to tell a manifest lie in the Bible is God himself, who plays the role of the father who does not want his children to do something and who scares them with a lie to keep them from doing it. Suppose he had told them the truth: there are two trees I don't want you to eat from because eating from one will make you godlike and eating from the other will make you immortal—and I don't want you to be godlike and immortal. Would that have kept his children away from the trees? Or would they have wondered all too soon why, if advancement to the rank of god is so easy, they are forbidden to take that step? Would they have gone further and asked themselves what odd insecurity on the part of their creator was to blame for his injunction, and what bad thing could possibly happen to them if they became god-like and immortal—not to mention why he put forbidden trees in the garden in the first place?

It is highly unlikely J's intention was to invite this manner of blasphemous speculations. He is among other things the original didact and standard-bearer for the society he lived in. Eve and Adam violated Rule One of any patriarchal society: If your father tells you not to do something, you obey him, and no explanation is required. Because I say so is the answer to any unauthorized why. If you don't obey, you're punished. As Adam and Eve were. One result of eating from the tree of the knowledge of good and evil is human misery: instead of life without a care in the world, their new existence means painful childbirth and subservience to her husband for the woman, and work by the sweat of his brow for the man. The serpent, God's lesser child, gets an even larger dose of divine wrath. From now on it will crawl on its belly and eat dust all the days of its life. So much for the wages of its subtlety.

The episode of the serpent in the Garden of Eden occurs in the older (by some 400 years) of the Bible's two creation stories. If we step back and consider it as a mythological anecdote, it falls into the worldwide tradition of the trickster tale. We'll become intimately acquainted with the trickster in the next chapter; for now a quick sketch will do. He is a supernatural animal or god who uses deceit or magic to have things his way. In the process he can play the role of fool or prankster, but he can also function as creator and destroyer. His résumé impresses. He has been known to thumb his nose at authority and get away with it and to have cheated those stronger and duller. He may bring light to mortals against the wishes of gods by stealing the sun or a box containing daylight (the Titan Prometheus, bringer of fire, is his kin). He can be the inventor of snares, traps, and nets, devices of trickery that give mortals the ability to feed themselves. He has knowledge that mortals do not possess, and he uses this knowledge to prompt change, often with no idea of the consequences of his actions to others or himself. He is an opener of unsuspected doors, a bringer of new things, a con artist often too clever by far for his own good.

The serpent is thus an archetypal figure. It is an ambiguous being, an animal possessing the power of speech and knowledge that God has kept from Adam. It tricks the first woman by making promises that, although true, give no hint of the repercussions of the action—namely, the punishment in store for its victims. It makes mortals more godlike by opening their eyes to the existence of good and evil. By the same token it also pushes them in the direction of becoming human, because, like gods but unlike animals, human beings know good and evil. This knowledge may seem a poor substitute for the light brought into the world by, say, Raven, who in the tradition of Pacific Northwest Indians stole the box of daylight from his parents' house, but knowledge is intimately connected with light in our symbolic imagination, just as darkness is with ignorance. (Note that the fateful tree is not the tree of good and evil but the tree of the *knowledge* of good and evil.) The serpent thus opens the way out of the Garden of Eden, with the unforeseen consequence of the path being a one-way street—return is warded off by cherubim and a flaming sword held against anyone attempting to approach the tree of life.

Deception working on human pride is held accountable for the Fall, and the serpent is a trickster. But although it appears at the beginning of human history according to the Bible, there is no trickster mythology worth the name in Judaism. Nor is there any in other monotheistic religions. The "beguiler" of the first woman is an import from polytheistic quarters, where tricksters share the stage with other divinities, more or less respectable, personifying human traits or actions (or nature or psychological states). The serpent is discarded as soon as it has done the job of alienating God's creatures from their maker. Although crucially important to humanity, it is given so little ink in the Old Testament that it rarely appears in catalogs of tricksters in mythology. Unlike in pagan myths, where the tricksters are fleshed-out characters who have their own histories and whose exploits brim with details and incidentals, the serpent has no past and all of its actions occupy a paltry five verses. So little emphasis is put on it that the reader who blinks may miss altogether the cataclysmic role it plays. Those of us attuned to Christianity's reading of the myth have been alerted to its significance, but Christianity's recasting of the serpent as the archfiend has also made it harder for us to recognize the serpent's trickster origin.

Why the animal tricking Adam and Eve is a serpent is another question. Traditional Near Eastern associations with the snake are danger and death, secret knowledge and magic, rejuvenation, immortality, and sexuality. Conversely, as a modern translator of Genesis suggests: God's curse against the creature may record "a primal horror of humankind before this slithering, viscous-looking, and poisonous representative of the animal realm."

The outcome, at any rate, is undebatable. Our first parents were torn from the placid stasis of life in the garden and propelled into a dynamic world of good and evil, with the ability to distinguish and choose between the two. And here are we, their progeny, eons removed, a motley gathering of more or less well-meaning sinners composed in unequal parts of near-saints, mean-spirited folk, good Samaritans, schemers and dreamers, the trustworthy, the hypocritical, the enlightened, the benighted, the virtuous, the depraved—a veritable bestiary of critters bearing all manner of moral stripes. All thanks to that subtlest of all animals.

Once Adam and Eve are driven out of Eden, the Old Testament becomes the story of a people, its generations, noteworthy members, places and events, its rituals, laws, and codes. As any tale of large scope concerning humanity must be, it is chock-full of rivalries, adulteries, bloodshed, revenge, and other conflict. This particular tale is also concerned with subjugation of the Israelites, and their conquests, and it contains the repeated cycle of God's chosen people falling away from him and worshipping other gods, followed by divine punishment, followed by reconciliation. Throughout, lies, deception, and treachery abound in the service of actions prompted by lust and greed, jealousy and envy, fear and hatred. Although less frequently, love, too, can motivate deception: Joseph's prolonged toying with the brothers who sold him into slavery—which includes a "stolen" cup planted on Benjamin, his youngest brother and the only innocent among them—comes out of his love for his father and his desire to awaken the remorse that creates the space for forgiveness and reconciliation.

So what does the Old Testament make of deception as practiced by the children of Adam, Noah, and Jacob, and by the alien races they trafficked with? By and large, not much. The attitude of the Old Testament writers is in general a pragmatic acceptance of lies as part and parcel of life in the world, necessary or even commendable at times, understandable always. This acceptance vanishes only at those particular moments when laws governing behavior are being presented. The commandment "Thou shalt not bear false witness against thy neighbor" does not have the subclause "unless thy neighbor has it coming to him (or her)," and neither do any of the other commandments Moses brings back from the top of Mount Sinai.

Curiously, this injunction against bearing false witness is the only way in which dishonesty is addressed on the famous stone tablets. But the constitutionally sneaky oughtn't to conclude from this that it is permissible to lie to (as opposed to about) thy neighbor. In Leviticus 6:1–5 God enumerates to Moses a variety of sins of dishonesty that a soul should not commit, all of which fall under the collective label of deceiving one's neighbor. In Leviticus 19:11 he bluntly commands, "Ye shall not steal, neither deal falsely, neither lie one to another." Again, no "unless this, that, or the other" waters down this rule of conduct. Still, the strict constructionist may argue that the members of a tribe who are being told not to lie "one to another" may well construe this to mean that they are allowed to lie to, say, the Canaanites or Midianites. Or, looked at from the other end, if universality was intended, then why not make the statement simply: "Thou shalt not lie." Period.

This quibble aside, laws forbidding deception were clearly in place according to Leviticus' P source not too many years after the Israelites' flight from Pharaoh. And Proverbs, attributed to King Solomon, keeps repeating precepts against lying with a frequency that borders on the maniacal. Proverbs is part of the rich body of wisdom literature found in the Near East. The typical book in that tradition is a set of instructions addressed by a father to his son. It contrasts the wise man and fools and knaves of all ilks and teaches by precepts and proverbs. The biblical version, in addition to reiterating warnings about not consorting with strange women or committing adultery, not killing the innocent, and not being proud or arrogant, or full of hate, or foolish, keeps hammering away at the wickedness of lying and deception: "He that speaketh truth sheweth forth righteousness: but a false witness deceit." "The lip of truth shall be established for ever: but a lying tongue *is* but for a moment." "Lying lips *are* abomination to the LORD: but they that deal truly *are* his delight." "A righteous *man* hateth lying: but a wicked man is loathsome, and cometh to shame." And so forth. A few early paragraphs summarize God's detestations: "These six *things* doth the LORD hate: yea, seven are an abomination unto him: A proud look, a lying tongue, and hands that shed innocent blood, An heart that deviseth wicked imaginations, feet that be swift in running to mischief, A false witness *that* speaketh lies, and he that soweth discord among brethren" (6:16–19).

All this said, it is one of the universal givens of all times and places that there tends to be a gulf between what people are told to do and what they do. In the episodes before Leviticus, the Bible's characters practice dishonesty; after Leviticus they do the same. Also, God's reaction is unchanged. It ranges from disinterest to implicit or explicit approval if the dishonesty is used to promote his single-minded cause, the Israelites' continual and perpetual service to, and adoration of, him.

Examples of pre-Leviticus lying are abundant. As we've seen, Genesis 2–3 chronicles the deceptions of supernatural agents. The first human lie appears a chapter later. Cain has murdered Abel. When God asks him, "Where is Abel thy brother?" he answers, "I know not." God is being disingenuous in asking the question, but unless we argue that Cain is being super-subtle (since he literally does not know where the souls of the dead reside), Cain's answer is a bald-faced lie coming out of his fear of punishment for the evil deed.

The first woman to lie to God is Sarah, Abraham's wife. When

God visits Abraham and her, both superannuated, and promises Abraham a son from his wife, Sarah overhears the conversation and laughs to herself, saying, "After I am waxed old shall I have pleasure, my lord being old also?" God asks Abraham why she laughed, and he adds, "Is any thing too hard for the LORD?" Sarah, fearful of having scoffed at divine omnipotence, denies it. "I laughed not," she says. God, unvexed but insisting on the facts, tells her, "Nay; but thou didst laugh" (Genesis 18:12–15). Note that Yahweh does not frown upon the lie; his only concern is that his ability to do the impossible is being called into question. He is similarly unconcerned about Cain's lie. The author of the story of Cain and Abel seems to have had a commonsense notion of lying, even to God, being so minor an infraction by comparison to the crime of fratricide that it would be bizarre to make God worry about it.

Many years before God visits Abraham, Abraham himself tells a lie, although not to God. Ordered by the Lord to go to a new land, Abram, as he is still called, takes his wife, Sarai (the later Sarah), and kith and kin and journeys to Canaan and on to Egypt. About to enter Egypt, he expresses to his wife his misgivings: She is "a fair woman to look upon." When the Egyptians see her, they'll say: "This *is* his wife: and they will kill me, but they will save thee alive. Say, I pray thee, thou *art* my sister: that it may be well with me; and my soul shall live because of thee" (Genesis 12:12–13).

When they come into Egypt, the Egyptians and the princes of Pharaoh indeed admire Sarai's beauty, and she is taken into Pharaoh's house to be his wife. Her "brother" is treated well— sheep, and oxen, and he-asses, and menservants, and maidservants, and she-asses, and camels (presented in this order of decreasing importance in the text) are lavished upon him. But the Lord inflicts plagues on Pharaoh and his house, and Pharaoh calls Abram and asks him: "What *is* this *that* thou hast done unto me? why didst thou not tell me that she *was* thy wife? Why saidst thou, She *is* my sister?" (Genesis 12:18–19). Abram's answer is not given, and the fear of God prompts Pharaoh to send him away with his wife and all his goods and chattel.

Two God-ordered name changes, wholesale circumcision, and the destruction of Sodom and Gomorrah later, Abraham and his wife, Sarah, travel south to Gerar. And there Version Two of the wife-sister story unfolds. Abraham tells people that Sarah is his sister; Abimelech, king of Gerar, sends for Sarah and takes her. This time Sarah's honor is not compromised: God appears to the king in a dream and tells him he's a dead man because he has taken another's wife. Abimelech, who hasn't touched Sarah, rightly objects: "Lord, wilt thou slay also a righteous nation? Said he not unto me, She *is* my sister? and she, even she herself said, He *is* my brother: in the integrity of my heart and innocency of my hands have I done this" (Genesis 20:4–5). God sees the point, and, as it turns out, he himself prevented Abimelech's sinning by keeping him from touching Sarah.

The next day early in the morning, the king calls Abraham and repeats Pharaoh's complaint of decades earlier: "What hast thou done unto us? and what have I offended thee, that thou hast brought on me and on my kingdom a great sin? thou hast done deeds unto me that ought not to be done." Asked why he did what he did, Abraham explains: "Because I thought, Surely the fear of God *is* not in this place; and they will slay me for my wife's sake" (Genesis 20:11). An embellishment follows: Abraham claims Sarah is really his half sister by the same father; when he was told by God to wander from his father's house, he asked her to tell people that he is her brother. Since no mention was made of this sibling relationship in the account of Abram's marriage to Sarai, Abraham is either making it up out of whole cloth or the author of this version of the story worried about the moral implications of Abraham's ruse and attempted to soften things by making Abraham not lie outright, as well as by keeping Sarah's honor intact. The later version is attributed to E, the earlier one to J, and the revision may be due to E being squeamish about the moral dubiousness of the "event." If so, he succeeds only in part. Even if Sarah were Abraham's half sister, the fact that she is his wife is the far more important piece of information, since God takes a dim view of a man taking another's wife. A lie is a lie whether it rears its false head in the deliberate statement of an untruth or coyly withholds crucial information. (My opinion, disputed by some of the guiding lights of the Church, as we'll see.)

What God is up to in all this is anybody's guess and falls into the category of "mysterious are the ways . . ." as do so many other things in the Old Testament. Pharaoh is punished for a sin he had no way of knowing he was committing. He is "plagued with great plagues" according to the King James Version (which, its celebrated majestic language notwithstanding, oftentimes nods). The case of Abimelech is more confusing. He takes Sarah, has his dream before he gets around to making a dishonest woman out of her, challenges Abraham about his dishonesty, returns Sarah to him, gives him sheep, oxen, servants, and a thousand pieces of silver, and allows him to settle anywhere he pleases on his land. Then Abraham prays to God and God heals Abimelech (we didn't even know he was ill!) and heals also his wife and maidservants, who now bear children. "For the LORD had fast closed up all the wombs of the house of Abimelech, because of Sarah Abraham's wife" (Genesis 20:18). The time frame is, to say the least, puzzling, a result probably of the "punishment" being thrown in as an afterthought to make the story conform more closely to its earlier version. Craven and lying Abraham comes out a very rich man, and neither his lie nor the fact that the lie compromised his wife's honor and exposed innocent people to the wrath of God are seen as sinful by J or E, who present it as a pragmatic solution to a threat to Abraham's life.

Lies told out of fear are treated matter-of-factly in Genesis, but what about lying for less creditable reasons—profit being an ever-popular one? One of the most disturbing episodes of Genesis, vividly remembered by anyone exposed to Bible stories at an impressionable age, has to do with deception for the sake of power and wealth. It concerns Jacob, grandson of Abraham, son of Isaac, a wily soul in anyone's book, who illustrates the sad fact that power-hungry bastards often thrive. Young Jacob, secondborn and twin to Esau, is first of all an extortionist. He refuses to feed his hunter brother dying of hunger on his return from the fields until Esau has sold him his birthright for bread and lentils.

Then Jacob takes part in one of the greatest underhanded masquerades of our storied past. Isaac, blind and dying, has asked his son Esau to go hunt and bring him venison, so he may eat and bless him before he dies. Esau and Jacob's mother, Rebekah, urges Jacob to disguise himself as his elder brother in order to receive his father's blessing. The disguise is necessary since Esau is hairy and Jacob is not, and, quoth Jacob, "My father peradventure will feel me, and I shall seem to him as a deceiver; and shall bring a curse upon me, and not a blessing" (Genesis 27:12). His mother has the answer. She dresses him in Esau's clothes and puts the skins of young goats on his hands and neck. Then she sends him to Isaac with meat and bread she prepared.

If there were a prize for the Bible's most meticulous rendering of the interplay between deceiver and deceived, the ensuing scene would be a shoo-in: Isaac asks, "Who art thou, my son?" Jacob answers, "I am Esau thy firstborn; I have done according as thou badest me: arise, I pray thee, sit and eat of my venison, that thy soul may bless me." His father is puzzled: "How is it that thou hast found it so quickly, my son?" Jacob is at no loss for an answer and has no qualms about involving a higher authority in the deception: "Because the LORD thy God brought it to me." Isaac is not convinced (he shortly tells why): "Come near, I pray thee, that I may feel thee, my son, whether thou be my very son Esau or not." He touches Jacob and comments, "The voice is Jacob's voice, but the hands are the hands of Esau." The narrator adds, "And he discerned him not, because his hands were hairy, as his brother Esau's hands." Still, a smidgen of doubt remains. "Art thou my very son Esau?" Isaac asks one more time. "I am," Jacob replies. Blind and duped, Isaac blesses him, making him lord over people and nations and over his brothers, who are to bow down to him.

The deed done and much (if unintentionally) blessed Jacob gone, Esau appears back from the hunt with savory meat, ready for his blessing. Too late! When he finds out what happened, Esau's plea could move stones: "He cried with a great and exceedingly bitter cry, and said unto his father, Bless me, *even* me also, O my father." Isaac cannot. He tells him, "Thy brother came with subtilty, and hath taken away thy blessing." Esau bitterly summarizes his brother's success: "He took away my birthright; and, behold, now he hath taken away my blessing." Predictably, Esau plots revenge, but years later the two brothers' joyful reconciliation becomes one of the Bible's greatest instances of forgiving.

If we double back, all of this may be seen as an example of God's will working mysteriously. Shortly before the birth of Esau and Jacob, their mother consults Yahweh at a sacred shrine and is given an oracle proclaiming that she will bear twins who will become two rival nations, the younger and stronger of which will dominate the elder. So Jacob's underhandedness may be seen as part of the divine purpose. The only problem with that pious interpretation is that it introduces a question theologians and philosophers have filled volumes answering: if a human action arises from divine purpose, does it have any moral meaning? The classical conundrum in that area is of course the question of how Judas could possibly have avoided betraying Jesus once Jesus foretold the betrayal. If he had *not* betrayed him, Jesus would have been wrong; if Judas, therefore, had no option but to betray Jesus, how could he be condemned for the act? St. Paul's answer to all such complaints is: "O man, who art thou that repliest against God? Shall the thing formed say to him that formed *it*, Why hast thou made me thus?" (Romans 9:20).

If the authors of the Bible register no disapproval of deception in the case of one brother defrauding another—either in commentary or by showing a wrathful reaction from high above—it is unsurprising that they find no fault when Jacob, in turn, is tricked by his uncle, Laban, into marrying the wrong woman. He travels to Laban's house, falls in love with his younger daughter, Rachel, and contracts to marry her in return for seven years' service. But the heavily veiled bride he marries and beds is Leah, the elder daughter. Asked by Jacob why he "beguiled" him, Laban answers that the tradition of his land is for the firstborn sister to marry before the younger (Genesis 29:25–26). To get Laban's permission to marry Rachel as well, Jacob has to obligate himself to another seven years of labor.

A marked discrepancy between sensibilities ancient and modern becomes glaringly obvious at this point. Our modern take on promises of any kind is that if they are extracted by fraud, the deal is off. Biblical folk, conversely, just as the characters of Greek or Teutonic mythology or of fairy tales, have no recourse if they are tricked. A blessing is a blessing even if obtained by trickery. (It is also clearly a thing that belongs to the physical as opposed to the spiritual world. In the case of Jacob and Esau, not the son intended is blessed but the one physically present. The words spoken are like a substance deposited on and adhering to the person they are addressed to.) Similarly, Jacob's being duped into marrying the wrong woman does not void his marriage to her. Caveat emptor is an unstated but ever-applicable motto in the Old Testament.

Unsurprisingly, the Old Testament shows categorical approval of deception in war or other instances of hostility. Spies, ambushes, and ruses have accompanied overt animosity from time immemorial. David's wife disguises her husband's flight from murderous Saul by hiding an effigy of sorts and a pillow of goat's hair under a blanket and claiming her husband is sick in bed (1 Samuel 19:13–14), and David himself feigns madness so convincingly, by scrabbling on a door and getting spittle in his beard, that king Achish throws him out rather than killing him (1 Samuel 21:13). A list of similar instances of deception for the sake of self-preservation would be lengthy even if pared down to chapter and verse.

Self-defense is one thing, but people have also tended not to be squeamish about lying if their aim has been to kill others. That in the Old Testament the ruse sometimes seems more contemptible than the killing has something to do with the peculiar cultural conditioning that makes us think of the slaying of an enemy in battle as an "honorable" thing but of deception as potentially slimy. Still, on many occasions God wholeheartedly approves, in one case even of the violation of a treaty and outright treachery. The captain of the army of Jabin, king of Canaan, while fleeing from a battle with the Israelites, comes to the tent of the wife of Heber the Kenite. There is peace between Jabin and Heber, and Heber's wife comes out of the tent and says to the captain, "Turn in, my lord, turn in to me; fear not." He does, and she covers him with a mantle and gives him milk for his thirst. Then when he falls asleep, she takes a tent spike and hammer and drives the spike through his temples into the ground. Her deception and treachery are lauded: "So God subdued on that day Jabin the king of Canaan before the children of Israel" (Judges 4:23). (That foundation of Machiavellian thinking, that the end justifies the means, is clearly much older than popularly maligned Niccolò M.)

Another instance of deception bearing the divine seal of approval was much cited by the fathers of the early Church when they were cobbling together a code of conduct for Christians and worried about under what circumstances, if ever, lying was permissible. Pharaoh, irked by the Hebrews' population explosion, has ordered their midwives to kill all male infants they deliver. They do no such thing. When he calls them before him and asks why they are not following his order, they claim that the Hebrew women are "livelier" than the Egyptian and give birth to their children before the midwives get to them. The lie is expressly condoned on high: "Therefore God dealt well with the midwives: and the people multiplied, and waxed very mighty" (Exodus 1:20).

Jews and Christians look to scripture for the explanation of where their sense of right and wrong comes from (Judaism, of course, exclusively to the Hebrew Bible; Christianity much more to the New Testament than the Old), and the Fathers of the Church spent their lives dissecting scripture to map out what human actions were to be deemed good and what bad, and under what circumstances.

In the Old Testament, deception is a relatively straightforward thing: something not to be practiced on your neighbor but permeating all aspects of a world in which the struggle between a jealous God and his errant people, and pride, lust, envy, and hunger for power and wealth lead to endless permutations of enmity and violence. It is sometimes rewarded by God if it is done for the "right" reasons. Mostly, though, it is ignored by him. The New Testament changes this cavalier attitude, and not merely because it lacks the epic qualities of the Old.

Our modern Western sense of lying as being—all concerns of its expediency and usefulness aside—intrinsically an evil, and our response to that evil, ranging from distaste to abhorrence, has a great deal to do with a shift in perception that came out of the New Testament. (For the reader asking what in blazes "modern sense" might mean, and whether it is allegedly shared by Evangelical Christians, atheists, assimilated Jews, Marxists, and corporate raiders, the answer is: Yes. The messages of Christianity have had an effect on anyone alive in the Western world and have seeped into the moral consciousness of even those who emphatically disavow the supernatural or think little of morals.) One of the clarion calls of the New Testament is the need to change people's perception of what constitutes the moral life. The demanded shift was from outward to inward, and it had profound effects on the ethos of Western culture.

The treatment that sinning in general receives in the New Testament illustrates the difference between old and new sensibilities and reflects a new way of looking at the self. Even though the prophetic strain in Judaism calls for spiritual repentance and renewal, the emphasis in the Old Testament is on outward forms. Sinning may be a breach of the covenant between God and his creature and therefore concerns the invisible world, but the ways of sinning are largely presented as external and perceptible. Hence the commandments against using the name of God in vain, not honoring the Sabbath, murdering, committing adultery, bearing false witness; hence the death penalty prescribed for major sins and the many ways to reestablish the covenant with God by way of ritual for minor ones: if the sin is X, the offering to be cleansed of it is two doves; if it is Y, the offering is one ram; if it is Z, one red heifer. The focus is not on the inner life or the spiritual state of the murderer, false witness, or man caught having sexual intercourse with a betrothed slave, but on the wrong done in sinning and on the penalty for it or the "trespass offering" necessary for atonement and forgiveness. Of the Ten Commandments, the only one not expressed in terms of physical action is that against covetousness: Thou shalt not "covet"—as opposed to "take"—thy neighbor's house, or wife, or manservant, or maidservant, or ox, or ass. (The shift here from prohibited physical to prohibited mental action may simply come out of common sense. As you well know, if you were to take your neighbor's wife, or ox, or anything else belonging to him, your neighbor would probably pay you a visit with a cudgel; no need to tell you to refrain from doing something for which retribution is at hand. Coveting conversely . . .) Leviticus does have the injunction to "love thy neighbor as thyself" (19:18), but the commandment, tucked away among hundreds of others having to do with the conduct of life in areas ranging from planting and harvesting, diet, skin disorders, clothing, and the selling of fruit to sexual taboos and the dos and don'ts of slavery, lacks the clout of the words on the stone tablets.

One of the fascinating things about the New Testament is how a change in psychological makeup, characterized by a far greater concern for the inner life, recast God and created a new way of relating to that colossal projection of the self. The Christian sense of God knowing at all times what goes on in every person's mind, for instance, turns him into a far more intrusive presence than the Yahweh of the Old Testament and makes Yahweh seem absurdly uninformed by comparison. He is forever sending angels among the people to find out what is *really* going on. Are Sodom and Gomorrah in as wrath-worthy a shape as he suspects? Are there fifty, or forty, or thirty, or twenty, or ten righteous souls to be found among the wicked? Although Yahweh, unlike, say, Zeus, cannot be tricked by lesser gods, his access to the inner life of mortals seems woefully limited. When he wishes to determine the depth of Abraham's devotion to him, he does not look into Abraham's heart but devises the ultimate test, the sacrifice of his beloved son. By comparison, Jesus *knows* that Judas will betray him; the kiss is nothing but confirmation.

As a rule, Yahweh can surmise only from the actions of people what goes on inside them. The idea of someone being culpable simply for having certain thoughts is quite foreign to the Old Testament, coveting being a conspicuous exception. Yahweh's wrath descends on those committing actions out of line with dogma; his jealousy is incited by the children of Israel being off worshipping yet another cast or graven idol or going a-whoring after Baal the moment his back is turned. For the God of the New Testament, the true drama takes place in the hearts of sinners, and actions are merely the outward expression of what goes on inside.

By the time of Jesus, Judaism had, with the emergence of the synagogue, evolved away from sacrifice toward prayer and Torah reading as the way to serve God. The New Testament's explicit concern for what is going on inside, where self-awareness and conscience reside, is revolutionary but it did not arise in a vacuum. Still, the New Testament jumped out of the Judaic groove in emphasizing concerns of the heart—to love, forgive, not to pass judgment—and in insisting on the consonance between actions and what goes on in the mind. Its demolition of old laws was part of this shift away from the physical aspects of reality to the mental ones and was in line with the new insight that "God *is* a spirit: and they that worship him must worship *him* in spirit and in truth" (John 4:24).

The question of diet is one example. When Jesus' disciples are found to be eating bread without first having washed their hands, in violation of the tradition of the elders, the Pharisees ask him why. He takes the opportunity to summon people around him and instruct them: "There is nothing from without a man, that entering into him can defile him: but the things that come out of him, those are they that defile the man" (Mark 7:15). The reason he gives is that what enters does not enter the heart but the belly and goes out again, but "From within, out of the heart of man, proceed evil thoughts, adulteries, fornications, murders, thefts, covetousness, wickedness, deceit, lasciviousness, an evil eye, blasphemy, pride, foolishness: All these things come from within and defile the man" (7:21–23). In other words, the world's evils issue from the mind, and the mind is what needs to be reformed if the aim is to reform actions.

Given this shift in emphasis, certain sins become perforce more grievous. Deception in all its forms is promoted from misdemeanor to felony since it is symptomatic of a discrepancy between what resides in the mind and what appears outwardly. Criminalized and exposed as an active evil, it is traced to its source: In the New Testament the devil as we know him makes his first appearance, and he is identified as a liar and the father of lies (John 8:44). To lie means more now than to break one of a hundred rules micromanaging the conduct of one's life. It means to follow the Evil One. As befits people performing acts that belong to the devil, the punishment of liars is explicit and severe. Not only the fearful and unbelieving, and the abominable and murderers and whoremongers, sorcerers and idolaters, but *all* liars will be cast into the lake that burns with fire and brimstone (Revelation 21:8).

Liars here means anyone who deceives in any way. Hypocrites are a prime example, and again the shift in perception is glaring. Hypocrisy is hardly mentioned in the Old Testament. Psalm 26:4 speaks of "dissemblers" ("hypocrites" in the NRSV) with whom the psalmist claims not to have consorted, but nowhere is there a commandment not to be hypocritical. By contrast, all three synoptic gospels address the issue, Matthew and Luke in the memorable instruction to "thou hypocrite" to cast out the beam in your own eye before worrying about casting out the mote in the eye of your brother (Matthew 7:5, Luke 6:42), Mark in mentioning Jesus' awareness of the hypocrisy of the Pharisees (7:6, 12:15). Matthew drives home the point with the formulaic refrain of Jesus: "Woe unto you, scribes and Pharisees, hypocrites!" repeated seven times when Jesus describes instances of false piety and charity (23:13–29). The message could not be clearer: it is sinful outwardly to exhibit, for the sake of appearing righteous, what is inwardly absent.*

The New Testament's most dramatic instance of lies being punished seems at first a straightforward comment on that evil practice, but its meaning is more complicated than that. Acts of the Apostles describes the alarming fate of Ananias and his wife Sapphira, members of an assembly of Christians. When the assembly is filled with the spirit of the Holy Ghost, it determines to let go of private possessions and to have all things in common. All those who have land or houses sell what they have and bring the money and lay it at the feet of the apostles Peter and John. "But a certain man named Ananias, with Sapphira his wife, sold a possession, And kept back *part* of the price, his wife also being privy *to it*, and brought a certain part, and laid *it* at the apostles' feet" (5:1–2). Peter, cognizant of the cheating, although the source of his information is not specified, confronts him: "Why hath Satan filled thine heart to lie to the Holy Ghost, and to keep back *part* of the price of the land? Whiles it remained, was it not thine own? and after it was sold, was it not in thine own power? why hast thou conceived this thing in thine heart? thou hast not lied unto men, but unto God" (5:3–4). Whereupon Ananias falls down stone dead.

Three hours later, his wife, not knowing what has happened, comes in. Peter asks her, "Tell me whether you sold the land for so much." She answers, "Yea, for so much," and he remonstrates: "How is it that ye have agreed together to tempt the Spirit of the Lord? behold, the feet of them which have buried thy husband *are* at the door, and shall carry thee out." The prophesy is fulfilled immediately: "Then fell she down straightaway at his feet, and yielded up the ghost" (5:7–10).

The punishment of the two cheats and liars, swift and devastating, has an Old Testament ring to it, but lying as an offense grievous enough to warrant the death penalty is a thoroughly New Testament idea. The cautionary tale was no doubt meant to instill

---

*The passage probably also reflects the author of Matthew having an ax to grind with the Jewish religious establishment.

in the early Christians a commitment to honesty in matters economic pertaining to the community: Cheat or lie and you may drop dead. The accusation that Ananias lied to the Holy Ghost rather than to men (presumably in pretending to be inspired like the others when in fact he was not) is puzzling, for one, because he obviously did lie to men too in implying that the money he offered was all he had gotten and, for another, because of the intriguing question it raises of what to make of people lying to God about being inspired by him. The author, sensibly, does not open the latter can of worms.

The most famous lie of the gospels—that of Peter denying three times before the cock crows (either once, in Matthew, Luke, and John, or twice, in Mark) that he is one of the disciples of the arrested Jesus—has by comparison very minor repercussions, although it is in the synoptic gospels a poignant illustration of human frailty and remorse. All three have Peter weep when he hears the rooster crow and remembers Jesus' prophesy that he will deny him (Matthew 26:69–75, Mark 14:66–72, Luke 22:55–61). The author of John is the only one who misses out on the narrative opportunity of having Peter's denial culminate in bitter remorse at his weakness and turning it into a moving experience for the reader (18:16–27).

Remorse at his own shortcoming is the only punishment Peter receives for his lie even though it is artfully executed, especially in Matthew, where the denial progresses from "I know not what thou sayest" to denial "with an oath" and the claim "I do not know the man" to a dramatic outburst: "Then began he to curse and swear, *saying*, I know not the man." The lie is clearly seen by the authors as understandable, coming as it does out of the instinct of self-preservation. That this forgiving attitude about a lie is at odds with much of New Testament preaching on the subject illustrates that a foolish consistency is not allowed to be a hobgoblin of biblical texts old or new. All liars may end up in a lake of fire and brimstone, but surely Peter won't. And neither should Peter's denial "with an oath" be construed as a violation of a direct commandment of Jesus, a commandment that, as it turns out, illustrates how radically the moral meaning of deception in the New Testament differs from that in the Old.

Jesus outright prohibits oaths even though he is well aware of their tradition. The Old Testament is full of instances of people swearing to do this or not do that. Leviticus adds to the commandments about neither stealing, nor dealing falsely, nor lying to one another "ye shall not swear by my name falsely" (19:12). God himself swears oaths to the patriarchs that they will be fruitful and that the land will belong to their progeny. In all cases the oath is seen as a solemn promise, and when mortals swear, the underlying threat is the same it has been in pagan societies since the earliest days of history: if they break the promise, divine retribution will follow. Compare this meaning of the oath with Jesus' lecture on the topic:

> Again, ye have heard that it hath been said by them of old time, Thou shalt not forswear thyself, but shalt perform unto the Lord thine oaths; But I say unto you, Swear not at all; neither by heaven, for it is God's throne: Nor by the earth; for it is his footstool: neither by Jerusalem; for it is the city of the great King. Neither shalt thou swear by thy head, because thou canst not make one hair white or black. But let your communication be, Yea, yea; Nay, nay: for whatsoever is more than these cometh of evil (Matthew 5:33–37).

The change is semantic and somewhat confusing since it blurs the difference between the promissory oath and the oath made to affirm the truth of a statement. Both are ancient ideas, but, of the two, the oath that promises is the far more common one in the Old Testament. Jesus' emphasis is clearly not on the solemn promise made and fear of retribution if the promise is broken but on the kind of oath soon to be uttered by Peter denying that he knows Jesus, the oath meant to guarantee that the one who swears it will speak truthfully. Jesus treats swearing as something intimately connected with the notion that anyone is capable of lying—and may well choose to lie under different circumstances—but that once someone is "under oath" what he or she tells now is the truth, the whole truth, and nothing but the truth. But the moment the oath assumes this function it becomes meaningless for anyone committed to absolute honesty. If you tell the truth at all times—as Jesus commands you to—you have no need of oaths. The shift in meaning again indicates the new concern for the truth and the new view of its opposite as the devil's spawn.

Why Jesus' straightforward condemnation of the oath (according to Matthew) was largely ignored in Christendom in the centuries to come is an interesting question. Most likely a widely perceived need is responsible for the persistence of the oath in even Christian societies. The New Testament calls all liars followers of Satan, but nominal Christians have been known to lie with little fuss. What was needed was ritual to solemnize those times when the truth was of crucial importance, in matters of life or death, or property, when the stakes were high and the temptation to tell a lie great. The solemn oath was meant to frighten the God-fearing into telling the truth. Small wonder it was a cornerstone of judicial proceedings in the Middle Ages, a time when belief in the possibility of direct divine intervention in human affairs appeared in such peculiar customs as the trial by ordeal (of which more later). The witness on the stand may well have feared that lightning would strike anyone who lied after swearing by Almighty God to tell the truth.

Modern common-law Anglo-American legal systems obligate witnesses to swear that they will tell the truth—so help them God. The threatened sanction for false testimony is no longer immediate divine retribution but imprisonment for the crime of perjury. (In the civil law of Continental Europe and much of Latin America the oath is voluntary and is taken after testimony.) As in the Middle Ages, the God sworn by is assumed to be the Christian one for the majority of those who take the oath—the selfsame who told the populace to "swear not at all." An exception is made for Quakers, Jehovah's Witnesses, and others who have conscientious scruples against taking an oath. They are allowed to use "affirmation" binding upon their consciences in lieu of the oath. Just like the oath, affirmation is intended as a safeguard against false testimony: Again, a false witness testifying under affirmation can be prosecuted for perjury. This said, the persistence of the oath in courts of law may be regarded as a resounding vote of no confidence regarding people's commitment to truth-telling. The consensus seems to be that the Old Testament's written-in-stone commandment against bearing false witness and the commandment in Leviticus against lying and the New Testament's condemnation of lying and its commandment to swear not at all are well and good, but let's make sure we have the clout to discourage would-be lying witnesses by threatening to make life miserable for them.

The oath is a serious matter, not only in the Judeo-Christian but, as we'll see, in other systems of belief as well, and its violation is doubly serious because it involves not only telling a lie but a false appeal to a higher authority or concept—such as one's father's grave—in order to have that lie taken for the truth. So what are we to do when told of a certain divine scoundrel who swore on the head of Zeus, mightiest of the gods, that he was telling the truth when he was in fact lying through his teeth? And who proceeded to swear and lie before Zeus himself, and—wonder of wonders!— lived happily ever after? The answer, as we'll see, is that we are to follow Zeus's example and laugh out loud. Another supernatural character who tangled with Zeus was less fortunate. Although he swore neither by nor before him, and never told an outright lie, his attempt to deceive the ruler of Olympus had grave consequences and his suffering for it became a recurring motif in Western thought. The two, Hermes and Prometheus, are two sides of the same coin minted in ancient Greece, a coin giving us access to a world that saw deception in a very different light.

Deception at First Light

"The net, the spell of Shamash would fall upon thee and seize thee."

A wise young eagle advising his father against eating the children of a serpent. When the father ignores the advice, Shamash, the god of justice, tells the serpent how to lure him into a trap to punish him.

> *What, you might ask, is the point of it all?*
> *Seduction, corruption, ruination—*
> *All this hard labour I put in,*
> *Day after night after day.*

"Lucifer Broods," D. J. Enright, *A Faust Book*, 1979

1

One of the great myths of the Western world is the Titan Prometheus, who stole fire from heaven and brought it to man and was punished for his kindness by Zeus. Fettered and pinned to a rock by chains and a spike driven through his middle, subjected to the torture of having his liver eaten daily by an eagle, he is a figure whose heroic potential was not lost on dramatists and poets. Aeschylus (525–456 B.C.) wrote a trilogy of plays about him, of which only the middle one survives. In that play, *Prometheus Bound*, the Titan flaunts an indomitable spirit that is ultimately exposed as foolish—he continues to rail against a god who can increase his torment at will. Byron turned him into a figure for the Romantic age, sign and symbol of the commingled greatness and wretchedness of humankind. Shelley, in his *Prometheus Unbound*, took even greater liberties with the material he got from ancient sources, giving Prometheus a Christlike charity for his oppressor from which springs the selfless love that regenerates heaven and earth. What the Romantics ignored, since it did not fit the meaning they wanted to draw from the myth, was that its first written version, attributed to the eighth-century-B.C. poet Hesiod and echoed by Aeschylus, features a more interesting Prometheus. That Prometheus reappears in other guises elsewhere in world mythology and is a complicated and intriguing figure.

Hesiod's *Theogony* describes how the gods and the world came into being. One of the poem's passages relates how Prometheus matched his wits against those of Zeus at the time when the details of ritual sacrifice were decided on. The question was which part of a sacrifice made to the immortals should belong to them and which part to mankind. Prometheus cut up a great ox and separated the pieces into two portions. The one he placed before mankind consisted of the meaty parts and the innards rich with fat, but Prometheus had hidden all of this in an unpalatable spot, the ox's stomach. The portion he placed before Zeus consisted of the bare bones, deceptively covered by a layer of gleaming fat. Zeus, inspecting both portions, pointed out how unfairly Prometheus had divided them. Whereupon Prometheus, "the devious-deviser, lightly smiling, answered him, quite well aware of his artful deception."

Prometheus' "artfully deceptive" answer to Zeus was an offer. Intending to dupe the greatest of the Olympians by shifting on him the blame for the gods being stuck with the inferior part of the sacrifice, he invited him to choose which of the two portions he'd rather have. Unfortunately, Zeus, who in Hesiod's theology is all-knowing, saw what was what.* Equally unfortunately, Zeus didn't settle for simply teaching Prometheus a lesson by choosing the meat hidden inside the ox's stomach. He countered the Titan's deviousness with his own.

Now Zeus's deviousness was in a league altogether different from that of Prometheus, who nowhere shows familiarity with the kind of deliberate self-deception practiced by people looking for an excuse for self-righteous indignation. Zeus's ploy was to *pretend* Prometheus had successfully hidden the truth from him and then to allow himself the reaction he *would have had* upon discovering that he had been duped. He chose the portion covered with fat.

---

*Zeus is by no means omniscient in all of the stories about him. In the matter of the birth of Heracles, for instance, his nibs was royally tricked by his wife Hera.

Then, after lifting up the fat with both hands, he let things take their course. "Anger rose up about his heart and the spite mounted in his spirit when he saw the white bones of the ox in deceptive arrangement."

The upshot is that, in his anger, Zeus takes away fire from mortal men, and Prometheus outwits him by stealing it back and returning it to them, and Zeus—livid now—retaliates by ordering Hephaestus, the divine smith, to make the first woman. Looking like a modest, beautiful young girl, dressed by Athena in gorgeous clothing, she is an evil thing from which originates the breed of women, forever a great sorrow to men. In Hesiod's other great work, *The Works and Days*, the evil thing is identified as Pandora, Zeus's gift to Prometheus' brother, Epimetheus, who foolishly accepts her despite Prometheus' warning that nothing good can come from Zeus. At Zeus's behest, Hermes—whom we'll meet again shortly—has put into the heart of Pandora "lies, and wheedling words of falsehood, and a treacherous nature," and Pandora's dowry is a jar full of sickness and trouble. Thus, Zeus's ultimate revenge on men for Prometheus' deceptiveness is to burden them with deceptive women, whose arrival spells the end of a golden age without misery or evil.

One intriguing facet of the tale of Prometheus' trickery is Hesiod's claim that it explains why sacrifices to the gods have from days immemorial involved burning the bones of the animals. An interesting theory, but one that should make uneasy anyone who sacrifices hecatombs to the gods. Is it really a good idea to give them what Zeus chose only because he *chose* to be tricked in order to have an excuse to harm mortals? Too modern a concern, probably, given the ancient world's view of any contract or oath as being carved in stone, no matter how fraudulently obtained.

Another intriguing thing is that Prometheus' trickery misfired very badly both for mortal men, who got stuck with mortal women, and for Prometheus, who spent some substantial length of time nailed to a rock, furnishing a daily feast for Zeus's eagle. As Aeschylus pointed out, the name the gods gave to Prometheus, "Forethought," ill suits him. Apparently deceiving all-seeing Zeus is not a good idea, even if the one doing it means well for humankind. (Zeus finally relented when he needed to give his son Heracles something to do that would make him celebrated and sent him to kill the eagle and free Prometheus; elsewhere things had clearly gone too far for anyone to rectify the harm done by Zeus's anger: womankind was on earth to stay.)

Note that Prometheus told no lie during his dealings with Zeus. His trickery relied on Zeus reaching the wrong conclusion from what the Titan had placed before his eyes. Rather than saying: "You're so right; on this side, obviously, is the better part of the sacrifice, and on that the worse. Pick what you like," he let the evidence speak for itself—and the evidence was false. But lie or no lie, Prometheus' intent was to trick the greatest of the immortals. That the story nowhere expresses outrage at the Titan's attempt to bamboozle Zeus defines it as pagan. There is nothing equivalent in the Old Testament. Biblical folk may on occasion lie to God because they are afraid of what God will do if he finds out the truth, but the vastness of the difference in nature that separates God from all other characters in the Bible, and especially from those whom most of the book is about—the human beings he created and the people he chose—makes it inconceivable for any of them to try to dupe him.

The reason Zeus can be tricked (Prometheus failed but others succeeded) is that the Greek cosmos teems with other godlike beings, many of whom are close family. Greek cosmogony is the story of legions of powerful immortals battling for supremacy, often by use of trickery. Zeus himself owed his life to his mother Rhea's deception of her husband, Kronos. Kronos was in the habit of devouring each of his children as it was born. Rhea, in despair, and advised by her parents, Ouranos and Gaia, went into hiding to bring forth Zeus. To her husband she presented a giant rock wrapped in swaddling clothes, which Kronos swallowed at once. As soon as Zeus reached manhood, he made Metis, wisest of the gods, concoct a draft that made Kronos vomit up all his children, and he drove his father from the sky. Zeus's relatives include the Titans, who were the sons and daughters of Ouranos and Gaia—which makes Prometheus Zeus's uncle. No wonder the immortals clashing in Greek mythology meet on equal grounds and behave accordingly—scheme against each other, wage war, trick each other. The grounds on which the Old Testament God and his creatures meet, on the other hand, far from being equal, are not even in the same world.

In the centuries following Hesiod, Prometheus acquired an impressive dossier. Aeschylus made him the original bringer, rather than the returner, of fire, which his Prometheus took from the smithy of Hephaestus. He identified him as a "crafty trickster" who needed to be bound in chains that could not be broken, but without mentioning any trick other than the theft of fire. Apparently he assumed his audience's familiarity with the deceptiveness of Prometheus, either because he knew that people knew their Hesiod or because his earlier, lost, play about the Titan elaborated on it.

In *Prometheus Bound*, the emphasis is on Prometheus as the savior of mortals at a time when Zeus decided that they had been a bad idea. New brooms sweep clean. Zeus, after banishing his father Kronos, putting down the revolt of the Titans (in which Prometheus prudently stayed neutral), and becoming the supreme ruler of Olympus, decided to destroy the human race and start another. He would have had his way if it hadn't been for Prometheus, who interfered, first by keeping men from passing into Hades after they were struck by Zeus's thunderbolt, then by giving them hope when they were ready to despair at the inevitability of death. He continued his good offices by teaching mortals to think, and see and hear clearly, to leave their caves and build houses, use numbers, understand the seasons and stars, tame beasts of burden and horses, make and sail ships, find and work metal, blend medicines for their ills. He also taught them those skills dearest to the ancient Greeks: the ability to prophesy by interpreting dreams, the flights of birds, the innards of sacrificial offerings, and other omens. In short, Prometheus gave men what separated them from the animals and made them human, and he was responsible for all arts, sciences, and crafts.

When Aeschylus wrote his tragedies, Prometheus had not yet been promoted to Creator of Mankind, but later tradition came close to doing so. By the time of Pausanias, that indefatigable Greek tourist and travel writer—ten books between A.D. 143 and 161—Prometheus' role in the origin of mankind had taken another leap in the popular imagination, probably courtesy of the biblical story of Genesis. He was held responsible for making mortals by molding clay into statues resembling the gods. Pausanias found in Phokis two large rocks that looked like hardened clay and smelled of human flesh, and he reported that the inhabitants claimed they were remnants of the Titan's workmanship. True, Prometheus was considered only the co-creator. His "men" made in the images of the gods were mere statues, and it took Athena, who was charmed by them, to breathe on them and bring them to life. Still, this trend of an ever more important role in human affairs played by Prometheus suggests that given a few more centuries without the advent of Christianity, he might have evolved into the sole creator of all things human in the Greeks' mythmaking imagination.

What Prometheus did evolve into in the poetic imagination of the Christian world mirrors the shift from a pagan to a Christian worldview. In that view, a "devious-deviser" would never do as a hero. If Prometheus was to be kept as a symbol for human advancement and heroic suffering, he had to lose certain characteristics. Anyone in whom the Christian notion of the evil of deception had been inculcated at an early age would balk at a tragic hero who practiced trickery. Byron's Prometheus is a figure of magnanimity and steadfast endurance whose "godlike crime was to be kind; / To render with thy precepts less / The sum of human wretchedness." Shelley's is the savior of humanity, who suffered unmerited punishment and forgave his oppressor. Neither fits the character of Hesiod's "artfully deceptive" manipulator.

As he appears in Hesiod and Aeschylus, the Titan is a fascinating figure, and one that reappears in world mythology in a large variety of guises and is held responsible for a great many things, good and bad, that are found in this world. Collectively known as the trickster, that figure pops up again in the Greek pantheon in variegated Hermes, and it is found in one form or another in most mythologies. In Teutonic myths he appears as Loki, in Hinduism as the child Krishna, in Shinto lore as Kitsune, a fox who is the messenger of the rice god, in the myths and folk tales of American Indians, Oceanians, Africans, and Australian Aborigines as a raven, hare, spider, tortoise, or other animal having magical powers. We've seen him make a cameo appearance in the Garden of Eden, and we'll see him again, giving a sinister, one-dimensional performance as the devil in Christianity.

2

A deceiver of gods and men, the trickster usually shows up not quite at the beginning of things but at a time when they have settled into a status quo. There are exceptions: Glooscap (or Gluskap) was a creator god, who made the sun, the moon, the plains, plants and animals, and human beings in the mythology of several peoples from North American forests, but he also featured as a trickster in hundreds of folk tales. Most of the time, though, the trickster is a disruptive force that changes the world, redistributes abilities and goods, reshuffles the deck. He is a thief whose theft can have enormous consequences. Like Prometheus, he may steal fire from the gods. The Polynesian god Maui stole fire from the keeper of the underworld and gave it to men. He also pulled land from the ocean so men had a place where they could live. Raven, the dominant trickster in tales told by Indians of the Northwest Pacific coast, stole daylight from the chief of heaven's house. Through the low trick of smearing dog feces on the buttocks of the petrel, who had to run off to wash himself, he stole water from a spring the greedy bird kept under a cover. When he flew away, water fell from his beak and turned into the great rivers and small creeks of Alaska.

Tricksters can help the gods achieve through deception what they cannot achieve on their own. Loki is not only one of the three creator gods in one version of his myth (the other two being Odin and Honir); he also helped the other gods by tricking a rock giant into rebuilding the wall around the Aesir's citadel after it had been destroyed in the war between the Aesir and the Vanir. He promised the giant the sun, the moon, and Freja, the goddess of love, if he finished the project by the first day of spring. At the same time, he reassured his fellow gods that the giant would not be able to finish the job by then. Unfortunately he had forgotten about the giant's mighty stallion, who tirelessly hauled boulders for his master. Helped by the great beast, the giant was dangerously close to finishing on time, and the gods were growing afraid of the chill that would attend the loss of love. Loki told them to trust him. He assumed the appearance of a seductive mare (among other things, Loki was a charmer and seducer of all creatures) and led the stallion away from his work and into the woods, where the stallion copulated with him/her, which resulted in Loki giving birth to an eight-legged foal that was the fastest animal in creation. The giant, unable to finish the work on time, was unable to collect. Enraged, he attacked the gods and was struck down by Thor.

At other times Loki turned his trickery against the gods. He used deception to murder beautiful, sweet-natured Balder, son of Odin and Frigg, the most beloved of all the immortals. When Balder began having dreams that seemed to forebode his death, Frigg asked all potentially harmful things to take an oath that none of them would hurt Balder. Fire, water, iron and all other metals, stone and earth, trees, sicknesses and poisons, and all four-footed beasts, birds, and creeping things swore. Balder was now deemed invulnerable, and the gods amused themselves by attacking him with arrows, swords, and stones, none of which had the slightest effect on him. Only Loki was displeased. He went to Frigg in the guise of an old woman and asked if all things indeed had sworn to spare Balder. Frigg told the old woman that east of Valhalla grew a plant called mistletoe which had seemed to her too young for the oath. Loki went and pulled the mistletoe* and took it to the assembly of the gods. The gods were once again entertaining themselves shooting and throwing rocks at Balder (never a dull moment in Valhalla). Loki approached the blind god Hother and asked him why he was not partaking of the fun. Hother told him the obvious: for one, he couldn't see where Balder stood, and, for another, he had no weapon. Loki was sympathetic and helpful: "Do like the rest and show Balder honour, as they all do. I will show you where he stands, and do you shoot at him with this twig." Hother followed the instructions, and the mistletoe struck Balder. More than that, it pierced him through and he fell down dead. And that was the greatest misfortune that ever befell gods and men.

After Balder's death, Loki compounded his crime by disguising himself as an old giantess who was the only being in all of creation who refused to weep for Balder, thus denying him return to life. This outrage and others finally caused the gods to chase and capture him. Loki's myth ends with the prophecy that he, as fire, and the frost giant Hrymir will jointly lead the forces of darkness

*The golden bough of Frazer's *Golden Bough*, incidentally.

against the gods. The battle will destroy all living things. At the end only fire and ice will be left and when they merge a new cycle will begin.

3

In Greek mythology, the trickster equivalent to Loki is Hermes, one of the sons of Zeus. He is a more faithful helper of the gods, a sunnier, less troubled, "luck-bringing" immortal whose disreputable traits are balanced by benevolent ones. As a trickster, Hermes is the new kid on the block, a junior schemer who in *Prometheus Bound* addresses the cunning Titan as "wise teacher." Not that Prometheus could tell the youngster a thing about deception. Hermes' versatility in that field is quite exceptional. Prometheus stole fire, but Hermes is the god of thieves—and of perjury, cunning, and fraud. He is also the god of eloquence and profit, a not too subtle hint that the latter may be helped along by the former.

Other roles include messenger of the gods, god of crossroads, and guide of the dead to the underworld. In addition, Hermes is credited with having invented the lyre and flute, the alphabet and hence writing, numbers, astronomy, music, weights and measures, the art of fighting, sacrifice to the gods, the technique of making fire by twirling a stick, and other useful or delightful things. Clearly, there is some overlap—with modifications—between what is attributed to Prometheus and what to Hermes. One brings fire, the other invents a way to make it; one apportions the sacrifice for the gods and for men, the other "invents" the idea of sacrifice to the gods. Mythmakers have never been known for a slavish adherence to a single story to explain the ways of things. Clearly, also, Prometheus and Hermes share the quality of combining deceptiveness with beneficence.

In the case of Prometheus, approval of his acts of trickery is implied in his myth: he used deception in the good cause of helping the human race. The view of Hermes suggests an altogether different sensibility. Mortals do not profit directly from his trickery, and, as we'll see, he is a liar as well as a thief. He very much has his own interest at heart in a famous prank he played in his infancy—no brownie points for promoting human advancement in that episode—but the lightheartedness at the core of the story about Hermes the scoundrel babe presents a view of deception that we haven't yet encountered. It is foreign to the Old Testament—where deception meets with somber divine approval if it furthers the cause of the Israelites and is otherwise treated with indifference—and it is even more foreign to the New Testament, where it is excoriated. Told in the *Homeric Hymn to Hermes*, the story shows Hermes to be a trickster literally from day one. And a lovingly spun tale it is.

A precocious appetite and a larcenous mind were to blame for Hermes' first feat. On the evening of the day of his birth, he longed to eat meat, and he sneaked out of his cradle and stole fifty heifers from the herd of cattle that belonged to the gods. A born rascal, to whom deception came as natural as breathing, he made them walk zigzag and backward so their tracks would mislead any pursuer. His own footprints he masked by making himself large sandals out of newly sprouted myrtle twigs and tamarisk. After hiding in a distant barn all but two of the heifers, he slaughtered those two, but rather than eating the meat, he partitioned it into equal portions for the twelve Olympian gods—one of whom he is, which means that Hermes not only invented the sacrifice to the gods but made sure that in the future people would sacrifice to him as well as to his fellow Olympians. Then he hurried back home and returned to his cradle in shape-changer fashion: he entered the chamber by flowing through the door's keyhole like a vapor.

When Apollo, his half brother and the guardian of the herd, discovered the theft in the morning, he tried to follow the baffling tracks, and he learned about the thief from a man who had seen Hermes in the night. Informed about the amazing cattle-herding babe, Apollo found the culprit in his cradle and accused him of the theft. Hermes, snug under his baby blankie, denied it.

In the *Homeric Hymn to Hermes*, his rhetoric and wheedling arguments are startlingly glib in one so young. Consummate liar, he is all indignant innocence one moment and fervent appealer to reason the next. How could I, a day-old infant, possibly have stolen cattle? he remonstrates with Apollo. I haven't seen them. No one has told me a thing. I can provide no information about any cattle, nor claim the reward for information. Do I look like a cattle driver? I was born yesterday. Plus my feet are too tender for me to walk on the rough ground. Still, if you insist, I'm willing to swear a great oath by my father's head that I haven't stolen the cows and haven't seen anyone steal them—whatever "cows" may be—to tell the truth, I know of them only by hearsay.

Apollo has to laugh at the fabrications of the crafty tyke. He says to Hermes: "My dear boy, I can tell you'll be a great nuisance to people, swiping their goods or cattle; the gods will surely call you the Prince of Thieves." He carries Hermes to Zeus, and the two present the case to their father. Apollo reiterates his charges: a thief, a sneak, a clever liar spinning falsehoods with the greatest of ease and making himself out to be a tender infant incapable of herding cattle. (Interestingly, he does not tell Zeus that Hermes swore a false oath by Zeus's head. The poet does not explain the omission, and we're at liberty to guess that Apollo has no desire to see his little brother thunderstruck by Zeus punishing a blasphemer.)

When Apollo is through presenting his case, Hermes has his day in court. He starts by telling Zeus the mother of all lies: "Of course I will tell you the truth, for I am an honest boy. I cannot tell a lie." Then he repeats that he is no cattle thief, couldn't be because he is too weak. For good measure he adds that he never even left the house. Finally he plays his trump card, considerably modified for his audience. He protests to Zeus: "You yourself know I'm not guilty. I will even swear this great oath: *Verily, by the gods' richly decorated colonnades, I am innocent!*"

Zeus, far from being insulted at this scheming babe "so smoothly denying his guilt about the cattle," laughs out loud, charmed by his son's nerve and cleverness (and possibly by his swearing by an architectural feature). He orders plaintiff and defendant to make nice and Hermes to show Apollo where the cattle are hidden. Hermes obeys. There is one more sticky moment: Apollo threatens to tie up the cunning lad to keep him from doing more mischief. But Hermes charms his brother by playing the lyre he made from the shell of a tortoise. When the sun god laughs with joy at the sweet sound, Hermes makes a gift of it to him, and

Apollo learns to play it and sing. Apollo, in turn, gives Hermes his shining whip and makes him keeper of the herd. The two half brothers become fast friends after Hermes swears he will never again steal anything from Apollo. Apollo then gives Hermes other offices. He appoints him tender of all the cattle and flocks of sheep and horses and mules, and lord of lions, boars, and dogs. He also bestows on him a minor prophetic gift by allowing him access to three sacred sisters, fortune-tellers known as the Bee Maidens, who tell the truth when they've eaten honey but lie when they've been deprived of the sweet stuff. Finally, he makes him sole messenger to the underworld. The hymn concludes on a cautionary note: Hermes moves among the immortal gods and among mortal human beings. And though he serves a few of the latter, most of the time, when night has fallen, he deceives mortals.

The attitude of the *Homeric Hymn to Hermes* toward deception ranges from lighthearted to ambivalent. Hermes' deception is ultimately unsuccessful because all-knowing Zeus sees through it, and Hermes, in proclaiming his own truthfulness, acknowledges by implication that honesty is a virtue and is what Zeus wants from him. But at the same time there is delight in the cleverness and ingenuity that go into a well-wrought and -executed bit of blarney. Both Apollo and Zeus are amused by the pint-sized rascal god and neither takes offense at his lies. Their attitude may be a reflection of the indulgence adults show toward the mischievousness of youth, but it also suggests the storyteller's delight in imagination and invention, faculties needed to make a story or a clever lie.

Delight in the clever lie extends into our own popular culture—that of yesterday and that of today. We'll meet Till Eulenspiegel, who, at a time of great official piety, was a celebrated liar and prankster, and Baron Munchausen, whose tall tales drew a large readership. Folklore relishes the clever rascal, and our own inclination is to view with amusement the hoaxes of our contemporaries and to admire the elaborate edifice of lies—the products of imagination, inventiveness, and ingenuity—that con artists construct to sting their marks. Even if we peg as scoundrels men like Clifford Irving, the perpetrator of the Howard Hughes "autobiography" hoax in the early 1970s, or Konrad Kujau, writer of the Hitler Diaries in the early 1980s, we're impressed by the cleverness of the lies they told while selling their bill of goods, as is attested by best-selling books on their exploits. The New Testament may tell us that damnation awaits liars as soon as they have shuffled off their mortal coil but if their lies are ingenious (and we ourselves aren't harmed by them) we're liable to derive as much pleasure from them as any pagan did.

4

Admiration for the clever lie or trick or prank and delight in it are found throughout the pagan world and in the myths of very different cultures. The baby Hermes, for instance, is mirrored in Hinduism in stories about the childhood and adolescence of Krishna, thief of dairy products and of the hearts of cowherd maidens.

There are hundreds of variations of the tale of Krishna the Butter Thief. In every one of them, the infant Krishna, a chubby, unruly, mischievous boy, steals butter, milk, or curds in one ingenious way or another. He pilfers with equal abandon from his own mother's store or from the stores of others. In the process he may have to be clever, climbing up to jars that are suspended from the ceiling or using a stick to reach them, and he may break them, get his hands covered with butter, smear it all over his face and body, feed it to monkeys. When he is caught, he offers a variety of clever denials, all of them to the effect that he did not eat the butter. No, he didn't. The reason he is covered with the sweet, creamy stuff is that he tried to keep ants from it, or was using it to cool the chafed skin under his bracelets, or the shepherd maiden accusing him of thievery is simply lying (talk about brass!)—how could he, with his stubby little arms, possibly have reached the butter? Disarmed by the clever rascal's inventiveness, his mother and other accusers have to laugh and forgive him.

This link between thievery and lying is standard in trickster tales. Tricksters are no respecters of property. One of their functions is to redistribute goods and surreptitiously pass on knowledge and skills by stealing them out of the hands of the haves and passing them on to the have-nots, in the process making things more equal. But the habitual thief also tends to be a habitual liar, not merely because theft is itself the fraudulent acquisition of property and anyone used to larceny tends not to be squeamish about violating the truth, but because the habitual thief is caught at least on occasion and will then use lies to try to wiggle out of a sticky situation. The plea, in time-honored fashion, will be: "I stole nothing; I found the thing; it was given to me; I have no idea how it got into my house, barn, bag, pocket." The trickster in mythology goes by that name rather than by the name "thief" or "liar" because those who invented him were drawing on real-life models and those models stole *and* lied—and cheated, bamboozled, and made false promises to have things their way. Not for nothing do we say "lie, steal, and cheat" in the same breath. In the case of the infant Krishna, lying is an integral part of the Butter Thief stories. Teller and audience are as delighted by the ingenuity of the lies as they are by the adroitness of the thievery.

A thief, a liar, an incorrigible prankster each moment inventing another trick, Krishna nevertheless charms. He is a glutton for sensual pleasure and ever ready to employ ruses to get his own way. At other times he steals the clothing of bathing maidens to get their undivided attention and multiplies himself a hundredfold to be able to dance with a hundred girls. But all his trickery is courtship of life and love. When he steals hearts and seduces he does so in order to transport, and the reward for those who allow themselves to be seduced is great.

The poet Sur Das composed a constellation of Butter Thief poems infused with such fondness for the trickster infant god that one cannot read them without smiling. In one of them, a shepherd maiden whose milk and curd Krishna has made a habit of stealing explains to Krishna's mother what happened when she finally discovered the thief. There he was, changing his shape before her eyes, one arm turning into four, dazzling her as he disappeared. Then in a flash he returned, his butter-spattered body sparkling, star-sprinkled by the chariot of the moon.

> *Then he laughs and laughs, this lad*
> *who protects the pious, warns the wicked;*
> *and all his fast adventures, says Sur,*
> *turn me and send me spinning.*

5

Tricksters turn the world and send it spinning. Advertently or inadvertently they turn things topsy-turvy—bones for the immortals, meat for men, but also sickness for mortals, courtesy of Prometheus, or access to a boundless reservoir of love, courtesy of Krishna, or knowledge of good and evil at the expense of struggle and pain for Adam and Eve, courtesy of the serpent.

Although tricksters sometimes play a role in the creation of the world and people out of raw materials, much more often their creativity lies in their transforming an already existing world into one that is different, sometimes better, sometimes worse, but always more interesting. After the transformation—the fall of man, the arrival of women, the invention of perjury and eloquence, theft and profit—the world is profoundly changed. Prelapsarian innocence is gone, the golden age a distant memory. People now have appetites and fears. They love and hate, propagate, suffer and grow old miserably. They hunt and harvest. They kill and they bury their dead. They make tools and weapons, sing and dance and play musical instruments. They study the stars and keep records of transactions. They tell stories. They ask questions and find answers, and change their minds about the answers. And they think and think and think. In other words, the world has become the world as we know it, grief and terror, heartache and loss, "desire and longings that wear out the body"—and the special glory that turns the first sin into *felix culpa*, "happy fault," despite all this.

Myths are stories, but they can also be coded expressions of subconscious awareness. The trickster is, in the words of Lewis Hyde, who wrote a dazzling and profound book about the connection between the trickster and art, "the mythic embodiment of ambiguity and ambivalence, doubleness and duplicity, contradiction and paradox." Hyde identifies the trickster as the personification of creativity itself, the inventor of potential alternate realities created, for instance, by talking about an event not the way it was but the way it might have been. Even the most mundane lie, say "I did not eat the butter; I tried to get the ants away from it," creates such an alternate imaginative reality. We'll reencounter the tie between deception and this kind of creativity.

Most tricksters (Prometheus being a notable exception) are liars. They use language, the means of communication, to furnish false information, with the intent to deceive. But false information can be conveyed in nonverbal ways as well. The outright lie is only one of the many ways of deception (although the least labor-intensive). A trap, for instance, is a visual lie. No one tells the intended victim: "Walk down this path; it's safe." But effort has been expended to make the path itself "lie" about its safety. Only when the leaf-covered twigs are stepped on does the flimsy structure give way and the victim fall into the pit. Tricksters use all the tools of deception—lies, traps, misrepresentation (the better part of the offering arranged so as to look unpalatable), disguises, and so forth—to get what they want.

The transformation wrought by the trickster can be on the scale of an altogether new world but it can be more modest as well. It can be as simple as the violation of an expected "natural" outcome. In folk tales, the trickster is invariably weaker, smaller, less powerful or ferocious than his opponent in a conflict. Yet he wins because he is more cunning or devious—that is, *because* he is tricky. In ordinary life, the same can hold. When relationships are characterized by an imbalance of power, a lie or other trick can win the day for the weaker player. It's easy to take candy from a baby, but try taking it from an adult, especially one who is stronger than you, and the challenge is obvious. A time-honored recourse is deception. Tell the strong-as-an-ox lover of sweets who is jealously guarding his stash that you're under orders from his superior to collect the candy, or that you've just found out that some of it is poisoned and you'll take it to the police for examination. Or divert his attention and substitute a bag filled with pebbles for the one filled with sweets. . . . A Colt .45 ("Your candy, and nobody gets hurt") may be an equalizer when it comes to naked aggression, but deception can be just as effective.

Given the efficacy of trickery when we're outmatched in terms of strength or power, it is small wonder that tricksters are the heroes of servants and slaves, and the disenfranchised in general, who can vicariously participate in the trouncing of some large, dumb, powerful brute by the underdog with quick wits and an inexhaustible bag of tricks. Brer Rabbit, New World incarnation of the

African trickster hare, outwits Brer Fox, Brer Wolf, and Brer Bear. He turns upside down the natural order of things, according to which superior strength and clout will always win. When he is caught by Brer Fox, Brer Rabbit's minutes are numbered unless he convinces his enemy that he'd prefer any mode of execution to being thrown in the briar patch. The West African spider, coerced by the lion to relinquish all his food, will go hungry unless he can make the greedy lion believe that the motley coat he desires will be forthcoming provided he allows himself to be tied up by the spider so tightly that he cannot move.

Although self-defense is often at the heart of these encounters, this is by no means always the case. The trickster can delight in mischief and pranks for the sake of a joke or use guile to satisfy his prodigious appetites—which can turn him into a glutton or a sexual predator—or can simply play tricks because he glories in his ability to outwit, dupe, and triumph over those who in the ordinary hierarchy of things are his superiors. As a glutton, he eats forbidden fruit; as a sexual predator, he uses lies and trickery to gain access to those sexually off limits to him—virgins, faithful wives, the daughters of his betters, the stallions of giants. He dupes or charms the ignorant and the unwilling, mates with them, impregnates them, and gives not a hoot about the consequences. Hermes sired Pan and, according to one tradition, he came to the mother in the guise of a he-goat. Iktome, the spider trickster of the Brulé Sioux, disguised himself as an old woman with a "growth" between her legs, which, Iktome told an innocent young woman, would only go away if he put it between her legs. The young woman thought this an unattractive idea but was willing to help. However, although the growth shrank after Iktome penetrated her, it always grew large again after a little while. Undiscouraged, Iktome suggested they keep trying, and the young woman, who had learned to like the curious procedure, agreed. Obviously, in this arena as in others, tricksters get through lies what they want from those who wouldn't give it if they knew the truth. Rape is not the trickster's way; making the unwilling willing by deception is.

6

So what of the "deceiver of all mankind," that great malefactor, horror of creation, enemy of God: Beelzebub, Lucifer, 'aduw Allah, Diabolus—in short, the devil? Does he fit into the trickster mold? Yes and no. Yes because he is obviously a supernatural entity devoted to getting his way by trickery, no because he is a one-dimensional fiend. A bare-bones history of him as he appears in Christianity alone would fill a book. One of his ancestors is the Persian Zoroastra's Ahriman, the prince of demons, god of darkness and falsehood, creator of death. Ahriman's first pleasure was the first lie spoken by the first human couple, and he is locked in continuous struggle with Ormazd, the god of light and truth and creator of life. But he is also related to the Satan of postexilic (after 538 B.C.) Judaism, who is no longer the prosecutor of God's heavenly court found in the Hebrew Bible but the spirit of perversion, darkness, and destruction.

The Christian devil derives his name from the Greek *diabolos*, "slanderous." He is renowned for his cunning and wiles, but unlike tricksters in the pagan world, he lacks all redeeming characteristics. An active force for evil, he was a figure custom-tailored for Christianity's view of the cosmos as it was developed by the Church Fathers. St. Augustine hammered out the dogma of Original Sin and the Fall and did it in terms of the story of Satan entering the Garden of Eden to tempt Eve. The Christian view early on cast things as either good or evil, with little shading, and by the late Middle Ages hyperdefined the world in those terms. Accordingly, the devil is the enemy of God and man dedicated to the world's ruin, which he strives to achieve through deception, being a liar and the father of lies (John 8:44). He was once a holy angel but fell away from God and became the tempter of mankind. To him and to the weakness of the first human couple do we owe original sin and the sorry state of affairs in which we find ourselves.

Christianity lacks the pagan world's capacity for ambiguity, and it is not surprising that its trickster figure is single-mindedly devoted to the spoiling and ruin of creation. Like pagan tricksters, the devil transforms through deception, but, unlike them, he is leached of all motives but one: to steal souls away from God. Although ingenious in matching temptation to the victim, he is uncreative. He turns the potentially saved into the eternally damned, blotted from the book of life because "the wages of sin *is* death" (Romans 6:23). The hellhound—all questions of his successes on the souls-snatching front aside—is a one-trick dog.

In folklore, the devil has some of the characteristics of pagan tricksters because Christianity incorporated pagan elements in its own symbolism. Old Nick owes his goat's foot, horns, and shaggy fur to Pan, son of Hermes, and he is a shape-changer, capable of appearing as a toad, a lascivious woman, a handsome demon lover, even as a priest preaching against sin in a church. One of the great evil documents of Europe, the *Malleus Maleficarum* (*Hammer of Witches*), codified the devil of folklore and gave him credentials among the literate. It became a vade mecum of witch-hunters for more than a century, and the harm its preposterous claims inflicted is incalculable.

Martin Luther, a strong believer in the Evil One, saw him as "a marvellous cunning workman," full of "subtle sleights." The devil, he claimed, deceives by planting false opinions against Christ in the heads of those he bewitches, who, as a result, turn to idolatry and are damned. If this sleight does not strike us as particularly subtle, it is because we have been exposed to the more interesting devil of literature, who gives knowledge and power to Faust in exchange for his immortal soul. Mephistopheles, bitter, articulate, sophisticated, tricks the man who already, by his own free will, has set foot on the road to perdition. He is a jester, ironist, and master psychologist. But the modern world has gone even further. In Mikhail Bulgakov's satirical gem *The Master and Margarita*, Satan appears as an amoral entity who deceives with glee and panache and whose ability to effect changes for the better turns him into a figure that bears a strong resemblance to the trickster of old.

7

Myths are the stories we tell ourselves to explain what we find in the world, to foster a sense—or illusion—of understanding regarding the enormous, unintelligible mass of things we find in the world and in ourselves. Water, land, sky, sun, animals, trees, where did they come from? Where did we come from? Why do we die and what happens after our death? How will the world end? How did evil first appear? Who gave animals their names? How did we get to be tool- and music-making, crops-planting, war-waging, talking, forward-thinking, remembering beings? Who or what gave us art and numbers and π and created the immutable fact that the square of the hypotenuse of a right triangle is the sum of the squares of the sides? Who invented writing and the ability to organize and categorize, create laws, record events? Where did we get the gift of fire? Why do women menstruate?* Why do Jewish males have to be circumcised? What is the ultimate answer to "life, the universe, and everything"? (Forty-two, according to Deep Thought, the supercomputer of Douglas Adams' sci-fi novel *The Hitchhiker's Guide to the Galaxy*.)

But myths do more than explain. They have also been used for propaganda purposes. Since long before modern myths like the divine right of kings, or the witches' Sabbath, or the Aryan superrace flickered on collective screens, stories have been invented to buttress the position of priestly castes and ruling segments of societies. Embodying the mythmakers' attitudes toward the world, myths have planted fears and discredited half of humanity. Hesiod and the tradition inside which he wrote classified women as beings intrinsically inferior to men and dealt with them as such. Obviously any myth accounting for the existence of women also had to account for their inferiority. At the same time the right myth could be used to maintain the status quo. A deeply misogynistic story like that of Pandora, the first woman—beautiful, treacherous, lying, and the bringer of all ills—did nicely. So, for ancient Persia, did the Primeval Woman of Zoroastrianism, also known as the Whore, who provoked Ahriman to kill the Primeval Man and thereby corrupt creation. (Still, the Whore was also something of a midwife, metaphorically speaking, since from the corpse of Primeval Man mankind was created.) Patriarchal Judaism, with its ethos of women as chattel, invented Eve, Adam's rib, weak, tricked by pride, responsible for all human woes. Christianity, via St. Paul and the

---

*Because Ahriman, the prince of darkness, kissed the female demon Jahi.

Church Fathers, accepted this invention of woman divinely appointed as inferior as unimpeachable authority, and it became a pernicious tautology, cited for centuries by men of the cloth to preach the sex's weakness, inferior intellect, and natural inclination toward depravity.

The infamous Foundation Myth section of Plato's *Republic* no doubt oversimplifies how myths come into being, but clearly Plato recognized their usefulness as tools to control the populace. In outlining the education of the Republic's Guardians, Socrates tells his friend Glaucon that in order to make the people in his utopian community accept their lot in life as members of different social classes, he will tell them a story of how God fashioned people by mixing gold, silver, or base metals in their composition, depending on whether they would be rulers or farmers or other workers. Socrates wonders whether there is any way to make people believe the ridiculous story. Glaucon's answer is no, not in the first generation, but the second and later generations may believe it.

Plato has been excoriated for this suggestion to use myth as a calculated lie in the service of propaganda, but his approach is understandable. He railed against the prevailing myths of lascivious, deceitful, shape-changing gods and called them nothing more than scandalous inventions of the poets. Small wonder he had no qualms about suggesting fighting invention with invention by the fabrication of a "benign" myth in the service of social harmony.

Explanation or propaganda, some myths are simplicity itself. Judeo-Christian Genesis makes one sin, that of aspiring to be godlike, the root cause for a great many other things. The ancient Greeks, compulsive storytellers and compulsive seekers of cause and effect, delighted in giving more particular answers: Hermes made the first lyre (and is—a pox on the pun!—the first glib liar); Prometheus taught people how to make medicines; the Judgment of Paris was to blame for the Trojan War; Mount Etna is the forge of Hephaestus; the mottoes "Know thyself" and "Moderation in all things" were the invention of Apollo; and so forth. They also compulsively personified nature and concepts: the Muses represent art and artistic inspiration, Hades the invisible presence of death, Aphrodite romantic love, the Fates inexorable destiny.

But the Greeks obviously did not have a monopoly on inventive theogony and cosmogony. World mythology is an immense tapestry of entities and their stories. Elephant gods and river goddesses, benevolent and malevolent jinns, avatars, and rock giants, primordial snake goddesses and prophets, drivers of the sun chariot and gods of war—supernatural beings have been tied from time immemorial to every observed physical and imagined conceptual niche in the world. Myths are also fluid. They can evolve slowly over the course of many centuries or change rapidly when merging with other myths brought by invading people or under the pressure of reform movements that sweep across the land. Two examples of countless instances: Zoroaster's reforms turned the Indian gods of light and truth into ancient Persia's evil and lying spirits, and in pagan Scandinavia, the medieval Christian conception of the devil preached by missionaries resulted in Loki acquiring some of the devil's traits.

All religions show such influences—Judaism incorporated elements of Assyro-Babylonian mythology and Zoroastrianism, and Zoroastrianism also influenced Christianity and Islam; Christ, like Krishna, is an avatar, a god incarnate appearing on earth at a time of crisis, and the virgin birth by which he made his appearance is common in Greek mythology. Even the most determinedly nonsyncretic religions have assimilated elements of other religions.

All this said, it is obvious that one of the great many things mythmakers of all times and cultures had to grapple with in their quest to explain the world was deception. They saw it in their fellow man and woman; it was obviously here to stay. So where did it come from? Well, one answer was that if mankind possessed the ability to deceive, supernatural entities had to represent deception in its purest state or had to excel at it. Enter Ahriman, the Lie, and Satan, the Father of Lies. If men and women used deceit for getting away with theft or for sexual conquests, or to destroy enemies, it would be absurd to assume the gods did not do the same, and more skillfully, by using abilities men did not possess. Enter Krishna as the Butter Thief, and amorous Zeus in the guise of a swan who bamboozles faithful Leda, and Loki as an old woman.

These two possibilities for the supernatural representation of deception—deception in its purest state or skillfully deceptive gods—respectively fit into mythologies that tell of a strong polarity and battle between good and evil and into mythologies in which any given god may have a mix of the two and hence be a closer imitation of a human being. The former assign supernatural deceptiveness almost exclusively to the forces of evil. The latter tend to be more lenient. Those who made them tolerated a larger degree of ambiguity and saw an admirable inventiveness in the clever lie or ruse. More than that, they were aware of the link between lying and the creative imagination and made trickery a metaphor for creativity. The abundance of tricksters suggests that mythmakers in a great many places and ages have said: "Let there be scores of deceptive gods and an abundance of lying and thieving supernatural scoundrels."

And there were.

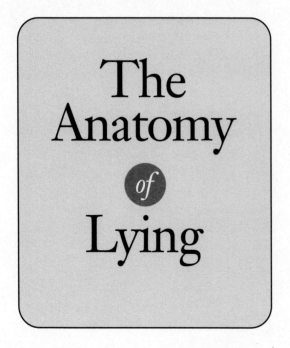

The
Anatomy
of
Lying

Why Liars Lie

"It is a far, far better thing I do than I have ever done."

Charles Dickens, *A Tale of Two Cities*

". . . an odious, damnèd lie.
Upon my soul a lie, a wicked lie."

William Shakespeare, *Othello*

1

On an unseasonably warm spring day in London in 1922, a young man named Theodore composes a telegram to a young woman named Emily: "Slight accident on way to station STOP not serious at all but a little indisposed STOP come same train tomorrow STOP." He pays a florin to have the telegram sent, then, gaily feigning a limp to amuse a female companion who has waited while he has been jotting down his note, he goes off to have lunch with her. Dinner follows, and then a nightcap with friends of theirs.

Meanwhile Emily, who is very much in love with Theodore, waits with a glad heart for the hour when she'll meet him at the station and take him to the cottage she has rented in the country for days of bliss with him. When his telegram arrives, her disappointment is crushing and she sees his accident as a sign sent by Providence telling her that the happiness she anticipated is an illusion and that her love for Theodore, and his for her, cannot last. The only way to avoid a heartbreak that will kill her is to leave and cut all ties to him. When he arrives the next day, the one person on earth who might have made him happy is gone.

Theodore and Emily are characters in Aldous Huxley's *Antic Hay*, a novel whose parade of fake artists, con men, pseudoscientists, dreamers, and schemers would be perfect in a book titled *A Short Encyclopedia of Deception*. The scene is particular but the point it makes is general: Somewhere in the great city of London, on an unseasonably warm day in the third decade of the twentieth century, a man lied to a woman.

Why did Theodore lie to Emily? Was it because he had once been in love with the notorious Vivian Viveash and caved in under her threat that she'd never speak to him again unless he stayed and had lunch with her? Was it because compared to that femme fatale poor Emily seemed entirely too homespun, the anticipated woodland walks and flower gathering too rustic, the candlelight supper in the cottage nestled in honeysuckle and hollyhocks, and the piano playing and cuddling in each other's arms too dull? Was it because he fooled himself into thinking that lying to the woman he loved was of little consequence—he could always pick up where he'd left off? Or was the reason more recondite? Did he subconsciously know that it was not in his nature to make happiness last (or that lasting happiness was not the way of the world)? Huxley, unfailingly aware of the complexity of people and their relationships, hints at all of the above. But if the reason Theodore lied is complicated, his motive was simple. He preferred spending the day with Vivian rather than with Emily and did not want to ruin his relationship with Emily by telling her the truth: "Cannot take train today because woman friend insists I lunch with her STOP will come same train tomorrow STOP."

The moral? In London and elsewhere on the globe, then and at other times, men have said to women things they knew to be untrue, with the intention of deceiving them, women have said such things to men, men have said them to men, and women have said them to women. And sometimes the motive (as opposed to the reason) has been simply to be here rather than there, or with X rather than Y.

What motivates people to lie? The answer—an infinite number of things—seems to shut the gate on further inquiry unless we can recruit the odd astronomer, inured to cataloging the uncountable, for the job. But the number hides a simple fact: when it comes to intention, any lie, from the plainest to the most intricately wrought, falls into one of just two categories. The glaringly obvious first intention is to keep the truth from being known. "It wasn't I who ruined your carpet, slept with your brother, inflated my expense account, committed the crime I'm charged with" fall into that category, and often suspicion by someone who smells a rat prompts the lie. Category Two is a variation on the same theme, the intention now being to make someone believe a falsehood when the belief benefits the liar. Examples: "I recommended you to the general, I spent twelve months in Antarctica collecting data on the ozone layer, I'm a direct descendant of the Duke of Wellington, my husband and I are separated." In either version, the unvarnished aim is deception, and the standard definition of lying—telling or otherwise communicating a falsehood with the intention to deceive—applies.

Equally obvious is the answer to why the liar wants the truth kept from being known or a falsehood believed. The fear of losing something—money, a job, a marriage, power, respect, reputation, love, life, freedom, comfort, enjoyment, cooperation, etc., etc.—is one reason; the desire to gain something—a better job, admission to a desired school, the chance to hang out with kids our parents tell us to avoid, sexual favors, money, revenge, love, cooperation, respect and admiration, control and power, comfort and convenience, and so forth—is another. Of course, depending on the liar's mental state, the desire for something may appear as the fear of not getting it; the intense desire to marry the adored creature can become the desperate fear of being thwarted, just as the wish for convenience can be the fear of inconvenience—millions have lied to avoid an argument.

Jonathan Swift, who anatomized evil as effectively as anyone before or after him, traced lying to the same two sources via his peripatetic ship's surgeon, Lemuel Gulliver. When Gulliver, that curious concoction—part mouthpiece of his satirical author, part naïf, part stand-in for European depravity—arrives in Houyhnhnmland on his fourth journey, his main challenge is to explain European society to the noble Houyhnhnms. The rational horses, in perfect harmony with one another and their world, are baffled by so many things, and Gulliver spends the better part of his stay trying to render comprehensible to his curious master such puzzling activities as murder, theft, gaming, whoring, war, perjury, rape, forgery, drinking, and so on. The despicable Yahoos, who bear an uncomfortable resemblance to Gulliver, help somewhat as an analogy, but lacking speech and intelligence, they can never aspire to humanity's thoughtful cruelties and refined perversions.

Among the human peculiarities Gulliver's master finds puzzling in the extreme is that of lying. "To say the thing which is not," is his semantic approximation of a concept that does not exist in Houyhnhnmland, and when Gulliver tries to explain lying and false representation, the sensible horse's objection is enlightened:

> The Use of Speech was to make us understand one another, and to receive Information of Facts; now if any one *said the Thing which was not*, these Ends were defeated; because I cannot properly be said to understand him; and I am so far from receiving Information, that he leaves me worse than in Ignorance; for I am led to believe a Thing *Black* when it is *White*, and *Short* when it is *Long*.*

Well put! And so wonderfully innocent and so entirely missing the point of lying, which is of course precisely to lead someone to believe the thing which is not. Gulliver's satirical comment? "And these were all the Notions he had concerning that Faculty of *Lying*, so perfectly well understood, and so universally practised among human Creatures."

Swift's point is that in a society of rational creatures not subject to fears or desires, lying would be an impossibility, and the passage is a small part of the Dean's attack on that pet eighteenth-century, Age of Enlightenment notion of man as *animal rationale*—an absurd piece of self-flattery by beings that are barely *rationis capax* (capable of reason) according to Swift's famed distinction.

The satirist was not interested in subtleties that would have di-

---

*Compare the Houyhnhnm's complaint with St. Augustine's thought on the subject from a religious point of view: "Now it is evident that speech was given to man, not that men might therewith deceive one another, but that one man might make his thoughts known to another. To use speech, then, for the purpose of deception, and not for its appointed end, is a sin." *The Enchiridion.*

luted the argument he was making—namely, that lying is an odd and contemptible way of dealing with others. Which is why he does not make Gulliver ponder whether lying may not be acceptable or even necessary under certain circumstances.

Gulliver also does not point out a fairly obvious problem with the Houyhnhnm's definition. "Saying the thing which is not" is a poor translation for "lying" since in the right context even the most determinedly truthful among us may do the former without qualms. Take irony. Saying the opposite of what we mean is certainly an example of saying the thing which is not, but it is just as certainly not lying since the aim to deceive is the furthest thing from our minds. In fact, irony misfires unless our listener recognizes the incongruity between our true attitude and what we are saying. And the same goes for all manner of verbal tomfooleries. Kidding, banter, understatement, etc., count on the joke—which is the discrepancy between the words and their intended meaning—being appreciated.

All of *Gulliver's Travels* and most of Swift's creative output in general are consummate examples of an author hiding behind a variety of guises and saying the thing which is not—albeit in the service of satirical attacks on very real abuses. From the mad "projectors" of *A Tale of a Tub* and *A Modest Proposal* to Gulliver, Swift's speakers are masks for the author in the service of satire. But Swift was also not in the least reluctant to engage in leg pulling for the sake of pure fun. Gulliver's invented publisher, his "cousin Sympson," professes in an introductory note to the reader that everything Gulliver wrote is the truth "and indeed, the Author was so distinguished for his Veracity, that it became a Sort of Proverb among his Neighbours at Redriff, when anyone affirmed a Thing, to say, it was as true as if Mr. Gulliver had spoke it."

The 1727 edition went one step further, with Gulliver writing to Sympson to express his contempt for people who suggested that his talking horses were "a mere fiction of mine own brain." Not so! In the two years he spent in the company of the Houyhnhnms he was able—although only with the "utmost Difficulty"—"to remove that infernal Habit of Lying, Shuffling, Deceiving, and Equivocating, so deeply rooted in the very Souls of all my Species, especially the *Europeans*." Swift is having fun, but the amusement generated by this kind of discrepancy between what is said and what is intended would be as puzzling to his noble horses as a garden-variety lie: the sense of humor of all of Houyhnhnmland wouldn't fill a thimble. Even if Gulliver were to use the most transparent irony, say he called the sight of brawling Yahoos charming, his master would not only *not* be amused but would think Gulliver had lost his mind.

Still, irony (from the Greek *eiron*, "dissembler in speech") *does* make its home in the same region of our minds in which the capacity for lying lives. Both take advantage of our ability to divorce our actual knowledge or attitude about a thing from how we communicate about the thing. And the same holds for much of humor in general. But Swift's concern as a satirist when he showed the Houyhnhnm baffled by lying was not to lambaste humanity for its use of irony—of which he was the great master—or its penchant for joking by saying what is known not to be so, but for its great facility with lying, and his innocent horses and their inadequate definition are merely devices in that attack.

"So perfectly well understood, and so universally practised" by us (or at least by us in 1726, when *Gulliver's Travels* was published), lying makes no sense in a society whose members have in mind the common good, are "naturally" divided into benign masters and contented servants, whose marriages are based on unvarying mutual liking, whose needs are simple and met by bountiful resources, and whose appetites are modest. The illicit desires that harrow humankind, represented in one scheme as the seven deadly sins— pride, covetousness, lust, envy, gluttony, anger, and sloth—are outside the Houyhnhnms' vocabulary, and the deception they invite is alien to creatures who desire nothing but what they can obtain without effort or conflict and whose imagination is, to put it mildly, limited. Fear, that other great engine for deception, is equally missing. The Houyhnhnms are threatened by nothing and see even death as part of the natural order of things no more to be dreaded than going to sleep.

Swift's picture of an idyllic place populated by beings that have a before-the-Fall innocence brings to mind another picture—one in the attic—that shows the real world, our world. In that picture all that the Houyhnhnms have is absent and all that they lack is present. They have unperturbed peace of mind and contentment. We do not. They live in a land in which little effort can satisfy the modest needs of all inhabitants. We do not (although we might if we put our minds to it, and if those of us with much became happy with less—not exactly a realistic prospect). They lack immoderate desire and fear. We have both and in an infinite variety. The environment required for deception is one in which desire, be it for people, objects, reputation, love, or the untold number of other things we want, exceeds satisfaction and in which fear is unavoidable and runs the gamut from minor anxiety to stark terror. Swift knew that it would take a cold day in hell for us to become like his fabulous horses. Quite apart from his official position as a theologian who had no choice but to accept the doctrine of the Fall of man and consequent loss of innocence, he knew that we are governed by desire and fear because our grasp will ever fall short of our reach and our fears are legion.

2

What ultimately concerns us as people living in an imperfect world is not the root causes of lies but the nature of any given lie—is it trivial or substantial?—the motive behind it—is it self-serving, is it intended to harm or be beneficial?—and its effects, both immediate and long-term. Deception is widespread, and it appears in so many different ways, and has so many effects—ranging from minuscule to fatal—that it can safely be said to be more complicated than anything else we do that carries a moral cargo. Moral philosophers and religious thinkers have grappled with it throughout the ages, typically categorizing lies according to underlying motive and effect on those lied to and on society in general, and according to the corresponding degree of moral failure or sinfulness. Opinions vary greatly: There are absolutists, who claim that any and all lies, under any and all circumstances, are evil, and utilitarians, who see deception by itself as morally neutral and judge it entirely by its consequences. The latter use common sense as a guide to determine which lies are reprehensible and which are "harmless" or even "beneficial."

Calling any action that needs to be justified "morally neutral" is suspect—we do not as a rule feel the need to justify, to ourselves or others, having told the truth—but most of us are utilitarians of sorts. Erasmus is our standard-bearer. He argued that the outright condemnation of all falsehood is futile and the idea espoused by many theologians that not even one harmless lie should be told, even if it saved the bodies and souls of all humankind, runs counter to common sense. Erasmus distrusted zealots, and his recourse to common sense breathed new life into sixteenth-century learning, but, as we'll see, common sense can be an erratic guide to moral judgment. When it comes to deception, it is easily swayed to lead different folk down very different trails and to very different locations.

The absolutists seem to have it easier at first glance. But, living in the world, they too tend to see the need for assigning degrees of severity based on motive and effect and to categorize lies accordingly. A few examples among many: In two seminal works on deception, St. Augustine's "On Lying" and "Against Lying," the methodical saint put lies into eight categories ranging, in order of decreasing severity, from the lie told in the teaching of religion to the lie harmful to no one and beneficial in protecting someone from physical defilement. Augustine's conclusion was that all lies are sins and hence to be refrained from. The fact that he called the lie uttered in the teaching of religion "a deadly one which should be avoided and shunned from afar" argues that he differentiated between lies in terms of degree of sinfulness, but his conclusion about even so-called beneficial lies—his example is the lie told to a gravely ill man that his son is alive, when in fact he is dead, in order not to imperil the man's recovery—is that they are wrong. If once it is granted that one ought to lie about the son's life for the sake of that patient's health, "little by little and bit by bit this evil will grow and by gradual accession will slowly increase until it becomes such a mass of wicked lies that it will be utterly impossible to find any means of resisting such a plague grown to huge proportions through small additions."

Thomas Aquinas, addressing St. Augustine's arguments, distinguished between officious, jocose, and mischievous lies. The first two, told, respectively, "for the sake of our neighbor's good" and for amusement "where some little pleasure is intended," are venial sins. The third, which is contrary to charity or told to injure one's neighbor, is a mortal sin. Needless to say, Christians are to eschew all sins.

Immanuel Kant, absolutist extraordinaire, took an even more extreme stance. He delighted in the categorical statement: if we are considered as moral beings, then "the greatest violation of man's duty to himself . . . is the opposite of veracity, lying." To lie is "a crime of man against his own person and a baseness which must make a man contemptible in his own eyes." His answer to the question whether a lie may not be permitted if it is told to save the life of a man hunted by someone out to murder him follows a tortuous (and eminently debatable) route to the conclusion: "To be truthful (honest) in all declarations, therefore, is a sacred and absolutely commanding decree of reason, limited by no expediency."

As we'll see, Kant is not a lone voice crying in the modern wilderness in claiming that all lying is evil, no matter the liar's motive. But the most thorough and thoughtful modern treatment on the morality of lying, Sissela Bok's 1978 work *Lying: Moral Choice in Public and Private Life*, parts company with him. Bok is no apologist for liars and finds suspect all lies, even those told in the "disinterested" wish to help someone in need (benevolent motives are easily mixed with less altruistic ones, she argues), but she concedes that, yes, there are cases in which lying is justified.

3

It takes the very peculiar mind of an Immanuel Kant not to be influenced by the motive behind a given lie in forming an opinion of it. Most of us do not have such a mind, and a telling exercise is to look at a random list of intentions hiding behind lies people have told and to monitor the deflections in a hypothetical approval/disapproval meter as the needle jumps from reading to reading in the range STRONGLY AGAINST, SOMEWHAT AGAINST, SOMEWHAT FOR, STRONGLY FOR. Let's say the liar in question is young Theodore (or a chameleonic version of him leading an excessively interesting life), freshly back in London after having lost the love of his life. Let's run down a list of Theodore's possible intentions in telling a variety of lies, keeping one eye on the approval/disapproval meter:

Theodore lies in order
- To get out of a tedious social obligation.
- To blacken the reputation of a business rival.
- To get out of helping a friend move.
- To keep from hurting his parents' feelings.
- To avoid an embarrassing admission of ignorance or lack of money.
- To keep from his wife the truth about a child he fathered before he was married.
- To have an excuse for missing a meeting considered important by his boss.
- To get a woman to sleep with him by claiming to be a marine biologist.
- To keep secret a crime he committed ten years earlier and deeply regrets.
- To protect himself from harm by the thugs of a police state.
- To remain a closet homosexual.
- To keep from his wife the truth about his having an affair.
- To keep his landlord from knowing he has a cat.
- To get a job at a law firm by claiming he graduated from an Ivy League school.
- To conceal from Emily preparations for her surprise birthday party.
- To cover for a teammate who missed practice and has promised to reform.
- To keep his I-told-you-so father from learning that he has been fired.
- To get even with someone who he knows has done him harm.
- To hide his drinking.
- To get a job by claiming he is a veteran.
- To sell as genuine a fabricated account of his childhood, alleging abuse and neglect.

- To save his young sister from the gallows by confessing to a crime he didn't commit.
- To get someone to have unprotected sex with him although he knows he has AIDS.
- To bring people around to his view on something by inventing supporting anecdotes.
- To keep one of his children from learning a distressing truth.
- To sell his romance fiction by using a female pseudonym.
- To get hired by a firm suspected of polluting in order to gather evidence.
- To pay less income tax.

The list is potentially endless, and the needle of anyone's approval/disapproval meter is likely to fluctuate wildly.

Not only will anyone's judgment vary from lie to lie, but different people may judge any given lie quite differently. Personality, morality, religious upbringing, view of the world—all enter into one's sense of right or wrong and influence judgment on whether or not a lie is deplorable, forgivable, or even laudable. Obviously, anyone who tends not to lie except under very special circumstances will in general be more inclined to disapprove on principle than someone who thinks of it as the coin of the realm, used hourly in dealing with people by anyone with any smarts. Someone for whom family loyalty is important will be more ready to approve of a man lying to save his sister from the gallows than someone with little family feeling and the pet peeve that criminals are getting away with murder. Plus, unless we are made of rarefied stuff indeed, we are in general less likely to come down hard on someone who lies to promote a cause we are in favor of. Environmentalists are likely to cheer the investigative reporter infiltrating a polluting chemical company whereas a major shareholder may find the action highly objectionable. Animal lovers are likely to forgive the cat owner lying about his pet. Homosexuals may approve or disapprove of lying to remain in the closet, depending on their own state or on how tolerant they are of the choice to hide one's sexual orientation.

Experience, too, enters the picture. The landlord who has been victimized by a tenant unclear on the concept of a litter box for his cat is liable to lavish severe disapproval on that lie even if he or she is fond of cats. Someone who was deprived of a decent education may be ready to forgive a lie about educational background on a résumé whereas a graduate from a demanding school may bristle at someone claiming false laurels. People who routinely cheat on their income tax are unlikely to disapprove of lying on tax forms— unless they disapprove of their own behavior or convince themselves that they have mitigating excuses that others do not have. And so forth.

Then there may be the question of gender. If Theodore were Theodora lying to cheat on her husband, using a male pseudonym to get published, keeping from her husband the truth about a child she had before they were married, judgment may be different, the slant having to do with personal or cultural biases.

But things are more complicated yet. Take Theodore's lying to get out of helping a friend move. Does he do so because he's a sluggard who wants to avoid the inconvenience? Or does he lie because he has a bad back and knows from experience that, no matter how resolved he may be to help only in the packing, he is bound to lend a hand lifting something, which will then lay him up for a week? Or because he has a deeply neurotic reaction to moving stemming from his rootless childhood that he can't bring himself to talk about and that years of therapy might just begin to address? Our approval or disapproval would certainly change depending on the why. Even the question about Theodore lying to his child to keep the child from learning a distressing truth becomes complicated unless we read it with the implied qualifier *generally*, as in "Generally, should one lie to a child if that's the only way one can keep the child from learning a distressing truth?" For any specific case we'd have to know background and details to determine whether we approve of Theodore's lie. How distressing a truth? How old a child? Judging from experience, how able to cope? Given the child's personality, what are the likely consequences if the truth should come out and the child discovers the father's dishonesty? Without the details we are at sea, with them we may have no doubt whatsoever. It would take a very odd view of life to censure the mother in *A Tale of Two*

Cities who told her daughter that the girl's father had died before she was born rather than letting the child know he had been locked up in a dungeon with no hope of rescue and might be dead or alive.

Finally, if we step back from the minutiae and consider the global picture, there is the question of what lies do to society. Any act of dishonesty carries the risk of being exposed. Every evidence of dishonesty decreases our general sense of trust in others. If our list were prefaced with the statement that Theodore's lies will be exposed, some of us, loath to see the world turn into an even more distrustful place than it is, might be more disapproving as a matter of principle than they would be if they assumed that Theodore's lies will remain a secret.

Still, most of us would agree that Theodore's lies range from the utterly deplorable to the innocuous or even humane. Only someone truly disturbed would disagree with the belief that telling lies in order to harm people is an unpardonable evil except under the extraordinary circumstances of warfare or other extreme hostility. Conversely, lying to a child to keep it from being distressed is generally considered pardonable even if perhaps wrong. Motive clearly is the most immediate thing on which we base our judgment. If malice aforethought motivates a lie we recoil. If it comes out of the fear of the truth hurting someone we may still think it misguided but will view it with understanding or even sympathy. Note, though, that while motive is the main thing, it is not the only one: the people lied to and the lie's effect on them also matter. The cliché villain of melodrama is the man who defrauds poor widows and orphans. Greed is his motive; the poor who suffer as a result are his victims.

4

If we categorize the lies attributed to poor Theodore according to motive, we quickly realize that labels exist for some of the categories. Many of these labels refer to lies that are meant to be seen as justifiable—do we detect a certain unease with lying that nomenclature is meant to dispel? The "noble lie" is one example. A staple of romance and melodrama, it often pits a hero's innate forthrightness against the even nobler need to lie for a greater good. It is the kind of lie that makes Sydney Carton pretend to be Charles Darnay before the Revolutionary jailers and go to the guillotine in his place in *A Tale of Two Cities.*

A sterling specimen appears in a book that manages to poke fun at romantic fiction at the same time it uses its machinery with awe-inspiring adroitness. When Tom Sawyer pleads guilty to Becky Thatcher's crime of accidentally tearing a page in the schoolmaster's cherished anatomy book, he honors a rich literary tradition. Tom lies to save her from the schoolmaster's rod and takes the whipping she would have gotten. Becky's father, informed by her about Tom's lie after Tom's perseverance has saved the two from death in Injun Joe's cave, is suitably moved. When she pleads grace for the "might lie" that Tom told to shift punishment for the mutilated book onto his own shoulders, Judge Thatcher bursts out in a fine piece of eloquence. "It was a noble, a generous, a magnanimous lie," he announces. It was "a lie that was worthy to hold up its head and march down through history breast to breast with George Washington's lauded Truth about the hatchet!" And so it is. It is the only lie Tom—who is not given to worshipping at the shrine of honesty—tells that is motivated by altruism: an instinctive response to Becky's distress at the approaching humiliation.

The noble lie is followed after a decent span (lest its ermine-trimmed train be trod upon) by that minor infraction labeled the "white lie"—often rendered as the even less offensive "little white lie" (not to be confused with its rascally young cousin, the "fib").* According to books on etiquette, it is the grease in the wheels of society, a must if the aim is to avoid bruising feelings and making enemies. Miss Manners (who must bear a banner with the strange device *Litotes!*) is a staunch defender:

---

*Historically there was an attempt to oppose the concept of the white lie with that of the black, but the term didn't stick. A 1742 issue of *Gentlemen's Magazine* tells its readers: "A certain Lady of the highest Quality . . . makes a judicious Distinction between a white Lie and a black Lie. A white Lie is That which is not intended to injure any Body in his Fortune, Interest, or Reputation but only to gratify a garrulous Disposition and the Itch of amusing people by telling them wonderful Stories."

The moral superiority of substituting "You look awful" and "I find your parties such a drag that I'd rather stay home and do nothing" for such sinful untruths as "How nice to see you" and "Oh, I'm so sorry, I'm busy then," is not apparent to Miss Manners.

("Sinful untruths" by the by is a synonym for lies that may have been coined by the whimsical Miss Manners; I haven't found it in any of the standard synonym finders.) This is the land of tact and diplomacy, where honesty can be thoughtless, inconsiderate, or boorish. In this delicate terrain, "brutal" honesty may even be a reflection of contempt: the truth teller's attitude may be "I think so little of you, I won't even do you the courtesy of lying." Note, though, that as a rule Miss Manners is far from cavalier about casual lying, say when answering someone's nosy question. A smiling "I never talk about _____" (fill in the blank) is the correct response in such cases. Note also that when it comes to important matters, neither Miss Manners nor the less ethereal Dear Abby tends to brook dishonesty for the sake of sparing feelings when family or friends are involved. Consider this Dear Abby query from a troubled reader:

> I have a problem and need your advice. My husband wants me to lie to his parents, and I would feel uncomfortable in this lie.
>
> We have been attending a church that is not the same faith as my in-laws'. If they knew it, they would be very hurt—especially since they want their grandchildren to grow up in their faith.
>
> Both churches are Christian churches, and there are more similarities than differences. Because of these similarities, I think my in-laws would get over our attending this church if they knew; my husband disagrees.
>
> —Anytown, U.S.A.

Dear Abby's response is blunt:

> Dear Anytown: You and your husband are adults and should not feel it is necessary to lie to his parents for any reason.

Lies told to avoid embarrassment to oneself or others tend to be seen as white lies. The excuse of a headache to leave a gathering is a time-honored tradition allowing a graceful exit for actual reasons as diverse as a panic attack, diarrhea, or the sudden realization that one is picking up the fleas of the hosts' huskies. And who would fault the hardworking boy in the movie *Willy Wonka and the Chocolate Factory* who lies to his teacher and classmates about the reason he bought only two Wonka Bars, when his classmates bought hundreds? He doesn't care all that much about chocolate, he claims. In fact, he and his family of invalids are too poor to buy more while the rest of the world goes crazy trying to find the five golden tickets that will admit the winners to Wonka's magical factory and give them a lifetime supply of chocolate.

When the white lie takes the form of pretending not to see, hear, or know something that would be embarrassing, it becomes "polite fiction" and is an example of tact. Depending on the circles we move in, this may mean feigning unawareness about someone passing gas or being an indicted embezzler, teacher dismissed under a cloud, artist turned down for a grant, neighbor whose husband has a drinking problem. The benefit of letting on in these cases that one *knows* is, to quote Miss Manners, "not apparent."

Another lie deemed acceptable under certain circumstances is one that has no special name in English, though, interestingly, it has one in German. The *Notlüge* or "lie of necessity" takes care of authoritarian thugs at your door. It is the lie you tell to keep the Gestapo from arresting you or to persuade the border guard to let you pass when your life is in danger. It is the lie of the people who aided the Frank family and friends hiding in the secret annex of an Amsterdam warehouse during the Nazi occupation. The fact that this type of lie has its own special term in German but not English suggests something about its relative importance to speakers of the two languages. (And the same may be argued for the white lie. It does *not* exist as a special term in German; those in search of an equivalent concept have to settle for the awkward *gesellschaftliche Notlüge*, the "social lie of necessity.")

The lie of necessity is the one told to fight a hostile world. We find it in war and other acts of belligerence, and we find it when obstacles threaten to thwart progress. Mary Ann Evans wrote under a male pseudonym for a very good reason: A George Eliot was more likely to be widely read and critically acclaimed than an author whose name was Mary Ann in a century in which pedagogues wrote treatises voicing their fear that educating women beyond the domestic sphere would induce "brain fever" in them and in which otherwise sensible men pondered such nonsense.

Another "justifiable" lie is the "tall tale" although, strictly speaking, a lie told to an audience that knows it is a lie violates the "intending to deceive" definition of lying and might be classified with irony. "Now haven't I lied enough?" the teller of Grimm's "The Tale About the Land of Cockaigne" asks the reader. The question comes out of the blue after the rogue has described seeing a young ass with a silver nose chasing after two hares, a large linden tree growing hotcakes, and a scrawny old goat carrying a hundred cartloads of fat on its body and sixty loads of salt. The answer is, apparently, No, you haven't lied enough, because he goes on telling about a plow tilling the soil without horse or ox, a one-year-old child throwing four millstones from Regensburg to Trier, and, my own favorite, two mice consecrating a bishop.

The typical tall tale is the frontier story in which the teller relates how he wrestled grizzlies, rode rapids on a log, or got the better of a dozen bloodthirsty redskins. The listener was meant to admire the liar's audacity and imagination. Where the tall tale enters myth—such as in gigantic Paul Bunyan, whose camp stove covered an acre and whose tarp was so big that when he spread it out ducks flying over it mistook it for a lake—it would have taken a greenhorn lumberjack of the first order to believe a word. The same goes for the cock-and-bull story, too absurd to be believed for a moment, the fishing story, in which arm span becomes inadequate to show the humongous length of the one that got away, the "lying sessions" of African Americans in the post–Civil War South, and so forth: the listener is expected to laugh and rib the teller for lying like a hound, rug, or tombstone.

For those of a mischievous bent, another justifiable lie is the "practical joke" or "prank," in which the lie is meant to result in laughter. To pull it off usually means ignoring the victim's distress and convincing oneself that the outcome will make it worthwhile. The risk that the joke will misfire is built in, and to play pranks on people who aren't practical jokers themselves is to ask for trouble. Someone who has never herself done the equivalent of convincing a friend that a fancy hotel at which she stayed is suing her for alleged damage she did to the granite floor in the lobby is unlikely to appreciate the humor of the bogus letter from a bogus law firm itemizing the necessary repairs and associated costs.

We have not yet met the most common lie, the everyday "lie of convenience." At its most basic, this kind of lie is the equivalent of the blink of an eye. Answering the chairman of the board's "How are you?" with "Fine, thanks" even though you're in a blue funk saves time and effort and is no doubt appreciated by someone who neither needs to know nor cares about your true mental state. The alternative—to answer "Rotten, but I'd rather not go into why"—would be inappropriate given the setting. As a matter of fact, when it appears as a formulaic response, the lie of convenience should more properly be called the "saying-the-thing-which-is-not of convenience" since it violates one of the basic premises of lying, the intention to deceive.

A more complicated form is found in the priceless 1997 novel *Killoyle* by Roger Boylan. A character taking stock of his own moral life enumerates his countless petty sins, among them

> the lies he told his wife on a regular, indeed, compulsive, basis ("I only had the one pint, dear," meaning two or three; or, "that's a low blow, acushla, the very idea of me skelping off to the races, haven't I avoided the ponies for donkey's years," meaning he'd watched the 3:30 at Leopardstown in Muldoon's betting shop at the far end of the town, sacrificing his monthly commission at the altar of the also-rans—this leading inexorably to the additional, redundant lies of "What monthly commission?" and "I never," etc.).

Small lies, one and all, hiding minor trespasses, but note the complications that creep into the picture uninvited but inescapably: Accused of things he is lying about, the husband has to adopt the role of the injured party feeling the smart of unjust accusations. He has to do so or violate plausibility, since people unjustly accused of what they haven't done tend to be hurt and resentful.

5

So far we've focused the investigation on lies told by people in a private setting. People, of course, also lie "professionally," and there are professions in which bending or otherwise deforming the truth is an ever-present temptation because of how much is to be gained by it. The legal profession is one example. Lawyers have been notorious for duplicity, if not bald-faced deception, for so long that the lying lawyer is a cliché even for those people—a happy lot—who have not required their services. Why the bad reputation? For one because Anglo-American common law is adversarial and turns trial lawyers into combatants using all available means, fair or foul, to win cases. But the universal complaint is the lawyers' skill at using language to confound in order to enhance their reputation and line their pockets. Anyone who has ever tried to phrase a law in such a way that it addresses all possible ramifications and anticipates all potential loopholes knows that it isn't easy. But anyone who wades through legal documents will also be assaulted by the suspicion that there are people who use the obscurest possible verbiage to make things indecipherable to all but members of their caste.

Distrust of lawyers can be found almost from the time of their first appearance in the law courts of ancient Athens. Plato's and Aristotle's view of the Sophists, who taught oratory and rhetoric to demagogues and lawyers, was that they made money by sham and were unprincipled cheats in arguments. The bad press has stuck: we do not call people sophists to express our admiration at how skillfully they present their arguments in the service of the Truth. Complaints echo through the ages. Jesus is unsparing: "Woe unto you, lawyers! for ye have taken away the key of knowledge: ye entered not in yourselves, and them that were entering in ye hindered" (Luke 11:52). Erasmus concurs, heaping scorn on "the most self-satisfied class of people," who "string together six hundred laws in the same breath, no matter whether they are relevant or not, piling up opinion on opinion and gloss on gloss to make their profession seem the most difficult of all." It's a short step from false arguments and the stringing together of laws for the sake of obfuscation to Swift's blunt assessment. There is, Gulliver tells his noble master in Houyhnhnmland, "a Society of Men among us, bred up from their Youth in the Art of proving by Words multiplied for the Purpose, that *White* is *Black*, and *Black* is *White*, according as they are paid."

Twentieth-century entries expressing a similar animus are as grains of sand on a very large beach. The opinion of the many is that lawyers use their finely honed skill at words to distort and mislead, that they are masters at violating the spirit of the law by finding verbal loopholes. Ask the man in the street (or the woman) whether lawyers ever lie, and the answer is likely to be: "This is a joke, right?" For lawyers lying in court is not merely unethical but illegal, but they can and do get away with manipulating known facts so as to make them seem to indicate one thing when another is the truth.

Other professionals renowned for dishonesty are advertisers. For a very good reason. The aim is to sell as much as possible. Modern advertising cut its baby teeth in the 1920s, and since then enormous effort has been expended on describing products in ways that make them seem indispensable, superior to other products, or just what the doctor ordered to cure anything from fallen arches to that annoying suspicion that we're still not having fun. What has been eagerly sought is ways in which products or services can be represented so that people reach for their wallets. And lying is one such way. To say that the soap one is manufacturing is as good as another soap already on the market may be true, but it is hardly likely to make people throng to stores. To say it is better, smoother, more effective, etc., is the ticket.

Outright lies in advertising have become a sensitive issue since the advent of consumer protection, and most companies have learned to steer clear of flagrantly false claims. If ads for Listerine now announced, as they did in the 1920s, that chronic periodontitis afflicts four out of five Americans (the actual number according to one expert source was one in twenty) and that Listerine is the answer, company executives would probably find themselves in a court of law for false advertising. But examples of false advertising still turn up. The "Vitamin O" scam exposed in 1999, for instance, bilked people of millions of dollars by making blatantly false claims about its benefits as "stabilized oxygen molecules in a solution of distilled water and sodium chloride" (a.k.a. salt water) and its use by astronauts.

The more savvy approach, though, is to use words and images to represent what is being sold in ways that are lies without being prosecutable for false advertising. "You can take Salem out of the country, but you can't take the country out of Salem" is one of countless examples furnished at one time by cigarette advertisers on TV. Read: "The menthol flavor will make it seem you're strolling down a tree-lined country lane, breathing all that wonderful country air." In the age of digital manipulation not a single object or living thing shown by advertisers is not in some way manipulated to make it more seductive and alluring, but airbrushes have eliminated wrinkles and shadows since the infancy of photography, light strategically positioned has created optical illusions, cropping has gotten rid of undesirable features—tricks of the trade to get people to buy.

Little needs to be said about yet another class of "professionals," who lie because not to lie would interfere with the conduct of their business and get them in trouble in a hurry. Deception is an integral part of crimes and misdemeanors, and, in terms of reprehensiveness, tends to be overshadowed by them. Seen from another angle, only a perpetrator who is repentant or out to be punished is honest. As any policeman will tell you, the answer to "Did you rob the bank, fire the shot, use the stolen credit cards, drink a bottle of scotch while driving?" is "No."

Then there are the deceptions that are in themselves criminal or subject to penalties. Defrauding, scamming, forging, cheating, plagiarizing, as well as cons of all kinds, are instances.

Finally there is the lie told with the intention to do harm. Malicious gossip, defamation of character, calumny, slander, libel, bearing false witness, sowing discord among allies or suspicion between lovers—human ingenuity in using deception as a weapon is limitless. Iago is the archetype in literature, but milder forms are found in the average mudslinging political ad around election time.

What is still missing is that odd thing, the pathological lie. Since its motive is murky, to say the least, it is best left to a chapter on the psychology of lying.

6

The liar's motive is the most obvious thing by which we judge lies. But if we want to anatomize deception, we run into another interesting feature, the liar's personality. Again things are complicated and it helps to start with a basic insight—which Michel Montaigne (who made a habit of it) expressed in the late sixteenth century. In his essay "On Liars" he complains:

> If, like the truth, falsehood had only one face, we should know better where we are, for we should then take the opposite of what a liar said to be the truth. But the opposite of a truth has a hundred thousand shapes and a limitless field.

Montaigne's complaint refers to the fact that if the lie were, say, "the horse that was stolen is chestnut," then the only information we could gather from the discovery that we were lied to would be that the stolen horse is any horsey color *other* than chestnut (always provided there *was* a stolen horse).

But the confusion also touches on another concern: the characteristics of a lie and the personality or psychological makeup of the liar. Is the lie "active," "bare- or bald-faced," "by commission" and told by someone who gives not a hoot about the risk of being exposed as a liar or "passive," "devious," "by omission," and perpetrated by someone who avoids as much as possible to tell a lie through his teeth but is a master at manipulating others into reaching the wrong conclusions? Modern consensus is that any act of communication with the intent to deceive is a lie, but liars of the manipulative kind have always made it a point that they did not in fact *tell* a lie and that the fault of misinterpreting rests with people jumping to the wrong conclusions. This kind of lowlife will tell you that her brother needs an eye operation, will ask you for money, and when you find she's spent the money on a cruise will inform you that she never said she would give the money to her brother for the operation—which, at any rate, he can easily afford. If you assumed a connection, that was *your* mistake. In such cases, the characteristics of the lie can tell us a great deal about the personality or psychological makeup of the liar even if we haven't a clue as to the motive behind the lie.

Equivocation is one version of this kind of lie, and the distant and not so distant past has seen lively debate about it. Theologians have done most of the heavy lifting, but the popular press of the last years of the twentieth century has contributed in innumerable articles analyzing equivocation in the light of the romantic life of an American President. An earlier example, however, sheds more light on the practice and its boon companion, mental reservation. Strictly speaking, we should reserve the discussion for the next chapter, where we investigate the how-to of lying, but the type of lying that concerns us here has as much to do with the why as with the how.

A short historical detour takes us to an exceedingly grim place. Suppose for a moment you live in England in the year 1605, on the eve of the Gunpowder Plot ("remember, remember, the fifth of November"). You're a loyal subject of James I, but as a recusant Catholic you refuse to attend the services of the Church of England or to recognize its authority. In spiritual matters you rather look to the Church of Rome. Priests are outlawed in England and, if caught, are treated as agents of the Pope and tried for treason. You look to these men, Jesuits disguised as ordinary subjects of the Crown, as your guides to salvation. They hear your confession, say mass in a secret room of your mansion, administer the sacraments.

The evil day comes when the authorities in the form of an officer and armed men pay you a visit. A disgruntled servant has informed them about your Popish practices, and they are here to arrest the priest. They ask you: "Where is he? Where are you hiding him?" Questions simple enough to answer if you're willing to lie. "I don't know. What are you talking about? There is no priest in this house," will do for a start.

The problem is that according to the doctrine in which you believe, you are *not* to lie under any circumstances; the penalty is to be cast "into the lake that burns with fire and brimstone," the fate of all liars come Judgment Day (Revelation 21:8). By the dictates of your faith you seem to have only two options: refuse to answer the questions, in which case your interrogators will quickly conclude that you are hiding a priest and will turn the house upside down to find him, or tell the truth: "He's hiding in the priest hole." Since this admission is bound to pique their interest and make them ask more questions—which, again, you are not allowed to answer with lies—you might as well continue: "Down the hall, to your left, push against the paneling and the door to the secret passage will open." The problem with that option is its outcome in *this* world: The priest will be arrested and chances are he'll be tortured. If he confesses to being a priest, he will be tried and sentenced to death for treason. Death means that he will be publicly hanged by the neck— but not until dead. Alive, he will be cut down and dragged to a chopping block. There his genitals will be hacked off and burned before his face. His bowels will be cut out, and then his heart, at which point he will die and not care about the continuing ig- nominy: his head chopped off and held up to the jeering spectators. Clearly, either outcome—your own eternal damnation as a result of lying or the priest's execution as a result of telling the truth—is ap- palling, although as a person of faith you should choose a priest's martyrdom over the death of your soul.

Human beings confronted by impossible situations tend to ar- rive at amazing solutions. Jesuits, caught between the rock of ages and a very hard place, were no exception. If neither they nor their flock were allowed to lie but telling the truth was suicidal, there had to be a way *not* to lie while keeping the truth hidden. Equivo- cation—speech fashioned to be deliberately ambiguous—was one answer, and Father Garnet, the alleged mastermind of the Gun- powder Plot, wrote a treatise on the subject. In it he explained how a good Catholic might use equivocation for dissimulating legiti- mately.

How is it done? Let's return to the officer and his men at the door: "Where is the priest? Where are you hiding him?" he asks. You look him straight in the eye and answer: "I don't know the priest of whom you're speaking." This may sound like a straight- forward lie, given that only minutes earlier you hurried the priest to his secret hiding place under the stairs. But, no, you aren't lying since what you *mean* by the statement is that sometimes you have the feeling you don't really *know* anybody—not even your wife or closest friend and certainly not the priest in question. Too bad for the officer that he jumped to the wrong conclusion rather than rec- ognizing the potential ambiguity of your statement. For emphasis you add: "There is no priest here." Knowing that the tenets of your faith bid you to speak the truth, the officer leaves, thinking that a malicious servant invented the priest. What he doesn't know is that not only was your first statement ambiguous but your second statement actually consisted of two parts, only the first of which you voiced. "There is no priest here," is what he heard; *in this hall* is what you added mentally. Between equivocation and mental reservation you managed to turn him away without uttering an actual lie.

Father Garnet recommends both equivocation and mental reservation in his treatise. The idea is that God knows what is in your heart and mind, and if the truth is there in an alternate or unvoiced meaning, you *cannot* be lying. The same would hold if you continued a sentence in a language unintelligible to your interrogator. What is important is that the truth exists in your mind. This is a rather amazing departure in spirit from the New Testament's insistence on consonance between what is outward and what is inward—thought and actions, thought and speech—but how else can you tell a necessary lie if such a thing does not exist in your conceptual vocabulary?

Father Garnet's treatise was originally titled *A Treatise of Equivocation*, but in a move that can be seen as either spin doctoring or clarification, he retitled it *A Treatise Against Lying and Fraudulent Dissimulation*. Despite the new title's indication that the treatise was meant as a manual instructing how *not* to lie, it was ridiculed by the prosecutor of the Gunpowder Plot and paraded as an example of Jesuitical duplicity. And of course strategies designed to keep others in the dark without tarnishing one's halo can seem more dishonest than a "straightforward" lie. Plus the intent behind equivocation is to keep the truth from being known, which, back to square one, *is* one intention behind lying. The Jesuits' defense was that if all they had wanted to do was lie, that would have been easy enough. *Not* wanting to lie was what created the need for equivocation. True enough, and the tension between not being *allowed* to lie and *having* to lie for self-defense is one that religious dissenters—Protestants in Catholic countries as much as Catholics in Protestant ones—had to deal with, and even the Church Fathers had found the question of legitimate lies heavy going. (Incidentally, his powers of equivocation did not save Father Garnet from becoming a victim of judicial murder.)

The Jesuits have gotten the brunt of the bad press—"equivoca-tion" and "Jesuitical" are commonly linked—but the notion that equivocation could be used in hostile circumstances was common among Roman Catholic clergy. Thomas Aquinas, a Dominican, found in his *Summa of Theology* (ca. 1269 to 1272) that lying to pro-tect someone from harm is illicit but "to conceal the truth pru-dently by means of an evasion" is permitted. The two Dominican friars who published the *Malleus Maleficarum* in 1486 went further, telling judges how to lie to accused witches to get them to confess if months in prison and torture have failed. The judge should "promise that he will be merciful, with the mental reservation that he means he will be merciful to himself or the State; for whatever is done for the safety of the State is merciful." It is not known how many people were burned at the stake because they mistakenly as-sumed that a judge telling them, "If you confess I will be merciful," meant that *they* would be shown mercy. The authors did point out however that other courses of action existed. A judge might prom-ise a witch that her life would be spared and then keep the promise for a while but burn her "after a certain period," or he might prom-ise her her life but in such a way that he could afterward disclaim the duty of passing sentence and deputize another judge to sen-tence her to death. Fighting the good fight apparently required buckets of deviousness in addition to an arsenal of engines of tor-ture.

A short step separates mental reservation from the lie by omis-sion. Just like equivocation, the latter takes advantage of certain as-sumptions and mental shortcuts we make in communicating with others, assumptions and shortcuts we've learned to make probably as infants because they allow us to process the flow of information that communication is. Mundane example: somebody tells you, "I went to Macy's to buy a pair of pants." The unquestioned assump-tion you make is that the *reason* he went to Macy's was to buy a pair of pants. If you should find out that he also went to buy towels, and indeed did buy towels, you are not concerned about the missing piece of information. But suppose you find out he went there to buy a $1,200 sound system, plus a pair of pants and towels? There is no way you wouldn't feel there was something bizarre about the I-went-to-Macy's-to-buy-pants conversation. Suppose now your friend owes you $1,000. Is there any way in the world you can avoid the thought that this withholding of information means you were for all intents and purposes lied to?

When it becomes just a bit more elaborate, this type of deluding goes under the name of misdirection or, more poetically, "leading down the garden path." The listener makes certain assumptions based on experience in communicating because most of the time the assumptions are correct. Unless you know you are dealing with a pathological liar, you would waste enormous amounts of energy if you consciously suppressed these assumptions every time anyone told you anything and asked yourself what it is you are *not* being told, what conclusions you're drawing, and are expected to draw, that may in fact be *wrong*.

Suppose the friend who owes you money tells you that he had maxed out all his credit cards and would have been evicted from his apartment for not paying the rent if his parents hadn't bailed him out. And suppose you assume this to mean that he didn't have the money to pay the rent and is, in his own way, apologizing for obviously also not having the money to pay you back what he owes you. And then you find out that shortly before the no-money-for-the-rent crisis he bought some pricey luxury gadgets because he (a) doesn't believe in living within his means and (b) has convinced himself that you really don't need the money he owes you. Don't you retrospectively smell the wisteria in bloom and marvel at the riot of color of the azalea bordering the path you were being led down?

For those who object to all this fancy prevaricating footwork, the final insult is that it is entirely possible for your friend to be dishonest without ever opening his mouth. All it takes is for him to know that you have the wrong idea about something and to remain silent and thereby keep you in the dark. Withholding information may not fit our standard notion of lying, but it certainly qualifies as deception. If the one doing it is a friend or family member, and the information withheld is important, the lack of candor will seem a hairsbreadth from a lie pure and simple.

7

We have drifted from an investigation of why people lie and the circumstances under which lies are justified to how they do it. The motive behind Jesuitical equivocation was to avoid harm without committing the sin of lying, but what fascinates is its execution. This overlap of interests—why versus how—is what makes generating a taxonomy of lying a challenge and confusion an ever-present danger. An example of yeomanly effort and considerable confusion is Amelia Opie's *Illustrations of Lying, in All Its Branches*. First published in 1825, the book is a product of that growth industry of the eighteenth and nineteenth centuries, the moral tract.

Opie was a minister's daughter, radical dissenter (from the Anglican Church), friend of Sheridan, Mme. de Staël, and other members of literary society, wife of the painter John Opie, and eventual Quaker. She was also a copious novelist, poet, and writer of moral tracts, one of which may bear the longest title in the history of English literature: *A Cure for Scandal; or Detraction Displayed. As Exhibited by Gossips, Talkers-Over, Laughers-At, Banterers, Nicknamers, Stingers, Scorners, Eye-Inflicters, Mimicks, Caricaturists, and Epigrammatists.* (Inhale.) Her novels languish in obscurity and will continue to do so unless we learn to read without the itch to edit passages like the following from *Adeline Mowbray*: " 'Gracious Heaven!' cried Adeline, clasping her hands and looking upwards with tearful eyes, 'When shall my persecutions cease! and how much greater must my offenses be than even my remorse paints them, when their consequences still torment me so long after the crime which occasioned them has ceased to exist!' " (Errant Adeline's crime was to have fallen under the spell of a philosopher who preached that the union of two virtuous lovers requires no marriage ceremony in a rational world; her cry is a fallen woman's remorse, continual even after her lover's death.)

Some twenty years after the publication of *Adeline Mowbray*, Opie took lying into her sights and the result was *Illustrations of Lying, in All Its Branches*. Opie's book is no longer in circulation in libraries but is sequestered in their rare-books collections—a somber reminder of the transitoriness of most literary achievement. The work was intended, in the author's words, to "promote the moral and religious welfare of mankind." A formidable aim, and one Opie hoped to carry out by defining, analyzing, and rendering abhorrent by illustrative anecdotes various types of lies. The result seems to have been a success. Between 1825 and 1856 at least three English and four American editions came out. The 1827 American edition on my shelf belonged to Mary M. Marshall of Rochester, whose penmanship was admirable, and it is well thumbed.

I discovered Opie two years into this project and read her attack on that shape-shifting monster, deception, with the same unhealthy gratification with which a builder might watch another's ambitious but wrongheaded edifice rise from a weak foundation. She starts out on firm enough ground:

> What constitutes lying?
>
> I answer, the *intention to deceive*.
>
> If this be a correct definition, there must be *passive* as well as *active* lying; and those who withhold the truth, or do not tell the whole truth, with an intention to deceive, are guilty of lying, as well as those who tell a direct or positive falsehood.

Sensible start, but the Introduction continues in a muddle:

> Lies are many, and various in their nature and in their tendency, and may be arranged under their different names, thus:—
> Lies of Vanity.
> Lies of Flattery.
> Lies of Convenience.
> Lies of Interest.
> Lies of Fear.
> Lies of first-rate Malignity.
> Lies of second-rate Malignity.
> Lies, falsely called Lies of Benevolence.
> Lies of real Benevolence.
> Lies of mere Wantonness, proceeding from a depraved love of lying, or contempt for truth.
> There are others probably; but I believe that this list contains all those which are of the most importance; unless, indeed, we may add to it—
> Practical Lies; that is, Lies acted, not spoken.

The list's inconsistencies leap fairly off the page—vanity is a person-ality trait, flattery an action; fear and interest are powerful motiva-tors that can prompt lies ranging from flattery to malicious slander; malignity, again, is rooted in personality. To categorize deception in this way complicates analysis from the start. But Opie was not inter-ested in a methodical treatment. Her aim was that of the didactic moralist, and the charm her book must have held for her readers is in the anecdotes she invents to illustrate the various lies.

The tales instruct. In most of them one or more liars are mildly chastised or severely punished, the punishment fitting the crime to a T. A family is ruined by a daughter bragging about its nonexistent wealth. Another loses an inheritance because a son facetiously flat-ters a would-be benefactor to get him to behave ridiculously. A man becomes the laughingstock of the community when he pre-tends he is the author of a celebrated novel. In other tales, those lied to suffer grievously even if the lie was meant to protect them. In the most poignant of these, a father dies after learning he has been charitably lied to about the fate of his son. (The death scene unfortunately concludes with the howler: "The paternal heart, bro-ken by the sudden shock, had suffered and breathed its last.") On the other side of the coin, those who tell the truth are rewarded, usually with handsome sums of money, always a convenient way to demonstrate God's approval. Those by nature virtuous but mo-mentarily errant resolve never again to tell a lie for whatever rea-son; the wicked suffer the loss of an inheritance or annuity, and they complain bitterly, never realizing that the sin of lying is to blame. Sentiment and didacticism rule and the homiletic sledge-hammer approach wearies after a while.

Note well, however, Opie's warning about the greasy slide, which echoes St. Augustine:

> If you allow yourself to violate truth—that is, to *deceive*, for any purpose whatever—who can say where this sort of self-indulgence will submit to be bounded? Can you be sure that you will not, when strongly tempted, utter what is equally false, in or-der to benefit yourself, at the expense of a fellow creature?

The answer is: No, you cannot be sure unless you keep much closer tabs on your moral life than most of us do. So if you lie, better be prepared to admit that there may be times when you are do-ing it at the expense of a fellow creature. And—a point Opie makes elsewhere—also be prepared to be lowered in the esteem of the people who catch you at a lie. Where reputation and respect are at stake, lying is not cheap.

We'll see just how expensive lying is in another chapter. First, though, a look at how that marvelous beast, deception, does what it does.

How to Weave, and Sell, a Tangled Web

Poets themselves, though liars by profession, always endeavour to give an air of truth to their fiction.

David Hume, "Of the Understanding," *A Treatise of Human Nature*

Tears in his eyes, distraction in his aspect,
A broken voice, and his whole function suiting
With forms to his conceit.

William Shakespeare, *Hamlet*

1

Montaigne was not the first to sound the warning, but he did it with his customary flair: "No one who is not conscious of having a sound memory should set up to be a liar." Ever committed to analysis, he outlines in his essay "On Liars" the difficulties confronting two kinds of liars: the kind that disguises and alters an actual fact and the kind that invents everything. The former are obviously prime candidates for tripping up, argues Montaigne, because it is hard for them not to mix up fact and invention when they refer to the same story again and again. Since the actual event was the first thing to lodge in the memory, and since it resides there with the vividness of something known, the details connected with it will readily jump into the mind and dislodge the memory of the invented details, which cannot have as strong a foothold.

Liars who fabricate the thing out of whole cloth are, according to Montaigne, only at first glance less likely to trip up. True, they have no memories of what actually happened potentially clashing with their invention, but since the invention has no hold in reality, remembering the details becomes a formidable challenge to anyone who does not have a very reliable memory. The liar lacking such a memory is liable to "recall" the same object being gray one moment and yellow the next. (Al Pacino in *Glengarry Glen Ross* expresses the same sentiment in advising that, when it comes to cops: "Always tell them the truth. It's the easiest thing to remember.")

To illustrate his point, Montaigne tells an anecdote about two great men, King Francis I and the duke of Milan (Francesco II Sforza), and an ill-fated third party—an undercover agent for King Francis at the duke's court. The unfortunate man, suspected by the duke of being the king's spy, had his head cut off on a false charge of murder. The duke's ambassador, swearing high and low to the irate king that the executed man's royal mission was utterly unknown to the duke, tripped when the king asked him why, pray tell, the duke had had the man executed at night and in secret. Because, said the ambassador, eager to put the best face on things, respect for the king made the duke reluctant to have the execution take place in daylight. Clank!

Forgetting for a moment the most important part of his story—that the duke was unaware of the agent's connection with the king—the ambassador introduced an inconsistency that made the lie glaringly obvious. The moral is that whether it involves misreporting a past event ("I was at the library all day" when in fact one went skiing or to the racetrack), misreporting something that is currently the case (one's feelings or beliefs, knowledge, the state of one's health, the amount of money in one's wallet or bank account), or misreporting one's plans (will be at a conference, on jury duty, at a funeral), lying is invention, and successful lying—lying that is believed by the people lied to—demands consistency, which, in turn, requires a good memory.

A successful lie also has other features, features less directly tied to memory. It has to be plausible and has to agree with facts wherever facts can be verified. No wonder writers of fiction have referred to their craft tongue in cheek as lying: it has many of the same requirements. In a lie, it has to make sense that one was at place X on day Y, doing Z; place X had better be described as pelted by torrential rain if the person lied to knows that on day Y torrential rain flooded X; one had better not explain the sunglasses one in fact bought at place A by referring to how bright a day it was (true at A but decidedly untrue at X). In "realistic" fiction, simi-larly, it has to be plausible that a character sold the most cherished of his possessions. He must have run out of money, be too proud to borrow, be in desperate straits. Having him sell the ring his dying mother gave him simply because the author needs a poignant mo-ment flooded with memories will not do.

The Greeks, who have the patent in perpetuity on all original ideas about art, recognized this consonance and expressed it with admirable economy. The word *pseudos* meant both "fiction"—sto-ries, tales—and "what is not true," which in the right context be-comes "lies." Of course we play the same verbal game: what politician charged with unethical conduct has not at one time or another called the allegations "pure fiction"?

Writing fiction requires imaginative effort, and one obvious question is: Does telling a lie require more effort than telling the truth? The answer is yes. Mental fabrication or invention, which may be defined as the imaginative amalgamation of memories from a vast number of sources, is intrinsically more difficult than recall-ing a coherent set of events connected with a given experience. Also, the further we depart from something that actually occurred, the more our power of invention is taxed. Any actual event com-prises numerous specific and concrete details which we draw upon when talking about it, usually without even being consciously aware that that's what we're doing. To be convincing, a fabricated account, too, has to have such details to make it seem like the truth. Clever liars strive to fill their tales with them. Odysseus is a sterling example: the false tales he tells about himself to people he meets in the course of his adventures are full of made-up names and rela-tionships. In the one he tells to Eumaios, his swineherd, he is the son of a rich man, named Kastor—the son of Hylakos—and a con-cubine, and was raised among the man's legitimate sons. When his father died, his half brothers gave him little of their father's wealth, etc., etc., etc.—details designed to make the tale seem real.

Keeping track of invented details is one challenge. Another arises because our invention may not prepare us for every eventual-ity. Unexpected questions have tripped up many a liar. What is wrong, for example, with the lie: "I tried calling twice from a pay phone, but the line was busy"? Nothing at all, provided the phone at the number called was off the hook on occasion. But what if the recipient of the lie asks: "Why didn't you try again? You knew I was waiting for your call"? And what if the answer is: "I ran out of change"? A clumsy oversight given that telephone companies have not as yet figured out how to pocket the coins of uncompleted calls without risking rioting in the streets; a lie most likely made up by a child or a drunk, but at any rate by someone who on the one hand did not think the details of his story through and on the other hand was not quick enough on his toes to come up with an answer that was not nonsense—"I got stuck in traffic; I couldn't find a phone; I lost track of time," would all have been answers that at least could not have been outright disproved. Add presence of mind to the abilities of a successful liar.

The quasi-heroic efforts of some liars may be a reason why we cannot help admiring them, but all lying takes effort; most people will no more lie unless something is to be gained by it than will get up and walk across the room unless the effort promises some reward. (Aristotle, who was much better at observing action in a Sophoclean tragedy than action in life, got this one as wrong as he got his natural science. He claimed in the *Nicomachean Ethics* that the truly truthful man is someone who tells the truth when nothing is at stake simply because of his love of truth. And if he tells the truth when nothing is at stake, he'll be "still more truthful" when something *is* at stake. More likely, the opposite holds: someone who is committed to telling the truth even when the stakes are high will also tell it matter-of-factly when they aren't.)

In order to tell the truth or, on a less lofty plain, to report facts accurately, we use the same faculty we use in lying—memory. We access and examine our knowledge of something—a past event, current state, future aim—with our thoughts (by what miraculous neurochemical processes we do this remains as unknown as the neurological nature of knowledge itself). We then report to the best of our ability on what we have found. To lie, we first cobble together something from memory, since no invention comes out of a vacuum, and then tell the fabrication as we remember it. To flesh out additional details as needed, we improvise—again drawing on things remembered. The lie most likely to succeed in terms of plausibility is a substitution of one consistent memory for another:

the remembered day skiing or at the racetrack, lied about, becomes a remembered day at the library—there was such a day, it just did not happen to be the particular day reported. Obviously, the further afield from a concrete memory we stray, the more likely the chance of tripping up.

Even if we stick to lies not far afield, though, the risk of tripping up remains. Let's take the case of an exemplary liar, call her Jane. Instead of the library, let's suppose Jane cites a number of errands she purportedly had to run on a day when she was in fact meeting the man she was having an affair with: She went, she claims, to an office supplies store, a copy center, a bookstore, where she bought a book, the post office, where she mailed a birthday present for a friend. Then she had lunch at a Chinese restaurant and after that bought a sweater at a department store. So far so good—she's done all of these things at various times in the recent past or intends to do them in the near future. Let's suppose nothing has changed about any of the places she claims to have visited—none of the stores have gone out of business unbeknownst to her and Yi-Chung's hasn't changed ownership and is now Giuseppe's; let's also suppose she was not seen a week earlier in the sweater she claims to have just bought. The likelihood is still high that a few days after the lie, when she has lost interest in the fabrication, Jane will slip, blurt out that she needs to buy the book previously announced bought, or mail the present previously announced mailed. In other words, carelessly spun yarns are easily snagged. Spun yarns, incidentally (as well as Sir Walter Scott's proverbial "tangled web we weave, when first we practise to deceive"), again hint at the similarity between lying and writing fiction, and as it turns out, much can be learned about deception by looking over the shoulder of the author.

First, though, it pays to set the dial to Attica. In Aristotle's prototypical lit crit text, *Poetics*, we find the useful insight that the function of the poet (Aristotle has in mind Homer and the Greek dramatists) is to present things that are "possible according to the law of probability or necessity," since "what is possible is credible." To do so, the writers of tragedy astutely choose historical or legendary subjects because "what has happened is manifestly possible: otherwise it could not have happened." A not unobvious point but instructive since it seems to provide one answer to the question of credibility with syllogistic ease: What is possible is credible; what has happened is, by definition, possible; therefore, if fiction deals with what has happened, then what it describes is perforce credible. Yes, but the argument would be more compelling if beginning writers charged with writing unconvincing fiction did not so frequently protest: "But this really happened!"

So far so good. But what about the Greek comedies, which are for the most part not based on history? There the playwright must construct his plot according to the law of probability or it fails. In fact, even the writer of tragedy, Aristotle rethinks, must pay attention to probability since not all people watching his play will be familiar with the history it is based on. There is, he tells us with no apparent appreciation of the conceit's delightful oddness, "no reason why some events that have actually happened should not conform to the law of the probable and possible." Indeed, there isn't. But leaving no stone unturned, the philosopher also reminds us that there is in the real world room for things that happen contrary to probability. This too is true. Life is under no obligation to convince anyone that a given event occurred or did not occur by ensuring that the event does not violate probability. Even fiction whose events seem improbable can seem a credible representation of reality provided the improbable is presented in a way to awaken our sense of "Who'd have thought it! Don't the most amazing things happen!"

Aristotle elaborates that when it comes to the question of credibility, the poet should prefer "probable impossibilities to improbable possibilities." In the *Iliad*, Achilles pursuing Hector is an example of the latter. The Greeks do not join in the pursuit, which is absurd and hence improbable. Probable impossibilities are trickier: the impossible must be justified by artistic requirements, such as making a scene more striking, or by invoking a "higher reality" or "received opinion." According to Aristotle, the appearance of gods in a tragedy qualifies as a probable impossibility: it seems probable because of people's exposure to tales about the gods even if the gods do not exist (and hence are impossible), as some have argued. The logic is somewhat tortured since if people believe in the gods, then Athena appearing to Odysseus in the guise of a man is not impossible, whereas if they don't believe, then her impossible appearance can hardly be probable—unless, that is, we practice Coleridge's willing suspension of disbelief, which handles with ease elves and giants, journeys to Mars and talking horses, and Pallas Athena, who sprang from the head of Zeus fully armed and brandishing a javelin.

2

At this point, a quick return to the tall tale is worthwhile. Populated by rational horses and giants, dragons and jackelopes, the terrain seems at first glance the least likely product of a teeming imagination to sell to an audience—unless that audience is also interested in Florida real estate or a bridge across the East River. But a look around shows just how fine the line can be that separates fiction and lie. A comprehensive essay on the tall tale would fill several books, a useful one of which, fortunately, was written in German in 1881 by Carl Müller-Fraureuth. The author traces it from the eleventh century up to that Old World prototype *The Adventures of Baron Munchausen*, and finds two intertwined traditions: the lying tale told with the intention of amusing a listener who knows it is fiction and the one told with the intention of convincing that the narrated exploits actually happened.

The historical Baron Münchhausen (with umlaut and two *h*'s) served with the Russians against the Turks in the middle of the eighteenth century and wrote stories of his fabulous exploits to amuse. Greatly enlarged with material from folk tales, the *Adventures* became widely known and popular in many languages. In their narrator, we meet a traveler whose luck and talents impress: When his horse is cut in half by a falling portcullis, the baron has it sewn back together with sprigs, with the marvelous consequence of the sprigs growing into an arbor shading the rider on his future journeys. At other times, he flies on geese, invents an early missile-defense system by using a cannon to shoot an enemy's cannonball out of the sky, lifts a carriage and jumps with it over a seven-foot hedge—not an easy thing even for him, he confesses. His most famous feat, that of hitching a ride on a cannonball, has been commemorated in enough illustrations to have become his trademark.*

The ingenuity and impossibility of the baron's adventures were meant to entertain, and they no doubt did, but many of them predate Münchhausen by hundreds of years and existed parallel to bona fide deception practiced by travelers in the Middle Ages and earlier. Hungry and in need of shelter and rest, they would stop at a village and tell the inhabitants about things they had seen in faraway places. Of course, the more interesting the tale, the more likely that the traveler would be plied with food and drink by news- and entertainment-hungry villagers. The villagers' ignorance coupled with the tale teller's urge to impress must have made for lively fare.

In the mid-sixteenth century, Hans Sachs, the Meistersinger idealized by Richard Wagner, expressed his irritation with this rigmarole. He wrote a satirical poem on liars who "reported" on kings and battles and lands they had never seen, making up whatever would interest an audience. Around the same time, a German count complained about "lazy fellows, who neither want to hew nor cut nor work in any way" and who went from village to village supporting themselves by inventing news about the world. "With lies many feed themselves," another, presumably well-fed, observer complained. A decent meal at day's end is not something to be sneered at but vanity must have entered as well. To describe one's exploits and see the eyes of the credulous grow big as saucers must have driven some of the "lazy fellows" into flights of fancy. Obviously, there is a fine line between the bald-faced liar and the "legitimate" inventor of tales—whose legitimacy rests on his listeners' sophistication in recognizing that what they are hearing is invention.

But by the Middle Ages this sort of thing was ancient. When Odysseus finally returns to Ithaca disguised as a beggar, the first

---

*The merry baron, sadly, has passed into the field of medicine. Munchausen syndrome affects people who fake, often after doing considerable research, physical symptoms in order to get the attention of doctors. In extreme cases, they injure themselves in addition to fabricating elaborate histories of their pretended illness. Even more distressing, if true, some researchers claim to have found a form of child abuse—Munchausen syndrome by proxy—in which a parent injures a child to get medical attention as the child's parent.

man he runs into is his swineherd, Eumaios. Odysseus claims he has news of Ithaca's long-lost king, but Eumaios is unconvinced. He admonishes Odysseus that "there are vain and vagabond men in need of sustenance who tell lies, and are unwilling to give a true story. . . . So you too, old sir, might spin out a well-made story, if someone would give you a cloak or tunic to wear for it." Odysseus (who tells no fewer than five false tales about himself in the course of his adventures) protests that he hates as much as he hates death "that man who under constraint of poverty babbles beguiling falsehoods." He then promptly proceeds to introduce himself as a Cretan, the son of Kastor, impoverished by his father's death, and so forth. The swineherd is not convinced but he does not seem to be overly bothered by this feature of travelers—which may or may not argue that Homer was not bothered by it. Lucian, in the second century A.D., on the other hand, was sufficiently irked by that particular brand of lying (as he was by pretty much every other example of human folly) to write a parody of fantastic travelers' tales. Titled *True History*, it describes a voyage that starts on the sea, continues in the sky, and includes stopovers in the belly of a whale and the Elysian fields. If anybody believed *True History*, no record of this simple soul exists.

3

Life, naturally, has fiction beaten all hollow when it comes to the question of credibility. No matter how outlandish or improbable something happening in reality may seem, if we experience it, or have a reliable report of it, we have no option but to believe it. One of your colleagues, unassuming, well adjusted, and with no apparent interest in religion, suddenly quits his job to heed the will of God by becoming a missionary in New Guinea. All you can do after your initial bafflement has worn off is accept the event as part of life's rich pageantry, especially once you start getting letters from New Guinea with photos of him and his flock. You cannot complain about improbability. But suppose your missionary colleague pops up in a novel. Do we hear wails (by book reviewers if no one else) that his behavior is insufficiently motivated and that he is unbelievable as a character?

Reading fiction aspiring to present some aspect of reality believably requires us to engage in Coleridge's willing suspension of disbelief, but the writer had better not assume this suspension to be an unshakable obligation. The characters encountered on the pages of "realistic" fiction, however slippery that label may be, cannot behave wildly improbably or the reader is liable to say, "I don't believe it," meaning that, given the circumstances presented by the author, no actual person fitting the profile of the character would do or not do this or that. Puff, vanishes the illusion, and, presto, enters the thought that bad writing is to blame. What this touches on is the question of how writers create characters that "come to life" and "jump off the page" in the argot of book-jacket copy. Consistent characterization is one of the things that turn a Tom Sawyer or Elizabeth Bennet or Anna Karenina into such a character. (Aristotle, covering all bases, got this far and further: if an inconsistent character does appear, he must be "consistently inconsistent.")

What does all of this have to do with lying? Plenty if the liar's aim is for the lie to be swallowed and kept down. Someone being told a lie is, for one, under no obligation to suspend disbelief. Try telling your colleagues you're quitting your job to become a missionary in New Guinea—it's the will of God, etc.—when in fact you're quitting because you decided to switch to a lower-level, less stressful job to have time to write that fictionalized exposé of the computer industry you feel you have in you. This even though you promised the people who hired you that you'd see the new model through from design to shipment. See if the thought doesn't cross their minds that you may be lying—the missionary story is too bleeping implausible given what they know about you. Quitting to move to another town in order to take care of an ailing sister may have a better chance of convincing because it is more plausible, but the best chance for success is lying by misdirection. "A mess; I'd rather not talk about it"—in other words, a matter too personal to be explained but tumultuous and dire—may be the ticket, one that has the added advantage of being impossible to expose as a lie since quitting a job to write may, after all, suggest a certain confusion of mind.

Back in the better-lit regions where a lie is a lie, plain and simple, the question remains how to make it believable. Elaborate pondering of the perennial challenge of making people swallow and keep down a bogus, self-promoting story occurs in *All's Well That Ends Well*, and the student prevaricator can learn much by paying attention. Unbeknownst to the young hothead Count Bertram, his companion Paroles is infamous for being "an infinite and endless liar, an hourly promise-breaker." (Note Paroles' name, which punningly hints at what he is and isn't: a voluble user of words—French *paroles*—and a breaker of promises—the root meaning of the English *parole* is a formal promise.) Paroles' self-proclaimed martial exploits are the empty boasts of an inveterate coward. When he accompanies Bertram to join the French contingent helping the duke of Florence fight a war, his luck as a braggart runs out. Set up by Florentine noblemen whose aim is to expose him to Bertram, he offers to recover a drum the enemy captured in the latest skirmish. He departs for this heroic feat, but, as one of the noblemen tells Bertram, he'll do nothing at all "but return with an invention, and clap upon you two or three probable lies."

The noblemen lie in ambush in order to capture Paroles and make him believe he has fallen into enemy hands, at which point the coward is sure to reveal his true nature by falling over his own feet in the haste to betray friends, comrades, and the duke to save his hide. They are in a position to overhear him debating with himself how to convince people that he made a heroic attempt but, alas, failed. Three hours' absence should be time enough to make them believe he'd gone to the enemy camp, done what he did, and returned. But then what? "What shall I say I have done? It must be a very plausive invention that carries it." Should he injure himself and say he was wounded during the exploit? The problem with that scenario is that slight wounds will not do the trick and he is understandably reluctant to inflict substantial ones on himself. How nice it would be if cutting his clothes or breaking his sword had the desired effect, but there was little chance of that. Or should he shave his beard and claim that was part of his strategy? Or suppose he threw away his clothes and claimed the enemy stripped him? Or what about telling everybody that he leapt from a window of the citadel? But that might not be believed since it is a thirty-fathom drop. If he could get his hands on one of the enemy's drums, he could swear he had recovered the lost one. . . .

He is interrupted by the ambushers jumping and blindfolding him. Back in camp, he promptly reveals to the "enemy general" all he knows about the Florentine army, gratuitously adding a bucketful of scurrilous slander about its leaders. Bertram, privy to the sorry show, is undeceived about his friend.

Shakespeare does not let Paroles decide on a story probable enough to be believed, and we are left with the question of how he might have pulled it off. The answer is: not at all, given the circumstances. Paroles knew that people doubted his courage and honesty. Short of his reappearing with blood flowing freely from one or more serious wounds, no one would believe he had made a heroic attempt to recapture the drum. The "very plausive invention" that would make people believe the derring-do of a man they suspect of not having enough nerve to say boo to a goose simply does not exist.

Plausibility is also the issue behind one of film's immortal lines, spoken by Peter Lorre as Joel Cairo in *The Maltese Falcon*, but the lesson to be learned is more complicated. The line comes after Cairo has spent the night at City Hall being questioned by the police about the struggle in Sam Spade's apartment. The struggle occurred when Spade took that cunning female Brigid O'Shaughnessy to his place to talk to Cairo, who was to pay him a visit.

Cairo arrives and things heat up in a hurry. He and O'Shaughnessy begin to squabble about some past pawn connected with their epic hunt for the glorious falcon, a man who proved impervious to her charms. They slap each other. Spade separates them, Cairo reaches for his gun, Spade disarms him and roughs him up. The doorbell rings. Leaving O'Shaughnessy and Cairo in the living room, Spade answers it. It's Lieutenant Dundy, the object of Spade's unreserved scorn, and Sergeant Polhaus wanting to come in to question Spade about his involvement with his murdered partner's widow. Spade refuses to let them in. They are about to leave when the sounds of a commotion and a cry for help issue from the living room. The policemen move in and find O'Shaughnessy furious, gun in hand, and Cairo bleeding from cuts on his face. She explains that he attacked her and she defended herself by hitting him with the gun. Not so, protests he. What really happened was that before the arrival of the police both she and Spade had assaulted him and that while Spade was talking to the police she had told Cairo that as soon as the police left the two of them would kill him.

The lieutenant is ready to take the three of them in when Spade, lying through his teeth, explains all: O'Shaughnessy is an operative he'd acquired a few days earlier; Cairo had tried to hire his services but he had said no. The three of them played a joke on the police. When the doorbell rang, Spade assumed it was the police. Tired of visits from the law, he enlisted Cairo and O'Shaughnessy in a practical joke. They were to pretend to be struggling and one of them was to call for help. End of joke. If the cops take the three of them in, the whole city will be laughing in the morning, when the story is in the papers.

The lieutenant doesn't believe a word. How did Cairo get the cuts on his face? Spade shrugs. They'll have to ask *him*, maybe he cut himself shaving. Cairo, seeing no advantage to spending the night in the company of inquisitive police, climbs on board, explaining that his face was cut when he and O'Shaughnessy pretended to be struggling for the gun and he tripped over the carpet. A valiant contribution, but he makes the mistake of leaving with the police and is promptly taken to City Hall and grilled all night. When he returns to his hotel in the morning, he finds Spade in the lobby. Did the police shake anything out of him? Spade asks. Not a single thing, Cairo says. "I adhered to the course you indicated earlier in your rooms." Then he utters his most memorable line: "But I certainly wished you would have invented a more reasonable story. I felt distinctly like an idiot repeating it."

Spade is smug: "Don't worry about the story's goofiness. A sensible one would have had us all in the cooler," he tells Cairo.

What is being touched on here is a higher order of deception where improbability itself becomes the trump card and the liar relies on his listener's sense that this is too crazy to be made up.

Lying in this manner is a tricky business, requiring a sense of the personality and degree of skepticism of the one lied to. The cop wearing a wire and joking to the hood he is trying to incriminate that they had better move away from the jukebox because he can't get a good recording in this din is counting on his or her ability to read others correctly. Robert Leuci, a New York police officer who went undercover in the late 1970s to obtain evidence of police and court corruption for federal prosecutors, is reported to have used this ruse to relax a corrupt bail bondsman who suspected him of being a government agent. The gamble paid off, but it might not have if his victim's suspicion had been stronger or if the man had himself been a skillful liar aware of that particular trick.

Back in that more pedestrian world where probability is essential to pull the wool over the eyes of the person lied to, a demand related to probability is factual accuracy. Liars have to worry about getting their facts right since nothing is more conducive to disbelieving what someone tells you than finding in his tale things that are manifestly wrong (remember our clumsy liar who allegedly kept getting a busy signal until he ran out of change). A good memory, presence of mind, and cleverness will all fail unless the liar is as good an observer and as knowledgeable about how things work as those he is lying to. Not getting the facts right is a surefire way of getting caught. Try claiming to have paid $25 for a cab ride from the airport when the listener knows that such a ride costs a minimum of $45, or try claiming that in the two peaceful years you spent in the army you rose to the rank of master sergeant, when your audience includes someone knowledgeable about promotion in the army. Or try convincing anyone but a small child that you held your breath underwater for ten minutes.

The same holds for writers of fiction, many of whom have slipped up in that area. Anachronisms are typical examples: on the pages of fiction, riders stand up in stirrups that weren't invented for centuries; people take photographs with cameras and ride in airplanes that didn't exist until decades later. They refer to historical events that are still in their future. The way things work (or don't) is another example: people die of poisons that do not kill, use weapons in ways they cannot be used, communicate fluently in languages they never learned. Yet another is the physical universe: the full moon rises at midnight, hinds have antlers (Aristotle's example of this kind of error), a ball of lead falls faster than a ball of iron, and so on. The knowledgeable reader cringes and disbelieves.

The point is that the world we live in does or does not permit certain things, and the author or liar who gets them wrong will get away with it only before people who are equally ignorant. Of course, there are types of fiction that thumb their noses at this concern. Action and sci-fi thrillers are conspicuous for violating not merely the probable but the possible. Things that cannot be done in reality are one of the staples of the genre and the envelope is constantly being pushed, the audience's leniency (or credulity) being assumed. Thus in the 1996 thriller *The Rock*, starring Sean Connery, Nicolas Cage, and Ed Harris, the ex-OSS man played by Connery flattens a quarter with one cuff of his leg irons, uses the sharp edge to score, with a single elegant sweep of the arm, a glass pane, and then pushes out the section of glass circled. Not bloody likely given that quarters are a rather soft copper alloy, but who cares or even has time to become aware of the absurdity while swept up in the moment?

A second requirement every bit as important to probability is consistency of habits, traits, aptitudes, etc. If in a novel the point is made in Chapter One that the character smokes only Camels, she had better not be found in Chapter Nine to be smoking Marlboros—unless we are somehow given to understand that Camels were not to be had or she has switched brands. If a character is described as spending her childhood vacations on a lake, where she once swam out to a small island to hunt for treasure, we better not find her twenty years later envying people frolicking in a pool for their ability to swim. A character having a Cockney accent must not lose it in mid-conversation unless a point is made of his doing so. If he does so without explanation, even the most forgiving reader is liable to be yanked out of the world of the book and to complain that the writer bungled.

Consistency, which in this case amounts to keeping track of details large and small, is equally demanded of the successful lie. If you lie that you're from Texas, it behooves you to keep monitoring y'all's diction; if you lie about the number of children you have, it's a good idea to memorize the number and sexes. All fraudulent claims about background, status, possessions, phobias, predilections, etc., etc., have to be kept straight. Liars indeed need excellent memories, and in innumerable comedies lies are exposed when memory fails and the pretended limp, or lisp, or aversion is forgotten and the truth comes out.

A winsome example is in the romantic comedy *How to Steal a*

Million. Peter O'Toole, playing a detective specializing in uncovering art forgeries, has been accidentally shot in the arm by Audrey Hepburn, playing the daughter of an art forger extraordinaire (the ever-delightful Hugh Griffith). Pretending the superficial wound is debilitating, he gets her to drive him back to his hotel. On the way there, he clutches his arm to elicit sympathy. Alas, he grabs the wrong arm, as she points out at once. (Undaunted, he explains: "The infection is spreading.")

When it comes to realistic art, verisimilitude (from Latin, *veri similis*, "like the truth") is the quest. The appearance of truth fostered by adherence to probability must be there, or the venture fails.

The funniest discussion west of the Atlantic regarding the question of how *not* to sell the reader on a piece of fiction is provided by Mark Twain via a treatise, unsubtly titled "Fenimore Cooper's Literary Offenses." Twain has a field day pointing out with let-me-count-the-ways thoroughness how dismally James Fenimore Cooper failed in the domain of romantic fiction. In *The Deerslayer*, Cooper got things wrong spectacularly often and to a spectacular extent in terms of the absurdities he thereby introduced. The ways are manifold; the reason is "Cooper's high talent for inaccurate observation."

> If Cooper had been an observer, his inventive faculty would have worked better: not more interestingly but more rationally, more plausibly. Cooper's proudest creations in the way of "situations" suffer noticeably from the absence of the observer's protecting gift. Cooper's eye was splendidly inaccurate. Cooper seldom saw anything correctly. He saw nearly all things through a glass eye, darkly. Of course a man who cannot see the commonest little every-day matters accurately is working at a disadvantage when he is constructing a "situation." In the *Deerslayer* tale, Cooper has a stream which is fifty feet wide where it flows out of a lake; it presently narrows to twenty as it meanders along for no given reason, and yet when a stream acts like that it ought to be required to explain itself. Fourteen pages later the width of the brook's outlet from the lake has suddenly shrunk thirty feet and become "the narrowest part of the stream." This shrinkage is not accounted for. The stream has bends in it, a sure indication that it

has alluvial banks and cuts them, yet these bends are only thirty and fifty feet long. If Cooper had been a nice and punctilious observer he would have noticed that the bends were oftener nine hundred feet long than short of it.

Cooper made the exit of that stream fifty feet wide in the first place for no particular reason; in the second place he narrowed it to less than twenty to accommodate some Indians. He bends a "sapling" to the form of an arch over this narrow passage and conceals six Indians in its foliage. They are "laying" for a settler's scow or ark which is coming up the stream on its way to the lake; it is being hauled against the stiff current by a rope whose stationary end is anchored in the lake; its rate of progress cannot be more than a mile an hour. Cooper describes the ark, but pretty obscurely. In the matter of dimensions "it was little more than a modern canal-boat." Let us guess, then, that it was about one hundred and forty feet long. It was of "greater breadth than common." Let us guess, then, that it was about sixteen feet wide. This leviathan had been prowling down bends which were but a third as long as itself and scraping between banks where it had only two feet to spare on each side. We cannot too much admire this miracle.

A hilarious description of the six Indians' attempt to waylay the boat from the perch of their bent sapling follows. By Twain's estimations, it takes the boat a minute and a half to pass the spot, one foot from the bank. The Indians' chief, "a person of quite extraordinary intellect for a Cooper Indian, warily watched the canal-boat as it squeezed along under him and when he got his calculations fined down to exactly the right shade, as he judged, he let go and dropped." And *missed* the roof of the ninety-foot-long dwelling that is the family's living quarters. It gets even better: The second Indian jumps and misses the boat altogether, landing in the water astern of it, then the third jumps and lands in the water farther astern, and so it goes for the fourth, fifth, and sixth.

The problem in this instance is human beings behaving unbelievably under the circumstances. Elsewhere "the eternal laws of Nature have to vacate when Cooper wants to put up a delicate job of woodcraft on the reader." Trying to find the lost trail of someone he is tracking through the forest, an Indian diverts a stream out of its running course, and there, in the slush in its old bed, are the telltale moccasin tracks, miraculously untouched by the current. Twain's verdict: "If Cooper had any real knowledge of Nature's way of doing things, he had a most delicate art in concealing the fact."

Then there is the matter of dialogue. Cooper, as hampered by inaccurate observation in this area as in others, failed to notice that "the man who talks corrupt English six days in the week must and will talk it on the seventh, and can't help himself." Twain compares Deerslayer's rhapsodic musing about nature: "the clouds that float about in the blue heavens—the birds that sing in the woods—the sweet springs where I slake my thirst" with his observation: "It consarns me as all things that touches a fri'nd consarns a fri'nd." Believable and consistent characterization, believable behavior, talk that sounds like human talk, "lifelikeness" and "seeming of reality"—Cooper failed spectacularly in all areas.

Twain on Cooper may seem to exhaust the topic of probability in fiction. But students of the lie as a fictional enterprise should take heed of one more complication: probability is both necessary and sufficient for the successful lie, but consistency, although necessary to make something probable, is not *sufficient* for a successful lie. In order for anything to be probable it has to be consistent, but consistency in no way guarantees probability. An entirely consistent tale can still be highly improbable. An example from the annals of crime makes the case.

The year is 1921. Henri-Désiré Landru is on trial at Versailles for the murder of eleven women. Monsieur Landru, married and with children, had the deplorable habit of approaching lonely women, courting them, promising marriage, and a short while later selling their furniture for tidy sums—not, however, before murdering them and burning their bodies in a stove at his country villa. At the time of his arrest, he had in his notebook the names of eleven women who had disappeared after being wooed by a suitor bearing not his name but an uncanny resemblance to him, and he was identified by various of the women's relatives and friends as the man who had been introduced to them as fiancé.

What did Landru, confronted by the evidence of eleven women who had vanished after being courted by him, do? He lied. But how? The women's names were in his notebook; witnesses identified him as the fiancé; other witnesses testified to his having sold the women's furniture; he himself admitted that the notebook was his and that he was the man identified by the witnesses. Surely the case was open and shut?

Non pas! Landru had, he testified, assisted every one of the vanished women in her aim to disappear. All of them had wanted to leave France for destinations he was not at liberty to divulge. By posing, with their consent, as their suitor, he had been able to make the necessary arrangements—which included selling their furniture so they would have money for a new start. A man of honor, he had no choice but to keep his oath of silence to them, and, added he, he was also convinced that their private affairs were none of the court's business. At any rate, he could offer no clues as to their whereabouts—even if his silence were to cost him his life.

Which it did. After a sensational trial attended by Paris' celebrities—actresses, poets, diplomats, all of whom paid scalper's prices for attending the spectacle—he was found guilty, and he ended his life on the guillotine in 1922. The jury may have been impressed by the consistency of a tale in which every detail fit (although there were some wrong notes, like his having strangled the three dogs of one of the vanished women), but it did not find it probable. This modern-day Bluebeard may have been admirably inventive in finding the one scenario that would account for all the facts and yet leave him innocent of the crimes he was charged with, but he discovered that, stretched too far, the bounds of credibility will snap.

Not that Landru's tale did not have other advantages. For one, it made it impossible for him to be challenged about factual inaccuracies that would most likely have surfaced—a ship purportedly taken that hadn't been commissioned at the time or purportedly sailing from a port that had never been visited by that liner. For another, it almost entirely dispensed with the need for a good memory. Since Landru provided essentially no details about his victims' alleged departures from France, not only was there nothing that could be checked and found wrong, but he also could not be caught at slip-ups à la "But you said earlier that Mme. Roubaud took the train to Le Havre, and now you're saying you drove her?"

Committed to his preposterous story, Landru cut a heroic figure after the death sentence was pronounced. He refused to sign the appeal for clemency drafted by his attorney. Being innocent, he had no need to plead for mercy or clemency, he insisted. Again, the consistency is admirable even if the pose is laughable—or would be if it hadn't been struck by someone so contemptible, a man who sought out his victims, wormed himself into their lives by feigning fondness, and murdered them.

4

Judging by his success with women, Landru seems to have been quite an actor. His impassioned refusal to beg for mercy after the sentencing probably convinced at least a few members of the court-room audience that here was a man willing to suffer the consequences of his gallantry to the bitter end. Which brings us to a concern not voiced by Montaigne. So far we have considered only the substance of lies and the attributes—a good memory, good powers of observation, the ability to invent a plausible tale, and so forth—that the liar must have to *craft* successful lies. We have not considered the delivery of these lies. "No one who is not conscious of being a decent actor should set up to be a liar," Montaigne might have said had he gotten around to it. Face to face with the person who is being lied to, the liar faces the challenge of mimicking the behavior of someone who is telling the truth under the identical circumstances, and the ability to tell the lie convincingly becomes every bit as important as the ability to concoct it.

Actors face this challenge of convincing all the time. Their intention to deceive is sanctioned, but they are liars in the sense that they try to make an audience believe (or make that "believe"), while the house lights are down, that it is seeing a distraught lover, angry lawyer, amused king, embattled president, desperate real estate agent, what have you. A good actor can convince an audience that they are watching a man baffled and enraged by his own hesitancy when he occupies the stage as Hamlet; a good actress can make an audience weep when Antigone talks about "the god of death who puts us all to bed" and who will claim her before a new day dawns. We believe the feelings and we believe the words even though we know that we are witnessing a performance. Invited to suppose for a moment that these are the premises—a prince grieving for the death of his murdered father, a girl condemned to die for burying her brother—we accept the invitation, and we judge what we see by how convincing it is.

The alchemy by which actors turn into characters is only partly understood even by them. Some emphasize technique—the ability to mimic the behavior of someone in such and such a situation—would he bend his head, frown, have a catch in his voice, raise his arms toward heaven, avert his eyes? Some favor Method—the ability to enter into the imagined mental state and thoughts of the character by drawing on memories of similar situations in their own lives. Method actors stress the need to believe, on some level, that *they* are in distress or pleased or angry or sad when the character is. Actors who practice technique are more likely to agree with Sir Laurence Olivier, who claimed in a 1980s TV interview that when Dustin Hoffman deprived himself of sleep to get the harried feeling of his character during the filming of *Marathon Man*, he said to him: "My dear boy, wouldn't it be easier to just act?" Simply put, an actor who uses technique alone will act *as if* he is sad whereas a Method actor will generate the feeling of sadness, which is then reflected in how the character he is playing behaves. Most actors use a combination of the two ways in order to get to the point where they believe in the character they are playing.

The liar's challenge when facing the person he is out to deceive is similar to the actor's: any successful liar has to come across to his audience as someone telling the truth. If his statement is "I mailed the report two days ago," he has to sound the way someone who has mailed the report two days ago would sound in the identical situation. If it is important for the report to have been mailed (and why else would he lie?), he has to sound reassuring. If the report ought to have arrived at its intended destination by now, he has to sound puzzled and has to conjecture that maybe it didn't go out on that day even though he made a special trip to the post office. Or is it possible the client gave them the wrong address? Or the secretary mistyped it? He has to do all of this thinking out loud the way someone telling the truth would do it and has to hide his panicky knowledge that he forgot all about the report, which is, even as he speaks, sitting on his desk.

Some people are excellent at this. They can project themselves into the role of the non-liar they are playing and use imagination to write the script and live the role. They are able to pretend convincingly that they are amazed or angry, bored or indignant, earnestly concerned for a friend, ignorant about a fact or event. They are able to do this because they have the abilities of good actors: they are good observers and mimickers of people and can also draw on their own memories of how they behaved under those circumstances when they *weren't* lying. The best liars probably make a psychological investment in the role by "believing" in the truth-telling character they are playing. George Costanza of *Seinfeld* fame is a self-confessed master at deception, and his talent is recognized by all his friends. In an episode in which Jerry Seinfeld wants to pass a lie detector test aimed at exposing a lie he told, George's words-to-the-wise reminder to him is: "It's not a lie if you believe it."

The lore and practice of "scientific" lie detection requires a separate chapter, but clearly any liar who manages in some murky region of the brain to believe his own lies will not provide any of the alleged clues by which experts claim to be able to ferret out liars. These clues—facial expressions, hand and eye motion, pitch of voice, posture, and so forth—are found in how-to books on "interpersonal relations," books that usually promise to make their purchaser an instant expert. The title of one millennial entry says it all: *Never Be Lied To Again* holds out hope for the kind of control over our fellow citizens that few of us can hope to gain—although I can see an entire shelf of books in the same vein: *Never Be Tailgated Again* and *Never Be Spoken To Rudely Again* come to mind. *Never Be Held Up to Public Scorn for Promulgating Simplistic Solutions to Complicated Problems Again* is surely a book crying to be written. (Its hype-driven and misleading title aside, *Never Be Lied To Again* has a modest aim. It is a manual suggesting strategies of deception by which to trip up spouses, colleagues, employees, etc., one already suspects of lying, and about a specific thing at that. All in a day's work for police interrogators, and often the quickest way to catch a clumsy liar, but it is disconcerting to find deception "taught" as a simple expedient without an inkling of moral qualms. Having found a quick-and-dirty way to solve one class of problems, we tend to use it for other problems as well. Of which more later.)

Actual experts on lie detection argue (and—what else?—studies have shown) that in general detecting lies is difficult. Even judges, trial lawyers, and detectives, people whose business it is to determine the truth and who may even have been trained for the task, cannot reliably determine whether a suspect is lying. Whatever clues liars do provide tend to be too subtle to be recognizable except by extremely close and careful observation of, say, taped interviews. And the better the liar, the fewer those clues.

5

The lies most likely to be successful must not only be believable; they must also take advantage of the prejudices, weaknesses, and fears of those lied to. Any lie custom-tailored to psychological makeup and biases, any lie that feeds vanity, jealousy, fear of rejection, or any of the ten thousand other goblins making merry in the twisted hallways of our brains, will be compelling in a way in which few other things are. Not many of us have the opportunity to conduct a meticulous study of someone truly accomplished at lying that is concocted specifically for the one lied to. But fortunately Shakespeare, who seems to have known more about how we do the things we do than anyone who lived before or after him, wrote *Othello* and gave us a perfect specimen in "honest" Iago.

Othello is traditionally taken to be Shakespeare's play about jealousy, but it is even more his play about deception. Shakespeare's comedies teem with characters in disguise and often make use of a stock notion of drama and fairy tales—that through deception the truth is unmasked. (Ariosto, Mozart, and Johann Strauss are a few of the many others who have based works on that notion, and in the typical plot the disguised lover sets out to find whether or not his beloved is faithful. Similarly, in fairy tales the disguised king or sultan finds what his subjects think about him and how his administrators administer.) But among Shakespeare's tragedies, *Othello* alone is permeated by deception, and it is a poison that kills. In Iago, Othello's right-hand man, the play presents the archetypal deceiver and villain. Iago murders with lies, using them so masterfully that to watch him is to have a crash course on deception—one that makes the blood run cold at the same time it teaches all there is to be learned about what works and how, under what circumstances, and for what victims.

Instruction begins with a short look at evasion and involves Cassio, Othello's lieutenant, cashiered by Othello after Iago took advantage of his poor head for wine and got him drunk. Pretending to be a good friend concerned for Cassio's well-being, Iago has persuaded him to ask Desdemona to intercede with Othello on his behalf. When Othello and Iago arrive on the scene, Cassio takes a hurried leave, and Iago strikes at once:

IAGO   Ha! I like not that.
OTHELLO   What dost thou say?
IAGO   Nothing, my lord. Or if, I know not what.
OTHELLO   Was not that Cassio parted from my Wife?
IAGO   Cassio, my lord? No, sure, I cannot think it,
   That he would steal away so guilty-like,
   Seeing your coming.
OTHELLO   I do believe 'twas he.

Between Iago's expression of dismay at Cassio's quick departure, evasion aimed at awakening curiosity, and assignment of guilt to Cassio's "stealing away," a laudable performance. But Iago has barely lit the kindling. A deft piece of insinuation to fan the flames is next. "Discovering" that Cassio used to accompany Othello when he wooed Desdemona, Iago begins to ponder:

IAGO   Did Michael Cassio, when you wooed my lady,
   Know of your love?
OTHELLO   He did, from first to last: why dost thou ask?
IAGO   But for a satisfaction of my thought,
   No further harm.
OTHELLO   Why of thy thought, Iago?
IAGO   I did not think he had been acquainted with her.
OTHELLO   O yes, and went between us very oft.
IAGO   Indeed?
OTHELLO   Indeed? Ay, indeed. Discern'st thou ought in that?
   Is he not honest?

> IAGO   Honest, my lord?
> OTHELLO   Honest? Ay, honest.
> IAGO   My lord, for ought I know.
> OTHELLO   What dost thou think?
> IAGO   Think, my lord?

Could there be a thicker broth of muddied waters, one richer in hints steering Othello's thoughts and in insinuations and make-believe pondering—all disturbing? And Othello *is* disturbed.

> OTHELLO   "Think, my lord?" By heaven, thou echo'st me
>   As if there were some monster in thy thought
>   Too hideous to be shown! Thou dost mean some-
>   thing.
>   I heard thee say even now, thou liked'st not that,
>   When Cassio left my Wife. What didst not like?
>   And when I told thee he was of my counsel,
>   In my whole course of wooing, thou cried'st
>   "Indeed?"
>   And didst contract, and purse thy brow together,
>   As if thou then hadst shut up in thy brain
>   Some horrible conceit. If thou dost love me,
>   Show me thy thought.
> IAGO   My lord, you know I love you.
> OTHELLO   I think thou dost,
>   And for I know thou'rt full of love and honesty,
>   And weigh'st thy words before thou giv'st them breath,
>   Therefore these stops of thine fright me the more;
>   For such things in a false disloyal knave
>   Are tricks of custom, but in a man that's just,
>   They're close dilations, working from the heart
>   That passion cannot rule.

The heartbreak here is that Othello is so close to catching Iago at his game but doesn't.

Iago proceeds to plant the barb but he does so with the consummate skill of the master manipulator: he won't relinquish it without help from his victim so it'll be sure to settle in Othello's flesh. He's loath to tell Othello his thoughts, he protests. He may be wrong, his suspicions may be vile and false. He may cause discomfort and jealousy where none are warranted. Othello, growing more worried and vexed by the minute, presses him to reveal what is on his mind. Iago, ever so reluctant, beseeches Othello not to allow a quite possibly misplaced suspicion to trouble him. He is a model of self-censoring scrupulousness: "As I confess it is my nature's plague / To spy into abuses, and oft my jealousy / Shapes faults that are not," he tells Othello, and he warns him: "It were not for your quiet, nor your good, / Nor for my manhood, honesty, and wisdom, / To let you know my thoughts."

Othello, hardly surprisingly, becomes more and more afraid of what Iago is hinting at. "By heaven, I'll know thy thoughts," he vows. Iago tightens his grip on the barbed lance and resists: "You cannot, if my heart were in / Your hand, nor shall not whilst 'tis in my custody." "Ha?" cries out Othello, and Iago yields—and plants the barb in the very act of cautioning Othello against jealousy, the green-eyed monster, and the agony of him "Who dotes yet doubts, suspects yet fondly loves!"

"O misery!" is Othello's response, and all his protesting that he could never be jealous, could never doubt his wife, and conversely would, if evidence of her infidelity presented itself, instantly stop loving her and therefore feel no jealousy—all of this is self-delusion. It is self-delusion Iago pretends to believe, which then allows him to advance to the next level in his monstrous scheme. He feigns to be making Othello privy to his worst thoughts and fears: "Now I shall have reason / To show the love and duty that I bear you / With franker spirit . . . I speak not yet of proof. / Look to your wife. Observe her well with Cassio."

He fleshes out the suspicion by enumerating causes: Venetians are by nature deceptive. Desdemona deceived her father. She strangely turned down many proposed matches with men "Of her own clime, complexion, and degree." Brutally honest, Iago gets to the point: "Foh, one may smell in such a will most rank, / Foul disproportions, thoughts unnatural!"

Truly, as neat a hatchet job as can be: Iago misrepresents a love so strong it triumphed over a father's objection and racial and class prejudice as something indicative of a lying, perverse nature. And

Othello accepts it as the truth, reaching the outrageous conclusion that "This honest creature doubtless / Sees and knows more, much more, than he unfolds."

In all of this, the archdeceiver taps into Othello's two greatest weaknesses: his hidden doubt that he—a Moor, rough of manners, an old soldier—could truly be cherished by a white, noble, young, lovely woman, and his sense that his honor and reputation are of surpassing importance. How puzzling, nay perverse, that Desdemona would choose such a match, Iago tells Othello. How likely that such an odd affection will depart in a hurry to alight on someone more suitable. The rapidity with which Othello accepts Iago's bogus logic suggests that Iago is repeating what an inner voice has told Othello all along: he is not good enough, light-skinned enough, refined enough, young enough for his wife. It argues that, for all his bliss, he never believed in his heart of hearts the great good fortune that befell him.

Still, there is as yet no proof of Desdemona's infidelity. Luck comes to Iago's aid in the form of Desdemona's loss of the famous handkerchief—Othello's first present to her, a keepsake he made her promise never to part with. Iago's wife, Emilia, finds it and gives it to her husband, who had urged her to steal it. Iago is delighted. He'll plant it in Cassio's lodgings. "Trifles light as air / Are to the jealous confirmations strong / As proofs of holy writ."

The trifle comes at the right time. Othello, wracked with jealousy, directs his anger at Iago, insisting that he prove Desdemona's guilt or suffer his wrath. Iago puts on a masterly performance of a good man unjustly accused by a friend.

IAGO   Is't come to this?
OTHELLO   Make me to see't; or at the least so prove it
    That the probation bear no hinge nor loop,
    To hang a doubt on, or woe upon thy life.
IAGO   My noble lord.
OTHELLO   If thou dost slander her and torture me,
    Never pray more; abandon all remorse,
    On horror's head horrors accumulate,
    Do deeds to make heaven weep, all earth amazed,
    For nothing canst thou to damnation add
    Greater than that.

IAGO   O grace, O heaven forgive me!
　　Are you a man? Have you a soul or sense?
　　God buy you, take mine office.

Self-recrimination, put on with a trowel, follows:

　　　　　　　　　　　　O wretched fool,
　　That lov'st to make thine honesty a vice!
　　O monstrous world, take note, take note, O world,
　　To be direct and honest is not safe!

We've seen such a display of wronged virtue earlier: the husband in *Killoyle* indignant about the "low blow," "the very idea" of his wife's charge that he's been betting on the horses. Purported outrage at false accusations is part of the liar's repertoire.

　　Othello, persuaded by Iago's self-recrimination about the folly of being honest, tells him, "Nay, stay. Thou shouldst be honest." He nevertheless repeats his challenge: Prove that Desdemona is false. Iago, still playing hurt and upset, is willing. But how—what proof does Othello require? Does he need to see Desdemona and Cassio in the act, him on top of her? That might be difficult since they're sure to take care not to be observed even if they're as randy as goats. What to do? How about this: "If imputation, and strong circumstances / Which lead directly to the door of truth, / Will give you satisfaction, you might ha't."

　　Imputation and circumstances (neither of which leads to the door of truth, directly or otherwise) follow: Iago reports how lying awake with a raging toothache he overheard Cassio talk to Desdemona in his sleep and how Cassio fondled and kissed him, mistaking him in his dream for Desdemona. Unsurprisingly, Othello is driven crazy by the lascivious tableau. He dismisses prudent Iago's cautionary "Nay, this was but his dream" with his own insight that the dream proves everything. But Iago has more substantial evidence: Does Desdemona not have a handkerchief with a pattern of strawberries? Indeed, she does, Othello acknowledges; it was his first gift to her. Well, Iago saw Cassio wipe his beard with it today and this "speaks against her with the other proofs."

　　Proofs of which, we might add, there aren't any! But Othello is convinced. "Now do I see 'tis true," he tells Iago. And now that he sees the truth, he is ready for murder: "Arise, black vengeance, from the hollow hell."

Iago, ready for the next level, urges calm. He does so in order to force Othello into committing himself to the most extreme position: "Patience, I say. Your mind may change." "Never, Iago," Othello vows, and he swears on his knees that he will never look back until "a capable and wide revenge" has swallowed up Desdemona and Cassio. Iago matches Othello's fervor by sinking to his knees and swearing by the "ever-burning lights above" to give up the execution of "his wit, hands, heart / To wronged Othello's service." Othello accepts and his first order is that Cassio be dead within three days. Iago promises, "My friend is dead." Step one, but Iago at once makes the next move in his lethal scheme, telling Othello,

" 'Tis done at your request; but let her live."

If ever there was someone who knew how to kill two birds with one stone, it was Iago. He is protecting himself against potential future recrimination, which he could answer with the simple reminder "I killed him at your request; I advised you against killing her." At the same time, his plea for Desdemona's life serves his master plan by having the intended opposite effect. Othello could banish and divorce her, but Iago forces him to seal his intention by putting it into words. "Damn her, lewd minx! O, damn her, damn her!" is Othello's response, and he goes to look for "some swift means of death / For the fair devil."

In calling blameless Desdemona a fair devil, her jealous husband could not be further from the truth. But the devil is indeed present and active in *Othello*. The play's biblical overtones are glaring and Iago's tie to the netherworld must have been plain as a pikestaff to an Elizabethan audience. Not that Shakespeare is in the least subtle about the connection: Iago sees his own actions issuing from the infernal quarters. "Hell and night / Must bring this monstrous birth to the world's light," is his final remark at the end of Act 1, and references to hell and the devil abound throughout the play. In the final scene, Iago becomes a "demi-devil," whose feet Othello sees as a fable disguising his hoofs and of whom he wants to know "why he hath thus ensnared my soul and body."

Iago's ancestry also appears in his motive, which resides in sooty depths indeed, and Iago hints at it in an aside explaining why he wants Cassio dead: "If Cassio do remain, / He hath a daily beauty in his life / That makes me ugly." This is the source of the devil's eternal vexation: the existence of things beautiful and good, compared to which he is doubly appalling. It is fueled by the self-hatred of the fallen angel turned ugly by sin and evil and despising all who remind him of his former state. Iago hates what is beautiful, and the depth of his malignity horrifies. In the play's moment of purest evil, Othello asks Iago to procure for him poison with which to kill Desdemona. Iago has another idea: "Strangle her in her bed, even the bed she hath contaminated."

Woe to Othello for not catching the whiff of sulfur. Strangle her in her bed? Kill the woman you love in the place where your happiness with her was at its most ecstatic? And find the fiendish suggestion agreeable? Apparently, since Othello's answer is: "Good, good, the justice of it pleases, very good." The devil would applaud—evil is good, monstrous injustice, justice. Sweet victory!

The reason we continue to marvel at Shakespeare with mouth agape is that, bluntly put, he was mind-bogglingly good at what he did, and it shows. Desdemona's lost handkerchief is one of a thousand examples. It is a token of love, private, simple, domestic, not a flashy jewel to woo a covetous woman but a piece of cloth with a pleasing pattern and the memory of the loving marriage of Othello's parents. Also a plot device, a trifle lost at the right time and put into the right hands to serve as proof of infidelity. Finally, when Othello tells Desdemona his lurid lie about its origin and purpose in order to frighten her—it was given to his mother by an Egyptian who could almost read minds; it would "subdue" his father entirely to her love, a love she'd lose if she lost it or gave it away; it was sewn in a prophetic fury by an ancient sibyl; it was dyed in an extract of mummified hearts—it becomes a sign ingeniously set before the audience. The sign reads: This way to hell. Not many hours remain before Othello destroys his love and, in doing so, his own life as well.

Shakespeare begins wrapping up his play with a scene of discovery as dramatic and effective as any to be found. Desdemona, dying, answers Emilia's question: "Who hath done this deed?" with the noble lie: "Nobody, I myself." Her last words are: "Commend me to my kind lord. O, farewell!" Othello disingenuously asks Emilia: "Why, how should she be murdered?" "Alas, who knows?" Emilia replies. Othello reminds her: "You heard her say herself it was not I." Emilia concurs: "She said so, I must needs report the truth." But Othello will have no further deception:

OTHELLO   She's like a liar gone to burning hell,
  'Twas I that killed her.
EMILIA   O, the more angel she, and you the blacker devil!
OTHELLO   She turned to folly, and she was a whore.
EMILIA   Thou dost belie her, and thou art a devil.
OTHELLO   She was false as water.
EMILIA   Thou art rash as fire
  To say that she was false. O, she was heavenly true!
OTHELLO   Cassio did top her. Ask thy husband else.
  O, I were damned beneath all depth in hell
  But that I did proceed upon just grounds
  To this extremity! Thy husband knew it all.
EMILIA   My husband?
OTHELLO   Thy husband.
EMILIA   That she was false to wedlock?
OTHELLO   Ay, with Cassio. Had she been true,
  If heaven would make me such another world
  Of one entire and perfect chrysolite
  I'd not have sold her for it.
EMILIA   My husband?
OTHELLO   Ay, 'twas he that told me on her first.
  An honest man he is, and hates the slime
  That sticks on filthy deeds.
EMILIA   My husband?
OTHELLO   What needs this iterance? Woman, I say thy husband.
EMILIA   O mistress, villainy hath made mocks with love.
  My husband say she was false?
OTHELLO   He, woman;
  I say thy husband. Dost understand the word?
  My friend, thy husband, honest, honest Iago.
EMILIA   If he say so, may his pernicious soul
  Rot half a grain a day. He lies to th' heart,
  She was too fond of her most filthy bargain.

Emilia calls Othello a gull, a dolt, as ignorant as dirt. Iago and a group of Venetian and Cypriot nobles enter. Emilia confronts her husband: he could not have told Othello that Desdemona was unfaithful to him; surely he was not such a villain. Iago is all virtue: "I told him what I thought, and told no more / Than what he found himself was apt and true." "But did you ever tell him she was false?" Emilia asks. Iago answers, "I did," and Emilia reveals for all those present her husband's viciousness:

> You told a lie, an odious, damnèd lie,
> Upon my soul a lie, a wicked lie.

A bloodbath ensues and ends the tale of "honest" Iago, who told not one odious, damned, wicked lie, but a hundred, and used them to get a man to murder what he loved best in all the world.

The High Cost of Lying

Every time you lie, deceive, or cheat, you lose a little bit of your soul.

Poi Dog Pondering, "I've Got My Body"

I hate, detest, and can't bear a lie. . . . There is a taint of death, a flavour of mortality in lies.

Joseph Conrad, *Heart of Darkness*

1

People lie because lying pays or at least promises to pay. One may gain something by doing it, or one may keep from losing something. Either way, the profit motive holds. But let the liar beware. What has been said about lunch holds for any lie of consequence: there is no such thing as a free one.

How expensive are lies? Very, by some accounts. In his improbably popular jeremiad, *Generation of Vipers* (all about the rot at the core of American society), Philip Wylie took the grim position that when someone deceives someone else, "he commits a crime as real and as destructive as the crime of deliberately running down a person with an automobile." The claim shows that the hard-line New Testament position was alive and well in 1942. The position is extreme, but lies clearly can harm and the cost of the harm they do ranges from moderate to high—where "cost" applies to what is spent by the liar as well as by those lied to and includes not only tangible and measurable things like time, money, or goods but a raft of intangibles like a guilty conscience, effort required to separate the truth from the lie, distrust, and ill will. And collectively society pays a high price for lies.

Aristotle identified one of the costs to the liar. Asked what a man could gain by telling falsehoods, he reportedly replied, "Not to be credited when he speaks the truth." Aesop illustrated the point: the shepherd's boy who entertained himself by alarming the villagers with shouts of "A wolf! A wolf!" to watch them scurry to save their sheep was not believed when wolves truly attacked the flock. We don't find out what happened to the merry lad when the villagers discovered that because they ignored his warning their livestock was mauled. A fair guess is that in an actual incident of this kind the practical joker who protests that *this* time people should have listened to him is not going to walk away without some indignities inflicted on his person.

But the penalty of not being believed when one speaks the truth—maybe at a time when being believed is important in securing someone else's aid—is only one consequence of being caught at a lie. Suppose you catch John Doe at a lie, and suppose the lie is not of a type you give your blessing to. In other words, you don't find it a necessary lie or evidence of commendable resourcefulness on the part of John. If you disapprove because honesty is something you value, and especially if you're not a dispassionate observer but the lie concerns something of importance to you, you'll probably think of John in terms in which you haven't thought of him before. In your eyes he is now *a liar*, and depending on what effect the lie had on you (did you lose time, sleep, energy, reputation, money, or anything else of value to you because you believed it or because others believed it?), he may be *a damn liar*, *a goddamn liar!*, or worse. Unless you have good reason to believe that John lies only under extraordinary circumstances unlikely to recur, you'll quickly move on to the truism that liars, by definition, lie and that you'd be unwise to assume that there won't be a repeat performance. Distrust is the result. From now on you'll question whatever he tells you and look for corroborating or contradictory evidence.

That beacon of morality Amelia Opie made the point:

> Admitting that perpetual distrust attends on those who are known to be frequent violators of truth, it seems to me that the liar is, as if he is *not*. He is, as it were, annihilated for all important purposes of life. That man or woman is no better than a nonentity whose simple assertion is not credited immediately.

A bit unrealistic in the past and present: neither the Borgias nor Shakespeare's Richard III, neither Stalin nor Hitler nor Richard Nixon can be called nonentities although all of them had reputations as outrageous liars. Still, to those of us who've been victimized by liars it's gratifying to think of the perpetrators as annihilated nonentities, especially if we doubt the even more pleasing prospect, threatened by Revelation, of *all* liars being cast into the lake that burns with fire and brimstone (21:8).

Once you've pegged John as a "frequent violator of truth," you may wonder how much of what he's told you about himself in the past is true. Skepticism about the actuality of claims he made or events he described may be the outcome. If you're charitably inclined, you may assume that *some* of the things he has told you *may* be true, but at any rate, you can be sure that anything he tells you falls into one of three categories: it may be the truth told to the best of his abilities, or it may be part truth, part lie (the relative percentages being unknown), or it may be all lie. One potential bad effect on your friend may be your reluctance to serve as a character witness in a courtroom since you may well wonder how much of what you think you know about him is actually true.

Other tangible penalties depend on the nature of your relationship with John: if you're his boss and the lie had to do with his job, you may fire him because you need someone you can trust about job-related things. If you're his dissertation advisor, you may have him thrown out of the graduate program if the lie took the form of plagiarism or faked research results. If you're his publisher, you may take him to court for deliberately selling you false information in a manuscript. And so forth.

The opportunistic liar may surmise at this point that all the penalties listed above result from being caught at lying rather than from the act itself and may wonder why this chapter isn't titled "The High Cost of Being Caught at Lying." There are several reasons, one of which should make sense to even inveterate liars, for whom honesty, presumably, is not a value and lying itself does not set up qualms, shame, or feelings of guilt—about all of which more shortly. One of the costs of lying *is* being caught. Not to be caught requires not only talent but luck, and no one is lucky all the time. Those who lie a lot are caught a lot, and unless they have a very high turnover in jobs, friends, and family, they will be known as liars and people will deal with them accordingly, with distrust, reservations, or outright contempt.

Tangible penalties aside, being caught at lying touches on that complicated question of how much our sense of self-worth has to do with what we think others think of us. If you esteemed John before you discovered him to be a damn liar, and he used your esteem to bolster his self-esteem (an odd thing to do since your esteem was based on an honesty he did not possess, but such mental acrobatics are not uncommon), your changed view of him will be a blow. Even if he doesn't give a hoot about your opinion of him, however, your calling him a liar may smart and he may perceive it as an insult, provided he has some passing acquaintance with prevailing moral standards. The Oxford English Dictionary expresses what used to be an unquestioned consensus rooted in ethics. The word *lie* "is normally a violent expression of moral reprobation, which in polite conversation tends to be avoided, the synonymous *falsehood* and *untruth* being often substituted as relatively euphemistic."

Nice, but by the end of the twentieth century this explanation had the potential of either inducing nostalgia or convincing anyone interested in the evolution of language that the word had in the meantime metamorphosed into something less fraught with reproach. In an age in which *lying* and the President of the United States appeared in the same sentence with nauseating frequency, and in which even supporters of the President used the word cavalierly, "violent expression of moral reprobation" seems too, well, violent a statement. The OED harks back to days when an upper-class English male called a liar to his face by another upper-class English male was liable to demand satisfaction, and pistols at dawn could be the consequence. Frederick Marryat, novelist and captain in the Royal Navy, summarized the sentiment in his 1834 novel *Peter Simple*: "All lies disgrace a gentleman, white or black." (The syntax, admittedly, leaves something to be desired.)

The idea of the gentleman not lying under any circumstances is in line with a society in which concepts like honor and virtue were on everyone's lips, if not in everyone's heart, and in which gentlemen were supposed to be men of honor. But note an entry in Queen Victoria's diary in 1839. She, her consort Prince Albert, and others were playing a game in which people tried to guess a word that could be composed from letters placed before them. Albert had picked the letters for making the word *pleasure*, and Victoria hinted that it was a very common word, to which Albert added, "But not a common thing." One of the company promptly asked, "Is it truth, or honesty?" and everyone laughed. Clearly, the very upper crust of British society had no illusions about an excess of honesty in the world.

Still, to think of an honorable, virtuous man or woman as a liar was impossible in Victorian England except in the high drama of romantic fiction, where the lie was either noble or impetuously spoken and quickly regretted. Hugh Trevor-Roper, in his biography of that inveterate rogue Sir Edmund Backhouse, talks about "the traditional virtues" of the great English public schools, which were "the virtues of the English gentleman, good manners and absolute truthfulness." (Backhouse concurred in thought, perennially professing a scrupulous regard for truth, but not in action. In the course of his piebald career as businessman, secret agent, scholar, and forger, he duped, among others, the British and the Chinese government, a British shipbuilding company, the American Bank Note Company of New York, and his alma mater, Oxford.)

The British upper-class insistence on the truth-telling gentleman descended from moralists like Cicero, whose widely read *On Duties* was a manual for gentlemanly conduct that stressed such qualities as fair dealing and honesty, and from the medieval code of chivalry. That code demanded of the knight to be without wickedness, to honor God and ladies, to protect the Holy Church, to be compassionate, generous, and without treachery, a just judge, a man of integrity who preferred death to dishonor. Chaucer's worthy knight of *The Canterbury Tales*, who loved "chivalrye, trouthe and honour, freedom and curteisye" (where *trouthe* is "integrity" in modern English and *freedom* "generosity of spirit"), is the perfect example.

The chivalric code influenced how men of noble birth thought of themselves, and it continued to influence how gentlemen thought of themselves long after hauberk, breastplate, and greaves had become ancestral relics. It also continues to influence the military ethos. The occasional cheating scandal is a black eye, but the military academies continue in their effort to inculcate a sense of honor in cadets and midshipmen, and the armed services' ceremonial swords are a reminder of the soldier's kinship with the medieval knight.

In everyday discourse, "honor" has a distinctly antiquarian ring to modern ears. The "honor code" continues at many private universities—students promise not to cheat or plagiarize or use other dishonest means to improve their grades. But anyone nowadays professing truthfulness with the expression "upon my honor" would turn heads. "Scout's honor" is still around and derives from the code of chivalrous behavior to which Boy Scouts promise to adhere when they take the Scout's oath, but non-Scouts use it jokingly and a modern-day Scout protesting his honesty thusly in non-Scouting circles would be an anachronism. Still, *honesty*, derived from the Latin *honor*, meaning—what d'ya know?—"honor," is in common use and so are a plethora of synonyms and related concepts. Truthfulness, trustworthiness, integrity, fairness, sincerity, uprightness are just a few. All of these qualities rule out that the person possessing them is a liar. (Trustworthy is something of an exception—a politician may think of a loyal aide or secretary who will lie *for*, although not *to*, him as trustworthy. Loyalty, for that matter, is another virtue that may be in conflict with honesty. To be honest, people have been forced to be disloyal on occasion, just as in order to be loyal they have had to be dishonest. At the time of the Vietnam War, some of "the best and the brightest" in U.S. politics had to choose one or the other: lie to the public to be loyal to the President or disclose the truth and be disloyal.)

2

As yet we've touched only tangentially on the effect of lying on the liar's inner life. Satan is the father of lies; lying disgraces a gentleman; deceit is shameful—any number of mottoes make it clear how we are to view liars, but they leave unanswered what really happens inside someone who lies and is not able to shrug it off. How, in other words, does lying relate to that complicated thing called "conscience" and to that related feature, one's perception of self-worth?

Volumes have been written about conscience and the moral

sense from which it springs. Definitions of conscience range from "the internalized admonitions and requirements of our society" to "learned modes of reaction to stimuli" (behaviorists are to blame for the latter). Consensus is that the edicts of our conscience—metaphorically transformed into an inner voice that guides us in the direction of right and reproaches us when the path taken is wrong—come from the moral principles of our society (which religion may or may not view as the universal laws of a deity) and are inculcated in us by parents, teachers, the clergy, and other figures and institutions of authority. Simple enough at first blush, but the particular rights and wrongs are of course subject to change. They are affected by the company we keep, books we read, experiences and epiphanies we have, as well as by internal affinities more difficult to pinpoint. Decorated war heroes turn into pacifists, Southern Baptists into Muslims, tax collectors into apostles, meat eaters into vegetarians, and their sense of right and wrong and the conscience intimately connected with that sense tend to follow their redefined selves. And society itself varies with locale and continuously evolves, declaring some moral or religious strictures (dietary, sexual, . . .) outdated while introducing others (concern for animals, the environment, . . .).

That said, what remains is the fact that to act against our conscience is to act against what *we* perceive to be right, which more often than not represents the moral principles of the society or segment of society in which we live. When we lie (or steal or cheat or murder) we violate those principles, which brings on feelings of guilt, shame, and remorse. Agenbite of inwit—remorse of conscience—has attacked many a sinner, and guilt has been a powerful motivator for all sorts of actions, from prayers for forgiveness to murder, but shame goes deepest since we experience it as a sense of having demeaned ourselves. The pain brought on by a loss of self-esteem cuts to our very core, and shame, more than any other feeling, attacks our sense of self.

All of this is part of being a social entity, brought up to hold certain values and on the one hand to understand very early on in our lives that disapproval and a lowering of us in the eyes of others attend our acting contrary to those values, and on the other hand to internalize those values and become our own judges when we violate them. Where the moral principles espoused by society come from is another question. Their most important purpose is to promote internal safety and harmony. Hence rules against indiscriminate bashing in of heads, theft, arson, rape, adultery, or saying or doing things meant to confound, mislead, or misinform. Hence the golden rule. All societies tell their members that it is wrong to commit certain acts against fellow members of the tribe, country, clan, whatever.

Clannish and xenophobic, most societies tend to be far more lax regarding the treatment of outsiders. The same Victorians who believed (or thought they did) in truthfulness deceived on a monstrous scale the people they colonized. Conrad's *Heart of Darkness* is among other things a clear-eyed indictment of the lies that sat at the core of the colonial enterprise: the incomprehensible laws whose purpose was to secure prisoner slaves, for instance, or the lucrative business of "trading" glass beads and snippets of brass wire for ivory.

The great thinkers, of course, have never settled for localized insights. Their quest has been universality. Prophets and saints, sages and moral philosophers have tried to apply the code of ethics and ideals of conduct that they developed from within their own societies to all the world. Edicts against doing harm to members of one's family or tribe or city-state became universal rules against such behavior. Blanket statements like "It is wrong to lie (or steal, cheat, murder, etc.)" are the result.

Most of us do not murder or steal, and the overlap between public and private inhibitions regarding those acts is large. Deception is another matter. "It is wrong to lie" is the axiom arrived at courtesy of Aristotle or Jesus or the *Bhagavad-Gita*. "It is wrong to lie to _____ ," those of relaxed virtue qualify, where the blank can be filled in with "my parents," "my wife," "a friend," "a brother officer," "a colleague." An English aristocrat may have made it a point of honor never to lie to a gentleman (a member of his tribe) while stiffing tailors and shopkeepers without the slightest qualms. A woman may never lie to a friend but feel no compunction about lying to her boss, neighbors, or husband. A man may never lie at his job but think that all is fair in love when romantically entangled. "You can't lie to a nun," Elwood Blues tells his brother Jake in that antiauthoritarian motion-picture fable *The Blues Brothers*. In all these cases feelings of guilt, remorse, or shame arise only when people violate a particular rule of their own making. Otherwise their conscience remains conspicuous for its absence.

Those who do have a general sense of unease when they break one of society's rules or violate their own conscience may nevertheless be very aware of the fact that lying can mean getting what they might otherwise not get. So the rule is broken and the advantage gained. After which, a bad conscience may kick in. But in the words of one philosopher who with old-fashioned charm claims to have absorbed the first edicts of his conscience at his mother's knee: "If a person persists in violating his conscience, it will grow decrepit, bother him less and less effectively, and it may soon cease to deter him at all." The insight is venerable. Anything done often enough becomes a habit, and it is difficult to feel habitually bad about anything we habitually do. Conscience seems to be an elastic thing. Stretched often enough or far enough it no longer returns to its earlier shape.

The nineteenth-century moralist's view was that in general any violation, no matter how small, of the dictates of one's conscience was dangerous. The small lie makes room for the bigger one, which makes room for theft, which makes room for robbery, which makes room for murder. The rapid descent down the slippery slope starts with a minor infraction. The model may be flawed—I know chronic liars who, as far as I know, show no inclination toward progressing to murder—but certainly the impulse to deceive in order to succeed can become as much a habit of mind as suspiciousness or greed, and once it has become routine, conscience is no longer an issue. Lying can become the maid of all work in dealing with others while the moral sense in charge of hindering it atrophies. The loss of conscience is probably not mourned by anyone who functions without it, but those who have lost the faculty to tell that it is wrong to harm others, or that deception is one form of harm, have been deprived of a humanizing feature and have suffered an impoverishment of their moral life.

So what is the cost of lying with respect to the liar's inner life, or, in more alarming terms, what is the harm done to the liar? For those with an unstretched conscience, the sense of guilt, remorse, and unease that comes with violating their own principles for one; shame and loss of self-esteem for another. For those whose moral sense in that area is gone, the cost is blindness (probably welcomed by them, but still a lost faculty) to the harm they do when they deceive others. The conclusion? "Th' expense of spirit in a waste of shame" may indeed be lust, but dishonesty, too, is a contender, harming those who practice it.

So much for the moralists' concerns. The Christian view is, of course, much less fraught with complications, and finds all this pondering about the dictates of conscience and the consequences of following or ignoring them so much wasted breath. The concept of sin handles with the greatest economy everything the moralist worries about. Yes, liars and thieves and adulterers and murderers harm themselves. They do so because they commit a sin. In sinning, they separate themselves from God and damage their immortal souls—and the day of reckoning cometh. The End.

3

Liars harm themselves, but if that were the only damage they do, we'd sleep better at night. The price we pay for lies we are told tends to be higher and the damage more painful. For those of us who value close relationships, lies can do harm to what is dearest to our hearts. They can utterly destroy a sense of intimacy, especially if one of the two people involved lies and the other does not. The shock of discovering that someone to whom you feel close deceived you can be tremendous, and the loss of trust and disappointment following the discovery can have a lasting ill effect on the relationship.

This last statement will strike some as an exaggeration. Anyone who lies frequently and is convinced that others do the same will find it difficult to believe that discovering a lie can be a shock. "What's the big deal; everybody does it" covers this and a great many other minor and not so minor sins (as in "everybody has the occasional affair, cheats on exams, runs red lights now and then, inflates expense accounts," etc., etc.). And if one should get caught at lying, what of it? One simply has recourse to any of the standard excuses. Classic examples: "I didn't want to hurt/worry/upset you." But, yes, to those who do not lie habitually, discovering that they have been lied to by a friend or spouse can be a shock.

The effect of lies is a complicated question. Let's start with a point about which there is universal agreement: serious lies usually concern something that matters to the one lied to. If what is lied about didn't matter, there'd be no point in telling lies. So if the liar is a friend or spouse, you're in the presence of someone you most likely feel close to, who, it just so happens, wants to hide from you information that matters to you, or wants you to believe something false when you'd rather know the truth.

Suppose the question is whether Jane has taken the car in to have it serviced, as she promised she would. If it doesn't make the slightest difference to John one way or the other, why would she tell him she took it in if in fact she didn't? And if it matters to him, how does he feel about her lying to him? And how does it feel to realize that if she lied about this, she may have lied about any number of other things in the past and may lie in the future?

Cut away unfashionable squeamishness about deception, turn on the laugh track, and this becomes the stuff of sitcom land. With Lucille Ball and Desi Arnaz or Helen Hunt and Paul Reiser playing the couple, we're off to a wonderful time had by all:

INT. JOHN AND JANE'S APARTMENT—EVENING
John is on the couch, reading the paper; Jane walks in.

JANE   Hi, honey, you're home.
JOHN   Hi, yourself. How are you?

He gets up and they kiss.

JANE   Homicidal. If Hazel asks me one more time whether I mean what I say when I say what I mean about the new layouts, I won't be held accountable for what I'll do.
JOHN   Can you make it look like an accident? I hate those strip searches before conjugal visits.
JANE   You'd visit me? Conjugally?
JOHN   Call me Mr. Loyalty . . . So how's the poor buggy?
JANE   Who?
JOHN   The car. How is it?

She had totally forgotten.

JANE   The car.

JOHN   Yes. Did you take it in?

JANE   Oh . . . Yes.

JOHN   What did they say?

JANE   Just the usual. Not much. They were pretty busy. I'm surprised there are any cars on the road, with so many of them in the shop.

She is on a roll, but John is not about to veer from the subject.

JOHN   Did the guy with the mole work on it? You know, the "Treat your car like a temple" nut?

JANE   I don't know. I didn't see him.

JOHN   Did you tell the guy you gave it to about the oil?

She hesitates, then goes for it.

JANE   Sure.

JOHN   What did he say?

JANE   You mean about it getting dirty so soon?

JOHN   Yeah, what did he say?

JANE   It happens . . . Hey, what do you think of this bumper sticker: "Manure Occurs." We'll get it copyrighted; make a million.

JOHN   Very classy. When does it happen? If the engine runs too hot or what?

JANE   I don't know. He was in a hurry. I didn't catch what he said. I think he just said they'd look into it.

JOHN   Did they adjust the brakes and check the clutch? Let me see the receipt.

She rummages through her bag.

JOHN   How much was it?

JANE   I don't remember. I must have left it in the car. What are we having for dinner?

JOHN   I don't know. Did you mention that sound, that weeeeee?

She bursts out laughing.

JANE   I didn't do that.

JOHN   You didn't tell him?

JANE   No, I didn't go "weeeeee."

JOHN   You think "weeeeee" is undignified.

JANE   Oh, no. "Chuckchuckchuck" is undignified. Or "kerplunk." "Weeeeee" is way beyond that.

He bristles.

JOHN   Well, it happens to be a precise rendition of the sound. What did he say?

JANE   He said they'd check it out.

JOHN   And?

JANE   I guess they checked it out.

JOHN   They didn't say anything? Didn't you ask them when you picked up the car?

JANE   I forgot. I don't think it's doing it anymore. The weeeeee.

She starts laughing again. He opts for dignity.

JOHN   I'd still like to know what it was. I'll go look at the receipt. Maybe it says. I'll look at the oil too.

JANE   Don't do that now.

JOHN   It'll only take a minute.

JANE   You'll get your shirt dirty. Let's figure out what we'll have for dinner.

JOHN   I'll be right back.

He leaves. She scurries to the phone, flips through the yellow pages, dials.

JANE   Hi. If I bring the car in at seven-thirty tomorrow morning, what time can I have it back? . . . Change the oil, fix the brakes, look it over. . . . Oh, and it's making this funny sound weeeeee . . . Okay, okay, I'll talk to you tomorrow. Bye.

She hurriedly hangs up just as John walks in.

JOHN   You won't believe this. They didn't do a thing! I don't think they opened the hood, those crooks. They must have thought they can pull a fast one on the little lady. I'm going down there right now.

He grabs his jacket.

JOHN   Oh, I couldn't find the receipt.

Etc., etc., etc., until the truth comes out, rueful explanations are offered, and all's well once again.

One of the idiosyncrasies of sitcoms and comedy in general is that very rarely does lying imperil marriages or friendships because (a) everybody does it, (b) the motives are harmless and the reasons amusing, and (c) there are no repercussions. (Amazingly, a departure from this rule is found in an episode of that blanket-bombing satirical cartoon sitcom, *The Simpsons*. When Marge, loyal spouse and moral compass of the Simpson household, discovers that Homer lied to her, she is hurt, and she makes the point that from now on she'll never know whether she can trust him.)

In sitcom land, husbands stereotypically lie to cover forgotten birthdays or anniversaries, wives lie to hide purchases, both lie about accidentally breaking things belonging to the other, running into a former flame, forgetting to run errands. Children lie about school, homework, broken lamps, girlie magazines under the mattress, sneaking out when they've been grounded. Friends lie to each other about dating each other's current romantic interests, damaging a borrowed car or jacket. Frasier, usually committed to the truth, will lie as glibly as unsuccessfully when love knocks on his door. Cultural icons like Jerry Seinfeld's buddy George Costanza, or Basil Fawlty (of *Fawlty Towers* fame), or Bart Simpson lie reflexively to keep people in the dark about any of half a dozen trespasses they commit hourly—the difference being that George and Basil have no conscience regarding lying whereas Bart suffers the occasional attack of remorse. Amusement derives from dramatic irony. The audience, let in on the truth, sees the liar perform with varying degrees of ineptness, and things can get hilarious when ever more elaborate fabrications are needed to keep an original lie from being exposed. Most episodes of *Fawlty Towers* are driven by the byzantine complexities of Basil's deceptions. As the incompetent owner of a third-rate hotel, who has first-rate pretensions, he has a good deal to be deceptive about—to paraphrase Churchill on "modest" Prime Minister Clement Attlee. If ever there was a fictitious genius at lying it is Basil Fawlty, George Costanza take note.

All of this has about as much to do with the lives most of us lead as car chases and Murder One, those other staples of popular entertainment. In reality, lying tends to be unentertaining even for people who'd rather walk barefoot on hot coals than be found judgmental, because when it comes to information, especially information we act on, we prefer the truth. Chances are that if you upbraid a mechanic for fraud, based on having been lied to that your car had been taken in for service, you won't be amused to discover the truth. And the same holds for any false information to which you have a reaction.

4

We've returned to the question: what does it feel like to be lied to by someone to whom we feel close? Disappointed is one answer. Lying opens a gap and the world becomes a lonelier, sadder place. Disappointment hurts, but the hurt can also be more directly connected with discovering a lie, and we can come away with the feeling that the lie itself has injured us.

The perception that we are harmed when we are deceived (and inflict harm when we deceive) is what turns lying into a sin or makes it morally reprehensible. The harm can take on many forms. If John—he of the car that goes weeeeee—rushes out of the house and makes a fool of himself in front of a mechanic, he can recite the grievances of embarrassment and waste of time when he confronts his lying spouse. If he goes further, say by consulting a lawyer before upbraiding the mechanic, his bank account suffers. But even if John does nothing more extreme than fume for an hour about scamming car repair shops, he will feel that the lie took from him something he values—a good mood perhaps, or mental energy he could have applied to other things.

Language reflects this notion of being harmed by deception: when we are undeceived, we are *disabused*. When we are deceived, we are *blinded, dazzled, misled, bedeviled, bewitched, baffled*. And, significantly, the harm is obvious even to people who find easy excuses for their own lies: they, too, tend to feel ill used when they discover that they have been deceived.

Depending on the circumstances, we can also perceive a lie as a sign of contempt—the liar has decided we do not deserve to know the truth—or, in milder cases, of a high-handed decision that we do not need to know what is really going on and are better off without knowing. Why? Because we wouldn't understand, or would come to the wrong conclusion, or would make a mountain out of a molehill. Parents worried about their children's smoking, drinking, or underage sex are prime candidates for being lied to for these reasons.

But if deception harms, then those who deceive us seem either willing to do us harm or do not care about the harm they inflict—dismal notions to entertain about a spouse or friend. Or maybe they are adroit at rationalizing deception and think of it as harmless unless practiced with the *intention* to harm. In which case they may wax puzzled when they find that someone they lied to feels injured after discovering the lie.

Such folk can endanger one's mental health, as can liars who use omission, misdirection, and equivocation to confound. We've met them as Jesuits two chapters ago, but there the focus was on the why and how. The effect these kinds of lies have on those lied to is another matter. As the prosecutors of the Gunpowder Plot showed, we can be more incensed at equivocation than at outright lies. One reason is that equivocation and other lies of that ilk are impossible to pin on the slippery characters who practice them. There is no satisfying "Got you! Here is what you said you did, and here is the proof that you lied!" Instead we get the equivocator's claim—usually accompanied by professions of hurt feelings—that there was no lie. If false conclusions were drawn, the "misunderstanding" was the fault of the listener.

But the roots of our anger at those kinds of lies go deeper. Falling victim to them threatens our sense of being competent at one of the things we most value—our ability to communicate, more specifically to make sense of what others tell us. To be told directly something that is not true, and to believe it, is no blemish on that ability. Unless we have reason to doubt, we tend to take people at their word; not to do so would be uneconomical and highly strenuous. If you questioned everything you were told, you'd lose the ability to function. "It's raining here," "The mail didn't come," "I'm in a meeting"—you're bombarded by an incessant flow of information from others. Respond to every statement with the thought "That may be a lie!" and you'll be in an institution by the end of the week. Depending on the context, the discovery that a given piece of information was a lie may be mildly irksome or highly upsetting, but that you believed it simply means you followed standard procedure.

The lie by misdirection, conversely, is far more likely to trigger feelings of insecurity. Unless we're familiar with equivocation, we're likely to ask ourselves a raft of questions: Was there something wrong with us in making the wrong assumptions? In jumping to the wrong conclusion? Would anyone else have done so, or are we dumber than the rest of the world? This is true especially when the liar is adept at the favorite hobby of the outdoor prevaricator: muddying waters and setting up smoke screens. A true master can go through life never once uttering an outright lie while being dishonest at the drop of a hat, and dealing with such a creature can be infinitely tedious. Much gnashing of teeth and hours of lost sleep can be the result while conversations are doggedly replayed in the hope of finding exactly how and where misdirection entered the picture.

On a grimmer note, when the lie takes on the form of a betrayal of trust—the deceiving of someone who had counted on the support of an ally or friend—things can get nasty. In *The Divine Comedy*, Dante reserves the ninth and lowest circle of hell for traitors, and he portrays them pitilessly. They are locked in eternal ice up to their necks, tormented by the bitter cold and by the lenses of ice that their tears have formed over their eyeballs. The cold reflects their coldheartedness when for the sake of gain they chose to betray those who trusted them. Judas is their archetype, and Dante depicts him being crushed eternally by the grinding jaws of Lucifer, but he punishes traitors of his own time as well, and with the passion of an enemy suffering from unhealed wounds. Forty years after the massacre of the Florentine Guelfs by the Ghibellines near

Siena in 1260, the Guelf Dante is bitter enough to have his alter ego rip strands of hair from the head of the traitor he holds responsible. The picture of his victim locked in ice, unable to defend himself and howling in pain, is among the most violent Dante paints.

Lies can disappoint and destroy trust, but they have another effect as well. Although lies meant to hide sins or misdemeanors are intimately connected with whatever they are meant to hide, they are also experienced by those lied to as separate from those sins or misdemeanors. Suppose the sin is adultery, always a good candidate. In the great majority of cases, having an affair involves a measure of active deception (in addition to the one implied because the party having the affair is not disabusing his or her spouse, who tacitly assumes that this is not the case). "I had to work late; I need to be out of town; how funny, I put my T-shirt on inside out this morning," are standard explanations for clandestine encounters or slip-ups. Someone fastidious about lying outright or aware that outright lies are the ones most likely to be discovered may go to extraordinary lengths to tailor the affair around actual events, leaving out only the more compromising details. A woman may keep her husband posted about her artist friend, with whom she had lunch, whose exhibit she attended in the evening, who is helping her design a Web page—the only thing missing in the accounts being the sex and romance before and after.

But suppose the husband begins to suspect something. Suppose he asks: "Are you having an affair?" And suppose the straying wife answers: "What? Of course not. Are you crazy?"

Look at the lie whichever way you want to—a correlative of the adultery, unavoidable the moment the question is asked, implied in the act—the fact remains that the stakes have been raised: a direct lie was spoken, the person spoken to is implicitly asked to believe what was said. The lie, in other words, is an offense separate from what it is intended to mask, and it will register as something apart from the adultery, not more grievous but on a different plane. When in the 1983 movie *Terms of Endearment* the young, pregnant wife (Debra Winger) realizes that her husband is spending nights with another woman and confronts him, he charges her with being paranoid. She tells him that if he is attempting to get out of admitting his guilt by trying to make her feel crazy, then "you may have just sunk to a point so low that you'll never recover."

This perception of a lie counting as another, added offense, separate from what it is meant to hide, is widespread and is deemed meaningless only in a court of law. There it is superseded by the right to defend oneself against criminal charges. No convicted criminal is tried for perjury even though he or she pleaded not guilty and testified to that effect under oath. A defendant's rights include the right to lie under oath. Outside a court, however, the accusations are along the lines of "You deliberately acted against my instructions, and now you're lying about it," or "You told our parents about my being fired and then you lied to me that they learned about it from a friend." Conclusion: What you did is bad enough and shakes my trust in you, but the fact that you also lied to me when I asked you about it adds insult to injury.

The rift in the great friendship between William Wordsworth and Samuel Taylor Coleridge had as much to do with Wordsworth telling a third friend, Basil Montagu, scandalous things about Coleridge as with Wordsworth denying that he had told Montagu anything of the sort. The actual events are muddled, as is usual when passion, insecurities, and things said behind people's backs and repeated out of context come into play. Apparently Montagu told Coleridge that Wordsworth had "commissioned" him to say that Wordsworth held no hopes for Coleridge, who had been "an absolute nuisance" as a guest in Wordsworth's household and was a "rotten drunkard." Naturally, Coleridge was deeply offended by what he was told. Wordsworth, finding out about his reaction, claimed that he was convinced Montagu had never said those words and that Coleridge had "forgotten himself." Coleridge, hurt and angry, wrote to Wordsworth that he was not "villain enough to have invented & persevered in such atrocious falsehoods," a thinly veiled attack on Wordsworth's own veracity in denying everything.

Later Wordsworth maintained that he had been misunderstood, and that what he *had* told Montagu had merely been intended to discourage him from taking Coleridge into his home because he felt it would do neither of them good. In other words, he *had* said what Montagu reported but with no intention of Coleridge finding out, and when Montagu blabbed, he promptly denied it by the amazing strategy of pretending to disbelieve that Montagu had said what he had said. It is not obvious that under these unfortunate circumstances the truth, "Yes, I told Montagu that you're a rotten drunkard," would have been any less disastrous to the friendship. But there is something unnerving and more than a little distasteful about a friend falsely accusing *you* of inventing the slurs he propagated about you.

5

Deception directly affects those who deceive and those who are deceived. But its ramifications spread further. Although Emerson anticipated Philip Wylie in overstating the case when he claimed: "Every violation of truth is not only a sort of suicide in the liar, but is a stab at the health of human society" (*every* violation of truth?), he touched on an indisputable fact: society pays for deception in an incalculable number of ways. Many of these ways are monetary— common frauds in all areas involve the transfer of legal tender from victim to perpetrator. The victim loses money; the perpetrator may put the money in a Swiss bank account or spend it lavishly, but will, at any rate, feel no compelling urge to pay taxes on it. People duped by shady stock or real estate schemes may lose their life savings or be forced to file for bankruptcy. There is no point in belaboring the obvious: vast sums of money change hands and the wicked flourish—financially speaking.

More interesting is the effort devoted by society to safeguard against deception. IRS agents, customs officials, intelligence agencies, the Securities and Exchange Commission, the Federal Trade Commission, consumer watchdog agencies, auditors, bunko squads, polygraph operators—in the United States alone the number of people whose job is to worry about dishonesty is large. Untold billions are spent, and, as in the case of military spending, one may wistfully wonder how much good all that money and effort might buy if it were expended on feeding and educating people and protecting the environment. Idle speculation, since, barring some major change in the moral climate, deception will continue to be lucrative for those who deceive and the need to police it will consequently continue.

Then there are the millions whose jobs, although not primarily devoted to it, include a concern for deception. Some examples: the notary who verifies the identity of people signing documents, the claims investigator for an insurance company, the systems manager on the lookout for the tricks hackers use to break into computers, the bartender and supermarket checker asking for ID, the teacher taking steps to make it difficult for students to cheat on exams, the doctor worried a patient may be concealing an alcohol or drug problem. Add to these occupational concerns for dishonesty the thousand and one institutionalized safeguards against it—the threat of perjury when testifying under oath, documents carefully worded to make people signing them subject to prosecution if they are caught at dishonesty, commandments prohibiting dishonesty under penalty of fire and brimstone, the Truth in Lending Act, the honor code at universities, with its threat of suspension or expulsion if it is violated, and so forth and so on—and what we get is a subtext to our daily lives that shows that human beings have been and continue to be infinitely worried about being deceived.

Where deception is tempting, sanctions are in place and punishment is threatened as a matter of fact. In the late 1990s, the simple act of buying a parking permit at Stanford University—$90 for twelve months—put into the hands of the permit's owner a flier in which the Office of Parking and Transportation Services informed him or her in no uncertain terms of the consequences of certain actions: "If you tamper with your permit or lie to receive it, we will seize your permit and you will remain ineligible for future permits for one year." Note the bracing sea breeze of noneuphemistic language. Someone at Parking and Transportation Services was tired of pussyfooting and opted for calling a spade a spade. "If you *lie*" rather than "if you misrepresent information."

Courts of law have historically made a great effort to discourage lying, for the obvious reason that lies can set criminals free or deprive innocent defendants of liberty or life, or can take money or property from legitimate owners and give it to fraudulent claimants. To discourage lying, courts force witnesses and prospective jurors to swear to tell the truth, the whole truth, and nothing but the truth. The penalty for those caught committing perjury can be jail. The voir dire, or "truth telling," of jury selection obliges potential jurors to answer truthfully questions put to them, the intention being to weed out those unfit to reach an impartial verdict. If you lie (and are caught) you can go to jail. Signatures on legal documents of all kinds attest to the truthfulness of statements made, and a lie on a signed affidavit is a felony.

The fear of deception affects how business is being done in places that we don't normally associate with deception. An example from the world of medicine can stand for the many other at-a-glance-improbable venues. From the early 1990s on, anyone who has donated blood has encountered certain peculiarities in the procedure, which are the result of a marked revision of an earlier protocol. The revision is a reflection of a concern for honesty—crucially needed and potentially lacking.

The actual procedure of phlebotomy has remained the same, alarmingly intrusive but harmless. What has changed is the pre-donation routine. The paperwork part of it used to be limited to circling the Y or N answers of a short questionnaire about the potential donor's history of contagious illnesses like jaundice or hepatitis, or treatments like rabies shots. The list was then checked in the donor's presence by a nurse.

In 1992, the questionnaire of blood banks was divided into two parts: the first to be completed by the donor, the second by a nurse. The Food and Drug Administration, the agency that regulates all blood donation practices in the United States, is responsible for the change. The first part now consists of about thirty questions inquiring tactfully about the donor's medical history. The second part is asked and checked off by the nurse sitting opposite the donor. It is indelicately and unapologetically concerned with the single issue of AIDS, and the questions concern sexual contact and the donor's knowledge and concern regarding AIDS. "Do you understand that if you have the AIDS virus, you can give it to someone else even though you may feel well and have a negative AIDS test?" is one of the questions. The blood bank's main worry, though, is the question: "Are you giving blood in order to be tested for AIDS?" Translation: "Are you afraid that you may have contracted AIDS, and did you decide that giving blood was a way to be tested without revealing this worry, and, by implication, revealing your sexual orientation, drug use, incautious promiscuity, or what have you?"

The great fear of blood banks is that someone afraid of having caught AIDS, and correct in the fear, may use blood donation for being tested and may do so before the test shows the disease— thereby passing on the virus. Bluntly put, the reason the AIDS- related questions are asked by a nurse, who circles the N or Y answer given by the potential donor, is the notion that it may be harder to lie to a person than to a sheet of paper when the dishon- esty endangers others.

An impressive amount of effort but not yet all. One final step is required before the donation. A slip of paper on which two stickers are pasted is handed to all donors. The stickers display a bar code only, but above them are the words USE and DON'T USE. The donors are sent to a confidential booth. Alone with their con- science, they have one more chance to consider the consequences of what they are about to do and, without anyone present knowing it, to put a stop to something that may prove fatal to the man, woman, or child who is given any component of their blood. The donor who pastes the sticker with the DON'T USE bar code on the questionnaire, which accompanies the bag filled with the do- nated blood wherever it goes, knows that the blood will be tested but will be disposed of regardless of the test's outcome. The USE sticker pasted on the questionnaire, conversely, guarantees that corpuscles, platelets, plasma, etc., will end up in the circulatory sys- tem of strangers unless the blood bank's tests detect that they should not be used.

In protecting from embarrassment someone who lied when an- swering the questionnaire, and at the same time protecting people in need of a transfusion from contracting a potentially lethal dis- ease, the DON'T USE bar code is a last-ditch defense against a dishonesty that is life-threatening. Someone too worried about em- barrassment to go to a clinic in order to get tested for the AIDS virus may use the blood bank for that purpose, but the DON'T USE instruction will keep the drawn blood from posing a danger in cases in which the test result may be negative but the blood never- theless contains the virus.

Since 1992, every potential donor has participated in this elabo- rate protocol designed to stop deception before it has appalling consequences. As an example of the defenses set up by society to protect itself against harmful effects of dishonesty this one shows remarkable sensitivity to human frailty. It acknowledges the possibility of people lying out of embarrassment or fear of disapproval and creates a moment in which, unobserved, protected by the anonymity of black vertical bars on white, they can tell the truth.

6

The cost of lying to society is high in terms of the effort, time, and money expended by institutions devoted to trying to safeguard against it. But there are areas in which deception is widespread and controls are practically nonexistent because it is subtle and unfortunately legal (unless the culprits happen to practice it while testifying under oath). They are hot spots of deception, and the harm they do in spreading distrust and cynicism is incalculable. As we've seen, the legal profession and advertising are two of them. But politics probably outdoes all others put together. We do not trust politicians because we fear that the public servant professing his or her commitment to a cause is more likely than not a self-serving hypocrite, an expert at ambiguity and spin, a manipulator far more concerned with self-promotion and jockeying for power than with anything else, and—need it be said?—a liar.

Language is the politician's tool, and one reason we've all become so distrustful of what "public servants" tell us is that we've been alerted by experts to "doublespeak," language aimed at distorting, misleading, and otherwise deceiving. The George Orwells and Philip Wylies of this world have sounded the alarm about that perversion of communication. More than half a century after Orwell published his classic essay "Politics and the English Language" (1946), not a word needs to be changed in the following:

> In our time, political speech and writing are largely the defense of the indefensible. . . . [P]olitical language has to consist largely of euphemisms, question-begging and sheer cloudy vagueness. . . . Political language—and with variations this is true of all political parties, from Conservatives to Anarchists—is designed to make lies sound truthful and murder respectable, and to give an appearance of solidity to pure wind.

Orwell's primary target was the totalitarian state with its well-oiled machinery of propaganda ("All Propaganda Is Lies" is the title of another of his essays), but he recognized the same kind of perverted speech in a democracy. The lies of Vietnam or the rhetoric surrounding the Iran-Contra arms-for-hostages affair as it was played out in 1987–88 would have been familiar stuff. Examples of doublespeak in these here United States are a dime a dozen. Take Secretary of State Alexander Haig's testimony before a congressional committee in 1982. A continued weapons buildup by the United States was, Haig said, "absolutely essential to our hopes for meaningful arms reduction." Or take the following bon mot, which Orwell would have been able to plug unedited into the stream of Newspeak, the official state language in his nightmare novel *1984*: "Capital punishment is our society's recognition of the sanctity of human life." The gem is one of Senator Orrin Hatch's arresting utterances, and it squares nicely with the *1984* slogan "War Is Peace." Exposed to such sinister drivel, the informed citizen hears the creaking machinery of manipulation and learns to distrust reflexively.

Distrust grows with every new discovery of dishonesty, be it evidence of yet another politician's bogus claim of a military career, be it the SEC's announcement that in 1998 Americans lost $1 million an hour to securities fraud. Once some critical mass of deception is reached, the first question that pops into one's mind in the presence of anything—a statement, report, documentary, what have you—is "Is this true or factual, or is it a lie?" Knowledge about deception obviously influences how suspicious we are. Politicians and advertisers lost the trust of the informed constituent or consumer long ago because their dishonesty has been well documented. But the more we learn about lies in all areas, the more trust leaks out of the world. Emerson's take on dishonesty as a "stab at the health of human society" is on the mark. If we run into the fifth article in a month exposing deliberately false reports written by journalists or footage faked by the makers of documentaries, we are likely to begin looking with a skeptical eye at everything we read in newspapers and magazines or see on TV. The exposure of one too many bogus memoirs or self-serving departures from the facts has the same effect on autobiography.

Once we find out about term-paper mills—one of *Doonesbury's* targets in January 1999, but they advertise in prestigious magazines like *Harper's* and on the Internet, and the college student who does not know of their existence has led a sheltered life indeed—we would be naive not to wonder about the origins of an A paper handed in by a student whose previous output was charitable C's. Was it the result of new diligence and effort or had it been written by, as one 1997 catalog promised, "professional writers, most with advanced degrees and all specialists in their field"? This treasure trove for "research assistance" listed over 20,000 papers, each available for $7.50 a page plus postage. Those truly in a hurry could get overnight delivery for $15 or fax transmission for $9.50. Which means that for $75 the undergraduate suffering those research paper blues could get prompt relief by requesting, say, "THE POPISH PLOT. Fictitious 17th Cent. political-religious conspiracy concocted by Titus Oakes [*sic*] to foment anti-Catholic backlash in England." Note that this and all other papers, including those custom-written for the student to the tune of $20 to $25 a page, were to be used "for research purposes only." Yeah, right.

If we catch our students, children, spouses, or friends lying to us, out the window goes trust and doubt and suspicion come in through the front door. One result is cynicism—the lazy person's response to the world's ills. But where deception is widespread and well known, suspicion and distrust are indeed the proper response: "Fool me once, shame on you; fool me twice, shame on me" reflects our feelings, as does our ready contempt for dupes, people who ought to know better and are too easily fooled, too gullible, too greedy to question scams promising fabulous returns on investment.

Clearly anyone's personal sense of how much deception there is in the world is shaped not only by personal experience but by information we acquire from impersonal sources: the more articles on fraud and deception we encounter in the media, the more we become convinced that shady doings are pervasive. Just as obviously, there would not be a great deal of reporting about, say, fraud, if there were not a great deal of fraud around (although here as elsewhere a bias is at work: sensational dishonesty gets reported, unsensational honesty is the story not told). Hard-core reported information aside, we are, and have ever been, influenced by "realistic" or "fact-based" fiction. Anyone who sees David Mamet's *Glengarry Glen Ross* on the stage or screen will have eyes opened and ears tuned to the unlovely tactics of agents selling real estate investments. As the man from "Downtown" tells it, it takes brass balls to get people to part with their money. But, note, it also takes a populace naive enough to swallow the unending stream of lies coming out of the man with the brass balls.

The result of excessive exposure to dishonesty is obvious: a ready distrust and fear of being taken advantage of. The consequences can be regrettable: we may encounter a perfectly legitimate appeal to our charity and be reluctant to give because we wonder whether it is a scam. Fearing a trap, people have refused to become Good Samaritans to stranded motorists. A stranger asking to borrow money for a cab because her handbag was stolen may have to ask quite a few people before one of them decides she "looks honest" or prefers to err on the side of trust. For honest souls a world in which distrust is pervasive is an undeservedly difficult place to live in, and we all daily pay the price of distrust: we are forced to carry proof of insurance in our cars, get affidavits notarized, sign documents "under penalty of perjury," show IDs when we pay with checks or, if young-looking, buy liquor, or rent X-rated videos. Prospective employers wonder how much of our résumé is padding or bald-faced lie and do background checks to verify our claims. We're suspected of malingering or calling in sick when we're not. One thing is clear: a world in which all our statements and claims are simply accepted as truthful would be a place very different from the one we live in.

7

The intent of this chapter and the two preceding ones has been to convince that except under extraordinary circumstances lying is an evil thing for those being lied to, for those doing the lying, and for that amorphous thing called society. It costs money, time, effort, reputation, and self-esteem, erodes trust, destroys intimacy, legitimizes suspicion and cynicism, and can make life exceedingly tiresome for those of us just trying to get along. It has had bad press galore, much of it provided by people in the throes of disgust about liars and lying. Proverbs' pronouncement that a lying tongue is "an abomination" unto the Lord and Meat Loaf's "Everything's a lie and that's a fact" bracket two and a half millennia of obloquy. (The latter appears in an orgy of weltschmerz that may just have the most memorable title in all of rock and roll, the 1993 single "Life Is a Lemon and I Want My Money Back.")

So what are we to make of one expert's untroubled assessment that lying can be useful in the conduct of one's life and that competent liars may be better than poor liars at certain jobs not traditionally assumed to be populated by liars? Paul Ekman, a professor of psychology and researcher in lie detection, makes this startling claim in his 1992 book *Telling Lies: Clues to Deceit in the Marketplace, Politics, and Marriage*. Ekman's book is a superb guide for anyone interested in how people mask their lies in face-to-face encounters, yet reveal them in subtle ways, but he has, I fear, gone over to the Dark Side of the Force. He describes in his book a series of experiments he conducted in the 1970s. The aim was to determine how people who had been instructed to lie behaved while doing so, and what, if any, differences there were in personality or background between good and bad liars.

The subjects were beginning students in the nursing program of the University of California at San Francisco, one of the nation's most prestigious. Each student was made to watch two films, one showing flowers in Golden Gate Park, the other highly disturbing scenes of burn victims and an amputation. They had to try to convince someone who could not see the films that, in each case, what they were watching was pleasant. The experiment was—they were told—meant to test how good they were at disguising from patients and family members the unpleasant feelings they would have to battle as nurses exposed to horrific injuries and suffering or to things that disgusted them. In other words, the claim was that they were being tested at how good they were at deception, which was presented to them as a skill essential for a successful nurse.

These student nurses were all highly motivated to succeed, and by making the stakes high, Ekman hoped to induce in his subjects a high degree of "detection apprehension" to verify clues to deceit he had discovered earlier. The greater this apprehension, he had found, the more difficult it is for someone to lie without sending clues detectable by a careful observer.

Ekman found that some of the students were superbly able to hide their feelings while others could not do so at all. He also found in follow-up interviews that those who had been unable to lie while watching the gruesome film always had trouble lying about their feelings because—he surmised—they had a great fear of being caught at a lie. On objective personality tests, the good and the bad liars scored similarly. "Apart from this one quirk," he concludes, the poor liars seemed no different from anyone else. "Their families and friends know about this characteristic and forgive them for being too truthful." (How nice to have people in one's life who tolerate such a shortcoming!)

Ekman identified those who "lied easily and with great success" in the experiment as "natural liars." They fare better in his assessment:

> *Natural liars* know about their ability, and so do those who know them well. They have been getting away with things since childhood, fooling their parents, teachers, and friends when they wanted to. They feel no detection apprehension. Just the opposite. They are confident in their ability to deceive.

(A confidence perhaps misplaced, considering that they are known to be liars by their nearest and dearest.) Ekman found them to differ in no other respects from the rest of the students in the experiment. A lack of apprehension at being detected at a lie is one of the hallmarks of the psychopathic personality, but these superb liars showed no psychopathic characteristics. They also had the same high grades, top scores on achievement tests, and excellent character references as the poor or average liars, and there was nothing antisocial in their makeup.

Interestingly, it was these "highly skilled in deceit" students who did best over the next three years of their training. Ekman does not explore the possible implications of this remarkable observation, which include cheating, possession of an excellent memory, or the ease that may come with the confidence that one can cover up by lies ignorance that might otherwise be exposed in the setting of a nurse's practicum.

Still, one may wonder where these people's frequent past need to lie to teachers, parents, and friends came from. What did these natural liars do or not do that made it necessary or useful to hone their skills at deception so finely? And what personality traits were connected with their confidence in their ability to deceive? Ekman makes the point that they showed no psychopathic characteristics other than lack of apprehension at being caught at a lie. As we'll see in the next chapter, the point needs to be made lest we quickly begin to suspect them of being sufferers of one or more mental disorders—in addition to being confident and competent liars.

The
Lying
Mind

Liars, Liars, Liars!

A fantasist and liar, one involved in large-scale confidence tricks as well as forgery, he seems the prototypical rogue willing to corrupt anyone or anything, including his own considerable gifts as a Chinese scholar, to turn a dishonest living.

Anthony Grafton about Edmund Backhouse

In his essay "On Liars," Montaigne writes: "I have a decent lad as my tailor, whom I have never heard to utter a single truth, even when it would have been to his advantage." Montaigne says nothing else about his truth-shy tailor, but modern psychiatry would diagnose him as a pathological liar and would venture that an aversion to telling the truth is not the only thing troubling this "decent lad." Pathological lying, according to a more recent authority on the subject, is lying that is compulsive or impulsive, occurs regularly, and either does not serve overt material needs of the liar or is self-defeating. It is, by definition, a sign of a clinical disorder. In four of the ten personality disorders listed in the 1994 edition of the American Psychiatric Association's *Diagnostic and Statistical Manual of Mental Disorders* (DSM IV) lying is identified as not only a characteristic behavior but the predominant one. People possessing an antisocial personality, or a borderline, histrionic, or narcissistic one, frequently deceive, although the situations in which they deceive, and how, vary considerably.*

*Pathological liars are an irritation to moralists, who'd gladly ship the entire tribe of liars to Mars and chafe at bad behavior being excused by mental illness (or, for that matter, at the disease model of the world's evils in general). Pragmatists have an easier time of it. They don't see the point of lying that is not to the advantage of the liar but can live with the reality of some people simply being nuts.

Take everybody's least favorite psychopath, the man or woman suffering from an antisocial personality disorder. Called in the past "constitutional psychopaths" or "sociopathic personalities," people who fit the diagnosis lead lives characterized by deceit, manipulation, and disregard for the rights of others. They tend to switch jobs, friends, and lovers frequently, exploiting and discarding people at will, and they may drink to excess and be sexually promiscuous. They have trouble with any type of authority and demand instant gratification. They blame others for their problems, cheat without compunction, lie with suaveness and aplomb, and are not in the least perturbed when caught at lying. They are often intelligent and superficially charming, and they convincingly feign contrition when contrition promises to get them out of trouble. According to one study, the male-to-female ratio is about four to one and there is a higher incidence among people who live in urban areas than among people who live in small towns.

Hervey Cleckley, who wrote the classic work on the subject, *The Mask of Sanity*, saw the sociopath as someone bored by "human life itself. In it he finds nothing deeply meaningful or persistently stimulating, but only some transient and relatively petty pleasant caprices, a terribly repetitious series of minor frustrations and ennui." The limited emotional capacity of sociopaths creates for them "a sort of quasi-life restricted within a range of staggering superficiality." Among the villains of literature, Don Juan (not Byron's more sinned against than sinning rascal but the earlier, nefarious versions Mozart's Don Giovanni is based on) might be diagnosed as a sociopath, but he also exhibits elements that fit into another diagnostic category, that of borderline personality disorder. Which is not to say that Mozart's librettist got it wrong. Every human being is a mix of traits, a fact that is not lost on the creators of fiction. A diagnostic manual can attempt to categorize prominent features, but any attempt at anatomizing someone in terms of a single disorder is guaranteed to oversimplify.

According to DSM IV, borderline personality disorder is characterized by hidden anger that can erupt into rage. The lies accompanying it tend to be correspondingly malicious. Sufferers of the disorder may start false rumors to discredit people toward whom they feel envious or jealous. They may feel wronged if someone breaks off a relationship with them and may use false accusations to exact revenge. They may try to set people against each other and derive a sense of power from doing so. Their relationships tend to be fragile as they first idealize and then undervalue a new friend or lover. They are impulsive, moody, and self-destructive. Their lying may take the form of pseudologia fantastica, the most picturesque kind of pathological lying. Pseudologues mix fact and fantasy in tales that glamorize them by providing them with a dramatic, flamboyant, or otherwise impressive past and present. Childhood tragedy, famous relatives, a heroic service record, torture at the hands of the enemy, advanced degrees from prestigious institutions are the kinds of fabrications pseudologues weave together with the facts of their lives until fact and fiction become a single, plausible tale. Daydreaming gone public is pseudologia fantastica, and after repeating their stories many times, pseudologues begin to believe them. Unlike psychotics enthralled by their own delusions, however, pseudologues *will* abandon or change their stories if a listener expresses enough disbelief or challenges them with contradictory evidence. Pseudologue or not, the borderline personality appears in mythology as the devil—angry, envious, malicious, a slanderer, the deluded angel who fell because he thought himself God's equal.

People who suffer from a histrionic personality disorder seem by comparison minor nuisances, but researchers have suggested that the disorder is the female version of male antisocial personality disorder and, like it, shares many of the characteristics of the borderline personality disorder. In other words, turn Emma Bovary into a man and we get Don Juan. Freud's ubiquitous hysterics fit the diagnosis, and *hysteria* is still a frequently used synonym for the disorder even though its etymological root in the womb and the misogynistic notions of early psychoanalysis have tainted it. People with histrionic personality traits are emotional, dramatic, and flighty, and they blur the line between wishing and reality. They lie frequently and without feeling guilty because they rationalize that they do so in order to keep people from becoming upset about trifles like their having an affair or not doing their job. They use their sexuality to manipulate. Flattery is second nature to them but they are very good at all kinds of lies that promise to create a dramatic effect and keep all eyes on them. They are masters at self-deception, excluding with ease unpleasant facts from their consciousness.

Finally, narcissistic personality disorder is characterized by apparent grandiosity that proves to be a bubble easily burst, by self-centeredness and self-involvement, and by the inability to experience reality as anything but a reflection of the self. It is allegedly the disease of the twentieth century. An "addictive and unrelenting narcissism" is "the archetypal pathology of our age," according to one observer of society and psychology writing in 1975. Astute naysayer, he would have found nothing surprising about the applause received by Ivan Boesky during his 1986 Commencement Address at the University of California at Berkeley's School of Business Administration. "Greed is all right, by the way," Boesky reassured those in his audience who had a vestige of doubt. "I think greed is healthy. You can be greedy and still feel good about yourself." (Small consolation, but Boesky was later convicted of conspiring to file false documents, involving insider trading violations, with the U.S. government; his being forced to pay $100 million in fines and the return of illicit profits must have smarted a bit.) No drastic change in the zeitgeist occurred at the turn of the millennium, and a day spent watching television should convince anyone that, according to public sentiment, narcissism is healthy and narcissists can feel good about themselves.

What the narcissist's self-confident facade hides is low self-esteem and extreme sensitivity to failures and slights. Narcissistically disturbed people are prone to lying because they need to define the world in a way that maintains their illusions of grandiosity or else their insecurities overwhelm them. Pseudologia fantastica is again a common symptom, granting the wish of a more interesting, captivating life or creating a personal myth of success. And again, deception of others and self-deception frequently go hand in hand, but now this is because of the challenge posed by the need to convince the self as well as the outer world of the narcissist's greatness. When they feel weak, narcissists may lie for the thrill of duping someone and the sense of power they derive from doing so. Glib manipulators, they tend to gravitate toward politics and entrepreneurship, but they are also not in short supply among performers and models. The object of desire in *American Beauty*, the film that swept the 2000 Academy Awards, is a prime fictional example. Her facade of poise and sophistication is shattered with ease by the insult "You're ordinary."

DSM IV lists one more personality disorder in which deception plays a large role, obsessive-compulsive personality disorder, but pathological lying is not one of its signs. As a matter of fact, those who suffer from it tend to do very little "bald-faced" lying, even though they can be masters at deception. Typically they use deception to keep secrets. Their lies tend to be lies of omission, carefully crafted to keep out essential information, and their bag of tricks includes equivocation and mental reservation. Accordingly, they tend to take great pride in their devotion to honesty and truthfulness while confounding all those around them.

So what causes these various disorders? Opinions on their origins vary, and there is the usual nature versus nurture controversy, with nature held responsible by the biologically oriented psychiatric community and nurture by the psychoanalytic one. Some studies suggest that a chaotic family life is the breeding ground for them. A high incidence of alcoholism, abuse, and other symptoms of dysfunction is found in the families of people suffering from antisocial, borderline, or histrionic personality disorder. Typically one of the parents was a heavy drinker and/or had extramarital affairs. Bitter, unhappy parents with low self-esteem, parents who are themselves sufferers of personality disorders, tend to raise children who follow in their footsteps. Narcissistic personality disorders are generally attributed to too little empathy and attention from parents who, often, were themselves narcissistically deprived in childhood and are emotionally insecure.

Personality disorders also seem to be hereditary and hence biologically based. The children of sociopaths are at greater risk for the disorder than children of nonsociopaths even if they are raised by stable and loving families. Biological explanations vary according to the different disorders. A deficiency in serotonin, one of the major neurotransmitters, has been identified as a common neurophysiological abnormality in the brains of people suffering from impulse control disorders (which include the more impulsive personality disorders such as antisocial and borderline personality disorder). One characteristic of people with antisocial personality disorder is a significantly higher rate of frontal-lobe dysfunction than is observed in healthy people.

Brain dysfunction also underlies pseudologia fantastica about one-third of the time. The dysfunction may take the form of dyslexia or other learning disabilities, and there may be a lack of "quality control" for the pseudologue's verbal production if the more logical and critical portions of the brain (the frontal lobes and nondominant hemispheres) do not adequately monitor verbal output and compare it to reality. Which leaves unanswered the question of where the two-thirds of pseudologues who show no evidence of brain damage come from.

Psychoanalysts of course see the various disorders and the deception that belongs to them as manifestations of unconscious processes. According to them, pseudologia fantastica is the result of unconsciously motivated efforts to preserve or create a sense of self and defend against overwhelming anxieties; narcissism stems from low self-esteem, which must be suppressed by a self-deceptive cover-up of grandiosity or else appears as depression; histrionic traits are the result of psychological issues that remained unresolved in the oedipal period of development, and the histrionic person uses ego-defense mechanisms (of which more later) to cope with life; people with borderline personality features use ego-defense mechanisms to perpetuate self-deception. And so forth.

Although each school of thought tends to emphasize one set of explanations over others, most psychiatrists and psychologists agree that biology *and* environment influence the development of personality. Which suggests that pathological liars are made by their genes and by their surroundings. At any rate, parents whose son or daughter lies frequently and about important things had better pay attention: a study done in 1989 found that persistent and extreme lying in a child is an important predictor of adult antisocial behavior and that lying is a fundamental underpinning of other types of antisocial behavior. There may, after all, be something to the old notion that lying can lead to more serious infractions. The emphasis is, however, on *persistent* and *extreme*. Nobody sensible would suggest that the occasional lie of claiming to have done all the problems in the problem set or not being the one who overturned the flowerpot is a predictor of adult psychopathology and criminal tendencies.

Psychology also looks beyond the possible relationship between adult mental disease or criminal tendencies and childhood lying to the function of lies in the development of children. One theory proposes that lying is an essential part of psychic development. Separation from the parents, and especially from the mother, must be not only physical but also psychological, and lying, the argument goes, becomes an important or even an essential means by which children can define themselves as autonomous beings separate from their parents. The lie that is not detected by the parent shows the child that it is not a part of the parent and has its own distinct identity. An early voice for this theory argued: "The striving for the right to have secrets from which the parents are excluded is one of the most powerful factors in the formation of the ego, especially in establishing and carrying out one's own will." The theory sounds good on paper but it would be more compelling if there weren't so many other ways by which children discover their separateness from their parents. Anyone who has ever watched an infant spit out what a parent lovingly put in its mouth will have little doubt that this bundle of contrariness is aware of its autonomy.

Another proposal regarding the psychic importance of lying by a child has to do with the child's realizing that its parents are not omniscient. If the child can lie successfully to its parents, then they are not as powerful as the child had imagined them to be. The Freudian analyst Heinz Kohut argued that the lost parental omniscience is then incorporated into the child's internalized controls and becomes an aspect of the omniscience of the superego. Lying, according to this view, plays a role in the growth of self-regulation. The number of adults of ordinary intelligence who have never once lied is probably zero, and since there is no never-lying group to which we could compare the liars in order to establish the two groups' degree of autonomy or self-regulation, these claims cannot be proven.

Freud himself treated lying as a common, everyday phenomenon like dreams or slips of the tongue. Like other acts, lies could be analyzed in the context of a patient's life and could shed light on pathologies. Regarding the lies of children, he objected to the accusatory, punitive attitudes of adults who more often than not were hypocrites in condemning what they themselves did. Rather than sharing the prevailing view of children's lies being a warning sign of a bad adult character, he saw them serving important functions in the child's mental life. In his analysis of "little Hans" in 1909, he commented on five-year-old Hans's fantasy that his little sister had been with the family the summer before her birth and "the countless extravagant lies with which he interwove it." The fantasy and the lies were intended as a revenge upon his father for having misled Hans with the fable of the stork, Freud concluded. It was as though Hans had told his father that if he really thought Hans was stupid enough to believe the story of his sister being delivered by the stork, then he expected his father to return the favor by accepting *his* inventions as the truth.

In a short paper Freud wrote in 1913, he reiterated his view that the lies of children are often their response to the lies told by adults. "We can understand children telling lies when, in doing so, they are imitating the lies told by grown-up people," he wrote. But he also warned that "a number of lies told by well-brought-up children have a particular significance and should cause those in charge of them to reflect rather than be angry. These lies occur under the influence of excessive feelings of love, and become momentous when they lead to a misunderstanding between the child and the person it loves." The two short case histories he used to illustrate his argument came out of the analysis of two female patients. Each remembered an instance of lying in childhood that had enormous repercussions on her mental life because of the way it had been dealt with by her father. In both cases unrequited love for the father lay at the heart of neurotic symptoms.

In one of the cases the patient had bragged "We have ice every day" in response to a schoolmate's boast that "yesterday we had ice at dinner." This even though she did not know what "ice at dinner" meant since she was familiar with ice only in the form of the long blocks in which it was carted around. She assumed that there had to be something grand in having it at dinner and refused to be out-done by the other girl.

Another lie she told had to do with her using a compass to draw a perfect circle, when the assignment in class had been to draw freehand. Challenged by the teacher, she refused to admit what she had done even though the marks the compass had left on the paper were evident. The teacher told her father of the lie and of the girl's refusal to admit to it. According to Freud, both lies derived from the child's unusually strong attachment to her father. She had ide-alized her father even though she had recognized that his actual achievements were minor—he had financial difficulties and was neither as powerful nor as distinguished as she had imagined. She found this departure from her ideal too painful and boasted about her father every chance she got in order not to have to belittle him. Freud wrote: "When, later on, she learned to translate ice for din-ner by '*glace*' [French for "ice"], her self-reproaches about this rem-iniscence led her by an easy path into a pathological dread of pieces or splinters of glass [*Glas* in German]."

The second lie came out of the fact that her father was an excel-lent draftsman and had often exhibited his skill to his children. "It was as an identification of herself with her father that she had drawn the circle at school—which she could only do by deceitful methods. It was as though she wanted to boast: 'Look at what my father can do!' " Freud being Freud, sex rears its untidy head at this point: "The sense of guilt that was attached to her excessive fond-ness for her father found its expression in connection with her at-tempted deception; an admission was impossible . . . [because] it would inevitably have been an admission of her hidden incestuous love."

The other patient's childhood lie, which she told when she was seven and bought paints for Easter eggs with money her father had given her for another purpose, required more complex analysis since it involved a more complex set of circumstances. Romantic trysts years earlier between the patient's nursemaid and a doctor, the child's silence bought with small coins, her betrayal of the cou-ple (she had probably seen them having sex)—all entered into it. The powerful mix of sex, money, love, and betrayal and, according to Freud, rejected erotic longings for the father (who had refused to give her the money for the paints, money which to her mind equaled love) were to blame both for the lie and for the dramatic change in personality that the girl underwent as a result of being punished for the lie. Punished for a set of circumstances that came out of her love, she went from self-confident to timid, and years later the trauma profoundly affected her married life.

In Freud's view, the reason these childhood lies turned out to be of enormous significance in the lives of both women was that the lies were told for a love the child herself felt guilty about. Being discovered at the lie added to the feeling of guilt because the true reason had to be kept secret even from the child herself. The lie became, in the words of John Forrester, who has written eloquently on Freud: "a turning point in the child's development, or an ineradicable source of guilt and self-reproach." It thus became "pathogenic because of the moralistic attitude of the parent." Again in this essay, Freud stressed: "It would be a serious mistake to read into childish misdemeanors like these a prognosis of the development of a bad character." Clearly, the lies Freud is thinking of are not the "persistent" and "extreme" lies in childhood that psychologists do see as predictors of adult antisocial behavior. And just as clearly there is a continuum between "normal" and pathological lying.

In several of the personality disorders, deception of others is closely linked with self-deception. The attempt to sell the outside world a bill of false goods seems to invite an odder transaction, in which the same false goods are unloaded on the seller. Since, as we'll see shortly, self-deception is purported to play a large role in the mental lives of people whose brains function reasonably well (read: you and me), it should come as no surprise that disordered brains practice it with a vengeance. A dramatic theory of how the minds of narcissistically disturbed people distort the outer world suggests how the process works for them:

> People suffering from the kind of grandiosity that is commonly termed "narcissistic" are compelled to invest large amounts of energy in defending against anything that might put their own

grandiosity in question. . . . One will usually find a somewhat tragic imbalance in their "psychic economy," as they unconsciously attribute their highest value to a special personality trait or a special talent they seem to possess. They tend, in other words, to project the self . . . on certain personal features and are not able to distinguish their wholeness as a human being from such a special, highly idealized attribute. Unconsciously they feel: I am great (in every aspect of my whole personality), since I am so exceptionally beautiful, attractive, clever, creative, etc. But the total of my self-value, and thereby of my self-esteem, would be destroyed if I were forced to realize that my beauty, my attractiveness, my intelligence, my creativity are not (or are no longer) exceptional.

In other words, unless they deceive themselves, people who are narcissistically disturbed cannot function. As we'll see, rumor has it they're not the only ones.

Deep Down, I Knew . . .

It makes sense to ask: "Do I really love her, or am I only pretending to myself?"

Ludwig Wittgenstein, *Philosophical Investigations*

It is as if you were running in a race. A sign-post stands at a fork in the road to indicate the route. You stop and twist the sign-post in the wrong direction, hoping thereby to deceive those following into running in the wrong direction. But how could you twist the sign-post round and thereby deceive yourself into running in the wrong direction?

T. S. Champlin, "Self-Deception: A Reflexive Dilemma"

The Big Book of Alcoholics Anonymous tells the story of Jim, a man with a wife and family whom he loved, intelligent, well liked, and the owner of a lucrative car dealership. Jim took to drink at age thirty-five and within a few years became so violent when he was drunk that he had to be committed to a mental institution. Released from the institution, he knew that he had to stay away from alcohol or be utterly ruined. But despite resolving to do so, he time and again found himself drunk. He related the last of these occasions to members of AA who had tried to help him in the past.

He had had a minor quarrel with his boss, the man who ran the dealership Jim had formerly owned, and decided to drive into the country to see one of his prospects for a car. But things took a bad turn:

> On the way I felt hungry so I stopped at a roadside place where they have a bar. I had no intention of drinking. I just thought I would get a sandwich. . . . I sat down at a table and ordered a sandwich and a glass of milk. Still no thought of drinking. I ordered another sandwich and decided to have another glass of milk.

Suddenly the thought crossed my mind that if I were to put an ounce of whiskey in my milk it couldn't hurt me on a full stomach. I ordered a whiskey and poured it into the milk. I vaguely sensed that I was not being any too smart, but felt reassured as I was taking the whiskey on a full stomach. The experiment went so well that I ordered another whiskey and poured it into more milk. That didn't seem to bother me so I tried another.

The episode ended with the experimenter's return to the mental institution.

Jim was a prime example of someone who although fully aware of the fact that he was an alcoholic—in other words, that alcohol was a life-threatening drug for him—was able with minimal effort to short-circuit that knowledge by a burst of illogical "reasoning," in his case that whiskey mixed with milk would have no effect on him and that if he felt fine after the first drink, he could have a second, and if he felt fine after the second, could have a third, and so forth.

In any AA meeting people will tell similar stories about how easy it was to overcome cast-iron resolutions, their fear of losing their families, of ruining their lives, destroying their health—all this by the feeblest of excuses, excuses they themselves found demented when recalling them after yet another drinking episode. And they will talk about the tricks they played on themselves before they finally accepted the cold, hard fact that for them taking a drink meant triggering a potentially fatal illness. To convince themselves that they were only normal drinkers, not alcoholics, they resorted to one or more "proofs" from a long list: they obviously had no problem with alcohol because they drank beer only, consumed a limited number of drinks, never drank alone, never drank in the morning, drank only at home, never had alcohol in the house, never drank during business hours, had switched from scotch to brandy, drank only natural wines, were exercising more, were reading inspirational books, and so forth and so on.

The first of AA's twelve steps to recover from alcoholism is the admission of powerlessness over alcohol and of the fact that life has become unmanageable. This typically involves breaking through an intricate network of bogus excuses by which the alcoholic distorted objective reality—the kind of reality that tells others that a woman unable to appear at a job interview or attend her daughter's birthday party because she is too drunk to stand up has a serious problem. An alcoholic, let's call him Jim in memory of the ingenious salesman who bought into his own harebrained notion that whiskey in milk was harmless, must realize that he is playing a dangerous game, self-deception by name, when he smuggles bottles into the house and hides them in his dresser, and masks the shot of vodka with orange juice, and is never without breath mints—all this because his wife foolishly worries about him having a drinking problem. He must recognize the discrepancy between what is actually going on inside him and the defiant pose he is striking—according to which he drinks not because he's addicted to alcohol but because he'll be damned if he lets himself be controlled by family members who urge him to quit, or the judge who orders him to, or a fed-up boss. Unless Jim recognizes that the attitude shown by others is a reflection of reality while the world he constructs for himself in order to be able to keep drinking is delusional, he has no hope for recovery.

Addicts tend to be masters at the kind of mental acrobatics necessary to distort the world to reflect a less troubling picture of themselves—the illusion of control, of being able to stop at any time if only they chose to, being the most conspicuous. And, as we have seen, self-deception is a symptom of several of the personality disorders. But we all have the ability to run rings around common sense or logic if the spirit moves us. A raft of self-reflexive expressions attest to widespread consensus about how good we are at the game: We *fool* or *kid* or *delude ourselves*, we *pretend to ourselves*, *refuse to admit to ourselves*, indulge in *wishful thinking*; we ruefully reflect on events and conclude that we *talked ourselves out of* what we *knew in our hearts* was the right thing, or *convinced ourselves* of the rightness of something we knew *deep down* was wrong.

Afterward, when we recognize the self-deception that had made us do or not do something, the sense we get from the experience is that we knew the truth, the facts, objective reality, what have you, somewhere, on some level, in some sense, but also knew how to apply tactics that suppressed our awareness of these things because they would have been inconvenient or troublesome to know. We convinced ourselves that worrisome symptoms had nothing to do with a serious illness. We wanted to believe the con artist's promise of a guaranteed high return on our investment, the benevolence of a mentor or therapist, a cure, an answer, a reassurance. So we overrode our doubts and shouted down the small voice that cried: "Watch out!" Sometimes a nagging sense of something being wrong—a thing we might as well call a bad conscience—eventually brought the truth to the surface and with it insight into our own mental machinations.

In other instances, the tactics become a mantra that has to be repeated periodically to keep the troublesome truth suppressed. Consider a creature from world literature, Giuseppe Baldini, Europe's greatest perfumer in Patrick Süskind's novel *Perfume*. By virtue of the miraculous nose of his apprentice Jean-Baptiste Grenouille, Baldini's business has flourished beyond his wildest fancy. When Baldini promotes his apprentice to journeyman and gives him leave, he can finally admit to himself that he had never felt comfortable with him in the house. A bad conscience had kept him ill at ease, and not a day had passed without his being haunted by the notion that in some way or other he would have to pay for having gotten involved with Grenouille. During those years, his constant anxious prayer had been for success without penalty. To keep his fears in check, he had let his thoughts run in the same groove morning, noon, and night:

> What I'm doing is not right, but God will wink His eye, I'm sure He will. . . . What wrong have I actually done, if there has been a wrong? At the worst I am operating somewhat outside guild regulations by exploiting the wonderful gifts of an unskilled worker and passing off his talent as my own. At the worst I have wandered a bit off the traditional path of virtue. At the very worst, I am doing today what I myself have condemned in the past. Is that a crime? Other people cheat their whole life long. I have only fudged a bit for a couple of years. And only because of purest chance I was given a once-in-a-lifetime opportunity. Perhaps it wasn't chance at all, but God Himself, who sent this wizard into my house, to make up for the days of humiliation by Pélissier and his cohorts. Perhaps Divine Providence was not directing Himself at me at all, but *against* Pélissier! That's perfectly possible!

How else would God have been able to punish Pélissier other
than by raising me up? My luck, in that case, would be the means
by which divine justice has achieved its end, and thus I not only
ought to accept it, but I must, without shame and without the
least regret. . . .

Baldini's desperate tactics to get from a feeling of guilt to one of
self-approbation in a few not overly subtle moves are perfectly obvious to the reader. And they are obvious to Baldini himself. Once
his uncanny apprentice is gone, he is relieved that "such sinister
thoughts" are now at an end. Of course Baldini has the fear of God
and a conscience honed by a Catholic upbringing throwing obstacles in his way on the road to self-deception, which is why he has to
put himself through the bad-Baldini-to-good-Baldini routine
thrice daily. His power to distort the truth about himself—he is
hourly sinning by breaking the laws of his guild and by lying about
his inventing perfumes he could not begin to imagine—is hampered by his background.

Baldini is a fictional character, not the John Doe of a carefully
documented case study, but he is one of countless imaginative cre-
ations to whom we owe our strong sense of knowing how the mind
works. Theater, film, even the odd insightful TV drama have given
us profound analyses of mental states and processes. Novels, in particular, are superbly suited to explore the inner life of their characters through literary devices like Giuseppe Baldini's interior
monologue, or the unreliable narrator (take splendidly demented
Charles Kinbote in Nabokov's *Pale Fire*), or the omniscient writer
(take George Eliot, who tells us in *Middlemarch* that Mr. Casaubon,
married to Dorothea, "did not confess to himself, still less could he
have breathed to another, his surprise that though he had won a
lovely and noble-hearted girl he had not won delight").

Famous fictional practitioners of self-deception are plentiful.
Jane Austen's Emma Woodhouse, victim of her own illusions,
which make her create a world as far from the real one as she can
get without being at once exposed as a vain, blind fool, is a prime
example. Emma learns from experience—and not before she has
done a good deal of fortunately repairable damage—that her opinion of herself is far too high. Other fictional geniuses at deceiving

themselves are not so lucky. Conrad's Kurtz, so full of noble schemes for the betterment of mankind and in fact an emblem for depravity, recognizes the truth when he utters his signature line shortly before his death in *Heart of Darkness*, but his insight comes too late. Anna Karenina, in her final hours projecting her own hatred on Vronsky and Kitty and Dolly—all of whom, she *knows!*, despise her—dies without the slightest notion about this and so many other tricks her mind played on her.

So far so good, but will any of it play before the Aristotelian Society or some other august body of Professors of Philosophy? Not likely. The problem is that this casual discussion of self-deception is based on commonsense observation and on the comparison of the facts—or those more complicated things called the truth or reality—with notions that contradict the facts, the truth, reality. Observation tells us that Jim the factual alcoholic and Baldini the fictional perfumer try to create their own versions of reality and that the versions they create are inadequate representations. The discrepancy between the world as it appears to them (or as they try to make it appear to themselves) and reality as it appears to us is what alerts us to their self-deception. Of course, anyone's representation of reality is idiosyncratic and debatable, but drastic departures from some normative version we agree on are easy to spot. Common sense, interpreting what we observe, tells us that what we are seeing is deception practiced by Jim on himself to give himself permission to drink and by Baldini on himself to be less afraid of divine retribution for his sins.

Philosophers, who have a carefully cultivated sense of disdain for common sense, rest far less easy with the concept of self-deception. The standard philosophical question about self-deception is: "Can you deceive yourself into believing what you know to be false?"

Yes, of course, Common Sense says; it's done all the time. Just look at the examples above. Plus, consider Nietzsche, who wrote, and I quote: "The most common lie is the lie one tells to oneself." Or consider Wittgenstein's aphorism: "Nothing is so difficult as not deceiving oneself." Surely we're talking about an open-and-shut case here.

Not so fast, Aristotelian Philosophy counters. Let me set one of our standard philosophical scenes, solitary confinement in a cell, and let me conduct a little experiment with you.

> You find yourself seated on a hard chair at a plain desk in a small, brightly lit, rectangular room. As you sit on your hard chair you hear the voice of your philosophical tormentor, who addresses you thus: "You see before you on the desk a packet of cigarettes. Take the packet and hide it from yourself! Obey me and I shall release you from this dungeon." Anxious to avail yourself of this offer of escape you pick up the packet and, holding it in your hand, begin to search for suitable hiding places. Eventually, you slide open one of the drawers of the desk—which proves, of course, to be empty—and slip the packet inside.

Have you met your tormentor's requirement for release? Not at all. Back on the intercom, he points out the obvious: although you may have hidden the cigarettes from him, you have not hidden them from yourself. He is right, of course. How could you have? If you hide a pack of cigarettes, you know the hiding place. How can one person be both the one who does the hiding and the one from whom the object is hidden?

Touché, says Common Sense, never one for prolonged cogitation. I must have been wrong when I thought I could hide anything from myself. Silly me.

What Common Sense ought to do instead is point out that the scene set by Philosophy not only does not allow Common Sense to hide anything from herself but also does not allow her to hide anything from her tormentor and is therefore meaningless. The tormentor, although a philosophical one and therefore capable of the willing suspension of the entirely obvious, presumably does know that the only place to put anything out of visual range in the cell is the desk, which means that the packet has to be in one of the desk's drawers. To be able to hide anything in such a way that it will remain hidden requires ignorance on the part of the one from whom it is hidden about the possible places where it may be found, and this is true whether I want to hide something from myself or from someone else. In other words, Philosophy's artificial setup ensures that no meaningful information can be derived from it.

Fortunately, philosophers, although no friends of common sense, do often see the need to bring their insights in line with it. The Professor of Philosophy responsible for the paper on the not-to-be-hidden-from-oneself packet of cigarettes, T. S. Champlin (the selfsame who posed this chapter's epigraphic query about the signpost twisted around to deceive the other runners in the race), does eventually warm to the possibility of self-deception. "You are guilty of self-deception if you mistake appearance for reality as a result of a deceptive appearance of your own making which counts as your being dishonest with yourself" is his verdict on the practice.

With his examples, Champlin does not show how "dishonesty" may work, but as we will see, given current psychological theories of mind, it is easy to propose a way. A prisoner ordered to hide something from herself or perish in the cell may literally forget where she hid it, *repression* being what her mind practices to accomplish the trick. The runner who twists the signpost around in order to deceive himself may run in the direction it now indicates by *rationalizing* that the sign must have been pointing in the wrong direction—no way would the organizers have charted a course that included a steep climb close to the end of the race! Both are being dishonest with themselves because although they *somewhere* know the truth, and also somewhere know that they know the truth, they have learned how to manipulate their conscious thinking in a way that makes life less painful or more convenient.

What lies behind the question of the existence, or lack thereof, of self-deception are conceptions of the mind. Any such conception derived from Descartes or Locke renders absurd the notion that we can deceive ourselves if we are sane. The mind proposed by the theories of seventeenth-century philosophy—the first philosophical theories we think of as modern—excludes the possibility of a person lacking self-knowledge. How could any man not know what is in his own mind? How could any woman? Our own minds are the easiest of all things to know, and only by virtue of knowing our own minds do we arrive at knowledge about other things. The ability to deceive ourselves would require the cognitive ability simultaneously to believe something to be the case and to believe it not to be the case, an ability surely rendered impossible by self-knowledge. Looked at from another angle, the possibility of self-deception attacks the very foundation on which the edifice of seventeenth-century philosophical thought rests. If it is possible for me to be mistaken about something that is directly accessible to no one but me, namely the operation of my own mind—what I believe about myself and the world, how I feel in the present about things, what I remember thinking or feeling in the past—how can I ever know the truth about anything?

The Lockean view of the mind does allow for the existence of people who lack self-knowledge but attributes any such lack to a failure of their will, which has somehow become diseased and corrupted. This interpretation squares with a traditional worldview that holds sane people responsible for the contents of their minds and its workings, and it is best illustrated in the works of satirists, who have ever taken a special delight in exposing mental rot. The satirical targets of a Jonathan Swift or Alexander Pope are examples of people in whose minds corruption has reached alarming levels. Dunces and fools, pretentious fops, harebrained scientists and fanatic preachers, dull critics, supercilious pedants, incompetent scholars, hacks with a hyperinflated sense of their poetic talent—one and all share a blindness to their own monstrous shortcomings. They deceive themselves on a monumental scale, and their self-deception is an integral part of a mind unhinged and out of kilter.

Seen in this light, self-knowledge becomes a sign of mental health as well as a "moral duty": the sane man knows himself, and his knowledge of himself includes knowledge of his faults and deficiencies. Pope's foil, the supercilious playwright or the poet who "strains from hard-bound brains eight lines a-year," has had his wits addled by a "secret standard in his mind, / That casting-weight pride adds to emptiness." Similarly Joseph Addison, the critic who damns "with faint praise" Pope's translation of the *Iliad*, is allowing himself to be blinded by jealousy. The critic is shirking his responsibility to know himself, and the repercussion of his moral failing is a false representation of the facts: Pope's *Iliad* is a poetic achievement of the highest order.

In this scheme of things, reason and madness become two opposite poles, but while reason is a relatively simple concept—it is the faculty controlling the thinking and actions of sane, well-balanced, *reason*able human beings, madness is a fluid concept. The satirist out to lambaste the vices of mankind applies it to anyone who veers from the civilized, decorous, modest behavior reason dictates, be he a pedant puffed up with a grotesquely inappropriate sense of self-importance or a vainglorious general sending troops to slaughter. Swift, whose "Digression Concerning the Original, the Use and Improvement of Madness in a Commonwealth" has been the glory and riddle of critics since *A Tale of a Tub* first appeared in 1704, used madness as a powerful metaphor for all things he found despicable in the world. What could be more crazed than warring monarchs, "enthusiasts," "projectors," and other fanatics whose earthshaking schemes for the improvement of their countries or all of mankind can be explained by a simple error on their part, the error of mistaking their own pustules, anal fistulas, or flatulence for divine inspiration? Were these people not every bit as "mad" as Tom O'Bedlam, raving and gibbering, exposing himself and screaming obscenities because of a diseased mind?

Well, no, they weren't. The confusion between the medical condition of a diseased mind and "madness" is a rhetorical strategy satirists have used to launch their diatribes against human vice and folly ever since there have been satirists. Swift knew that poor Tom couldn't be held responsible for his actions, but his transforming mind collapsed the difference between the raving madman—who could be viewed in rags and chains for a small fee on weekends by the moral set out for a bit of edifying frisson—and the fanatical preacher spewing the venom of dissension from his pulpit.

In the real world, and on a medical scale of mental aberration, those suffering from a severe mental illness are farthest removed from objective knowledge and reality. The paranoiac, with his delusions of grandeur, reference, and persecution, is vastly mistaken about the importance he thinks he has in the lives of others or in the grand scheme of things. When he tells himself: I am the True Emperor of the world and this is why I'm being kept prisoner and constantly watched and slowly poisoned, he is wrong, as is the schizophrenic who hears a voice tell her to kill her family. If we step back and look at the larger picture, one thing becomes clear:

to say that these people are deceiving themselves is true, but the diagnosis ignores the larger problem of their radical dissociatedness from all reality.

The changing perception of the mind in the history of the world and the roots postulated for its disturbances—variably found in the supernatural, an immoral way of life, the enfeebling effects of civilized living, masturbation, the uterus, organic disease, and so forth—are complicated subjects. Antiquity found explanations on terra firma and in the clouds. "Know thyself" is one of the mottoes inscribed on the temple of Apollo at Delphi and attributed by Plato to the Seven Wise Men. (Another inscription is "Nothing in excess"—talk about a "*so* not millennial" sentiment!) Not knowing oneself can arise from ignorance as much as from self-deception, just as not knowing a fact about the world can mean never having experienced it or been reliably informed about it, or can mean the refusal to accept the evidence. But either way, the injunction suggests a moral obligation, and a moral view of the world lies at its heart. Small wonder it was on the temple of Apollo, the god who presides over the intellect and the moral sphere.

Compare this philosophical view with that of Greek drama. Fatalistic rather than moralistic, it unapologetically attributes people's blindness about themselves to the gods. Creon, the accursed uncle of Antigone, who punishes his niece with death for her pious act of sprinkling earth on the corpse of her brother, is easily identified as someone whose absolute devotion to a law created by him arises from a distorted perception of himself and his role in the world. In Sophocles' *Antigone*, Creon accuses himself of "the wretched blindness of my counsels" when he learns about the fatal consequences of his actions: the death of his son and wife. His actions are "the sins of a darkened soul, stubborn sins, fraught with death." In a more modern translation, they are "senseless," "stubborn," "insane," "stupid," "deadly." In any event, he finds the cause in some god having descended from above with crushing weight and having driven him down a savage path into cruelty.

Masters at metaphor, the Greeks used deceptive and destructive gods as emblems for the self-deceptive and self-destructive elements in the human mind. The gods drove men mad with pride, anger, or lust, beguiled them with visions of their own greatness or justice, ensnared them in traps from which there was no escape. If we look through the opposite end of the spyglass, the gods are projections of human impulses and mental structures. The question "How could I have been so blind?" can obviously be answered just as easily by referring to some malevolent entity outside oneself as by finding the fault in the machinations of one's own mind.

Christianity, similarly, can have recourse to a supernatural entity to explain instances in which one is apparently deceived, deluded, or blinded by oneself into following an evil path. The devil, "the deceiver of all mankind," can be blamed. Without the devil's aid, the concept of self-deception poses a problem for a scheme that metes out reward or punishment based on what we *truly* know, or believe, or think rather than on what we have convinced ourselves we know, believe, or think. Suppose a Catholic confessing his sins is fooling himself when he thinks he is feeling contrition? Suppose, unbeknownst to her, a regular churchgoer does not truly believe in Jesus Christ? Honesty in these matters is essential for salvation. If it is compromised by self-deception, things become murky indeed. Ultimately, the Christian has no choice but to believe that what truly goes on in one's own mind is accessible by an honest inventory.

What is still missing from this survey of self-deception is the modern psychological explanation for this odd phenomenon of one part of the mind hiding things from another. When did psychological theory part with the view that self-delusion is a sign of mental aberration? Interestingly, a challenge to the very idea of self-knowledge can be found in the same century that saw the heyday of the English satirists, archconservatives who milked the old concepts of what constitutes a stable, sane mind even when, like Swift, they had a disturbing sense of how easily the mind is corrupted. The philosophical underpinnings of self-deception as we think of it can be found in the conception of the mind proposed by David Hume, very much a man of the age that shaped a new way of thinking about mental processes. With Hume, we begin to see the "nor-

mal" mind as something not far from chaotic, and it is a small step
from his view to the realization that we can and do deceive ourselves. Hume's claim is that for any and all of us "what we call a
mind, is nothing but a heap or collection of different perceptions,
united together by certain relations, and supposed, though falsely,
to be endowed with perfect simplicity and identity."

Hume wrote his *Treatise of Human Nature* before he was twenty-
six, a sobering thought for late bloomers and other slackers, and by
his own words it "fell dead-born from the press, without reaching
such distinction as even to excite a murmur among the zealots."
Dead-born or not upon its publication in 1738, the *Treatise* gives us
a conception of the mind that approaches that of much of modern
psychology. The most elementary insight of psychoanalysis is precisely that the mind lacks perfect simplicity and identity but rather
consists of a conscious and a subconscious (or unconscious) part,
and that much of the work done by the mind occurs on that second
level.

The proposed relationship of the conscious to the subconscious
varies. Freudian and Jungian theory—both highly influential—
draw very different pictures, although both Freudian and Jungian
analysts agree on one fundamental thing: we do not know consciously what we know subconsciously, feel consciously what we
feel subsconsciously, have consciously the correct answer to the
question of why we do what we do. Psychological theory solves the
problem of self-deception by positing a self composed of these two
separate agents, the conscious and the subconscious, and holding
the latter to be in the know about what is actually going on deep
down inside. Not only is the subconscious privileged to a view of
an inner topography the conscious cannot see but it is also perfectly capable of deceiving the conscious about that topography by
keeping information hidden or garbling it, for what it perceives to
be the greater good of the self.

In Freudian theory, the issue of self-deception is not a moral but
a medical one: it is unavoidable but when it becomes extreme it appears as a neurosis. Treatment involves finding the roots of the
neurosis. Fortunately, no matter how committed the subconscious
is to hiding it, the truth can be unearthed. The garbled words of
the Freudian slip, the forgotten appointment, accidentally hung-up

phone, inadvertently crumpled photo—all of these can help find the truth because they express the way we *really* feel about something or someone. What also helps is the psychoanalyst's recognition of the various ego-defense mechanisms by which the subconscious tries to keep the conscious self from knowing the truth. In the Freudian model (originally developed by Anna Freud), the means by which we fool ourselves to make life more agreeable or less anguished are multifarious and ingenious. To list only the ones that involve deception:

- *Denial* is the ego's way to protect the self from un- pleasant reality by making it refuse to perceive it.
- *Repression* prevents painful or dangerous thoughts from entering consciousness.
- *Displacement* discharges pent-up feelings, usually of hostility, on objects less dangerous than those that actually aroused the emotion.
- *Isolation*, or *compartmentalization*, cuts off emotional charge from hurtful situations or separates incompatible at- titudes by compartments impervious to logic; it does so by never allowing connected thoughts about conflicting atti- tudes or about their relation to each other.
- *Rationalization* is the attempt to prove to oneself that one's behavior is rational and justifiable and thus worthy of the approval of oneself and others.
- *Projection* places blame for one's difficulties on others or attributes one's own desires to others.
- *Sublimation* gratifies or works off frustrated sexual de- sires by substituting for them nonsexual activities socially accepted by one's culture.
- *Fantasy* gratifies frustrated desires in imaginary achieve- ments, most commonly through daydreaming.
- *Reaction formation* prevents dangerous desires from be- ing expressed by exaggerating opposing attitudes and types of behavior and using them as barriers.
- *Introjection* incorporates external values and standards into the ego structure so the self is not at the mercy of them as external threats.

Additional ego-defense mechanisms, suggested by later researchers, are:

- *Distortion*, which grossly reshapes external reality to meet the inner needs of the one doing the distorting.
- *Hypochondriasis*, which transforms anger toward another person into anger toward oneself and then into the perception of pain and other physical symptoms.
- *Passive-aggressive behavior*, which involves hurting or defeating oneself in order to make others feel guilty or thwart their wishes.
- *Dissociation*, which moves ideas, memories, or experiences that may elicit intolerable feelings out of conscious awareness.
- *Suppression*, which excludes thought or feelings from the conscious but differs from repression in allowing retrieval of memories at a more appropriate time.

What all of this suggests is that our subconscious is much like the Marine colonel in *A Few Good Men* (Jack Nicholson at his obnoxious best) berating that fancy lawyer in uniform (Tom Cruise) who insists that he tell the truth: "You can't handle the truth!" What it also suggests is that the notion of self-knowledge is itself an illusion about something that is impossible to attain and, if it were somehow miraculously attained, is highly hazardous to any number of things we value. To foil our ego defenses may mean raising not only the forgotten wrecks of illicit desires and wrenching experiences, or even just shameful ones, but also the anguish and pain that cling to them. It may mean saying goodbye to a favorable self-image, to a sense of safety, to illusions and pipe dreams, unrealistic perceptions, wrong conclusions.

But of course the purpose of psychoanalysis is precisely to uncover truths the subconscious has hidden. Those years on the couch are meant to help the patient break through bulwarks of ego defenses that have kept the truth confined, allowing it to sneak out only heavily masked—be it in the latent content of a dream or in the obsessive-compulsive acts or other symptoms of full-blown neurosis—and become consciously acquainted with it. To have any hope of recovery, the patient kept in thrall by her own subconscious has to be brought face to face with painful ideas, desires, and experiences that were hidden and has to deal with them rationally. The self-deception must stop and the truth be acknowledged. Or so much of psychoanalytic theory goes.

How is the truth to be brought to the surface, unmasked, and introduced to the conscious? By free association in Freud's original view of the therapeutic process. Freud assumed that if patients reported without inhibition the stream of conscious thoughts and associations that flowed through their minds, verbal clues would bring him close to the repressed memories that were at the core of their illnesses. Then, once he abandoned the seduction theory, according to which the illnesses of many of his patients stemmed from sexual abuse in their childhood, Freud shifted analysis away from the excavation of buried memories—that is, the patient's actual experiences—toward transference. In the new theory, it made no difference whether the analyst worked with actual memories or with wishes and fears that had been transferred from the past to the present and that appeared in the form of thoughts and feelings about the therapist and resistance to the therapy. Objections can and have been raised to a theory that assumes that actual but repressed experiences are adequately addressed in this way.

C. G. Jung, the founder of analytic psychology, saw the battle of self-knowledge waged on a more dramatic field and considered it as much a moral as a medical one. Enter the shadow, a psychological composite of the dark characteristics of a person and a moral problem that poses a challenge for the entire "ego-personality." To become conscious of the shadow glowering in the subconscious demands great moral effort. It demands "recognizing the dark aspects of the personality as present and real." This recognition is, according to Jung, "the essential condition for any kind of self-knowledge, and it therefore, as a rule, meets with considerable resistance. Indeed, self-knowledge as a psychotherapeutic measure frequently requires much painstaking work over a long period."

To achieve self-knowledge, a measure of assimilation of the shadow into the conscious personality is necessary, and Jung argues that with "insight" and "good will" this partial assimilation is possible. But the shadow can resist the attempt at moral control through projections of one's dark characteristics onto others. Since the unconscious does the projecting, the conscious is unaware of it and is only too happy to see the evil that lurks in the unconscious allocated to another being. Accordingly,

> The effect of projection is to isolate the subject from his environment, since instead of a real relation to it there is only an illusory one. Projections change the world into the replica of one's own unknown face. . . . The more projections are thrust in between the subject and the environment, the harder it is for the ego to see through its illusions. . . .
>
> It is often tragic to see how blatantly a man bungles his own life and the lives of others yet remains totally incapable of seeing how much the whole tragedy originates in himself, and how he continually feeds it and keeps it going. Not *consciously*, of course—for consciously he is engaged in bewailing and cursing a faithless world that recedes further and further into the distance. Rather it is an unconscious factor which spins the illusions that veil his world. And what is being spun is a cocoon, which in the end will completely envelop him.

The shadow has a lot to answer for in Jung's picture, but the source of projections of a certain destructive kind is no longer the shadow—the negative side of the personality, which is always of the same sex as the "subject"—but a "contrasexual figure." The *anima* of the man and the *animus* of the woman, both autonomous and subconscious, both capable of projections that are far more stubborn and difficult to recognize than those of the shadow, can wreak havoc on the ignorant ego. Jung traced these "archetypes" to mythology and hypothesized their connection with the son's relation to the mother, the daughter's to the father, with Eros and Logos, and Maya, the "Spinning Woman" of the East, who creates illusion by her dancing. According to Jung, dissolving animus/anima projections requires enormous moral and intellectual effort and the self-knowledge resulting from doing so is exceedingly rare. And Jung worried about the ultimate outcome. To his mind, a profound doubt arose as to "whether one is not meddling too much with nature's business by prodding into consciousness things which it would have been better to leave asleep."

Jung's worry about whether it is always wise to bring into consciousness things hidden in the subconscious is a mere murmur.

Louder voices have been heard claiming that, first of all, of course we keep things hidden from ourselves and deceive ourselves but, what is more important, *not* deceiving ourselves is impossible if we wish to remain alive. Unless we continue to deceive ourselves, any sense of self-worth or achievement that we are currently nurturing will shrivel. Only by thinking of ourselves as more decent, generous, competent, smart, respected, loved, in control, etc., etc., etc., than we really are do we function. In the words of one voice for self-delusion: "individuals deploy strategies for the achievement of personal wholeness, and . . . some of these strategies involve deception and/or self-deception."

This bliss-through-self-deception claim is supported by studies that have looked for a relationship between self-deception and depression. The authors of one such study, in which subjects played games that were secretly manipulated by the experimenters, found that nondepressed subjects overestimated their responsibility for the outcome of a game if the outcome was favorable and underestimated the degree of control they had if the outcome was unfavorable. Depressed subjects, on the other hand, were consistently more accurate in their assessment of how much control they had over the results. The authors suggested that seeing themselves responsible for good but not for bad results is an adaptive mechanism by which nondepressed people maintain or enhance self-esteem. Other researchers, who reviewed numerous studies dealing with self-delusion, came to the conclusion that "the mentally healthy person appears to have the enviable capacity to distort reality in a direction that enhances self-esteem, maintains beliefs in personal efficacy, and promotes an optimistic view of the future."

This is a startling departure from the view that ego-defense mechanisms separate us in an unhealthy way from reality or that the failure to perceive reality without distortion is a sign of mental illness. It nevertheless intuitively makes sense, provided we define appropriately what constitutes a "mentally healthy person" and what constitutes "reality." Let's follow humanistic psychology in defining as mentally healthy someone who sees life as rich and meaningful and the world as populated by other beings who have needs and wishes that are valid, someone who has the capacity to love, who assumes that events are not entirely governed by random chance but that some control over them is possible and can produce desired results, someone who derives from these assumptions the strength to continue living and a measure of happiness. Let's in addition follow the nihilists in defining reality as a random succession of meaningless events. Combining the two views, we now have a working model of self-deception as the prescription for mental health—and possibly for the survival of the species.

The full-blown thesis is that only by believing, against the evidence, that our lives have meaning and that there is hope for the future do we keep having children, or washing the windows, or spending twelve hours a day designing software that will be obsolete six months after it hits the shelves. Take away the thousand and one delusions we weave and we will be paralyzed by apathy, or run screaming for the hills, or turn to stone while staring into the unblinking void of a Godless, purposeless, blind universe, vast beyond all comprehension, old beyond all reason, which will expand possibly forever or will possibly collapse, but which certainly lacks any human characteristics or higher purpose.

The thesis, furthermore, is that we are deluded when we reinvent the cosmos in our own image, and endow it with gods or spirits of all ilks, but that the delusion is necessary for our survival. One staunch advocate for deception, a nihilist with a plan, goes even further. Loyal Rue, professor of religion and philosophy and author of a book aptly titled *By the Grace of Guile*, postulates that, of course, the meaningless universe is the truth, is, in fact, "a monstrous truth." But there is a way to deal with this truth without dismay. By reinventing an old myth, that of the *anima mundi*, the soul of the world, we can make life bearable once again. Retold, the myth is that all life is linked in a biological web, and the myth's benefit is that by focusing on our interconnectedness with all other forms of life we will expand our affection for the world. Even though this myth, like all the others, is a lie, it can give new meaning to existence and can save us from the truth.

An intriguing thought, but one that ignores two things. The first is the simple fact that we can no more prove that the universe has *no* meaning than we can prove that it *has*: to call the empty universe the truth makes as little sense as claiming a monopoly for the One True Deity presiding over human affairs. The second is a pronounced quirk of human nature—we desire to know the truth and loathe being deceived. We may in a patronizing mood be able to say: "Let others believe in what we know to be a lie as long as it makes them happy." But we don't consciously urge ourselves to engage in this kind of trickery. Our reluctance to be deceived is too strong. But even if we could somehow overcome this reluctance, an unsurmountable barrier remains in the form of a logical impossibility: We cannot believe something we *know* to be a lie.

What all this leads up to is a question as old as human thought and voiced in a variety of ways, some more economical than others. What is truth? we ask (or What is *the* truth?). *Is* there such a thing as certainty about anything? Aren't all observations biased by what we wish to see and incommunicable because of the limitations of language? Isn't all memory pliant and forever altered by wishful thinking and suggestion? Aren't all things relative, and isn't all knowledge that isn't factual or objectively verifiable mere opinion?

Religion, of course, begs to differ. Pilate's famous question to Jesus: "What is truth?" is a cynical man's quip in response to Jesus' claim: "To this end was I born, and for this cause came I into the world, that I should bear witness unto the truth. Every one that is of the truth heareth my voice" (John 18:37). Pilate does not wait for an answer to his question but goes outside to tell the Jews that he finds no fault at all in Jesus. If he had waited, Jesus would no doubt have reiterated the claim that appears in John over and over, the claim that *he* is the truth, that those who believe in *him* believe in what is true, that those who do not believe in him are the children of the devil, who *is* the father of lies.

Fine and good, but those who do not believe in Jesus—by the latest count several billion people—do not, of course, think that whatever religious or nonreligious view they have of the cosmos is a lie. If they are fundamentalists or resolute atheists, they rather believe that their conception of the divine—Yahweh, Allah, Vishnu, Buddha, the Goddess—or of a godless universe is the true one.

Things become interesting when conversions occur. Moving toward a new faith is usually attended by the sense of a change from a state of ignorance, blindness, deludedness to one of knowledge, vision, the truth. St. Augustine, that great observer of the self, speaks of his "false conceptions of God." In his *Confessions* he tells God: "My conception of you was quite untrue, a mere falsehood. It was a fiction based on my own wretched state, not the firm foundation of your bliss." My eyes saw only material things, my mind saw only their images; I did not know, I was ignorant, I was blind—the *Confessions* are studded with these kinds of self-assessments concerning Augustine's earlier false, deluded state.

The profound spiritual transformation that Augustine underwent involved an equally profound feeling of having arrived at the truth after decades of error and after a battle with his own mind, which had insisted that the truth be revealed by rational thought. Among self-confessed former self-deceivers, he stands out for his analysis of the fear that attended his conversion, the fear of taking the wrong path. He tells God:

> I wanted to be just as certain of these things which were hidden from my sight as that seven and three make ten. . . . If I had been able to believe I might have been cured, because in my mind's eye I should have had clearer vision, which by some means might have been directed towards your eternal, unfailing truth. . . . [M]y sick soul, which could not be healed except through faith, refused this cure for fear of believing a doctrine that was false.

Even when God had stood him face to face with himself to make him see how sordid, deformed, and squalid he was "so that I should see my wickedness and loathe it," Augustine had resisted. "I had known it all along, but I had always pretended that it was something different. I had turned a blind eye and forgotten it."

This feeling that conversion has led to superior knowledge and to a shedding of delusions is widespread among converts. Even a man as committed to reason as John Henry Newman concluded that his earlier thinking, although that of a rational, informed mind, had been in error. When Newman began to doubt that the Anglican Church was the true successor to the original "Catholic" Church of the fifth century he asked himself what to do. He found: "I had to make up my mind for myself, and others could not help me. I determined to be guided, not by my imagination, but by my reason." Guided by his reason, Newman became convinced that the Roman Catholic Church was the true modern representation of the original church, whereas the Protestant churches represented a breaking away from the true doctrine of that church. Again, as far as the convert was concerned, error—belief that the Anglican doctrines were true and the Catholic ones false—was replaced by truth—the belief that the opposite was the case. Newman recounted "that great revolution of mind" that made him convert from one faith to another in his *Apologia pro Vita Sua*. The task before him was formidable, he stated. "For who can know himself, and the multitude of subtle influences which act upon him? and who can recollect, at the distance of twenty-five years, all that he once knew about his thoughts and his deeds, and that, during a portion of his life, when . . . , though it would be most unthankful to seem to imply that he had not all-sufficient light amid his darkness, yet a darkness it emphatically was?" (Read: the move from Anglicanism to Catholicism equaled the move from darkness to light.)

For Newman, reason ruled. But even converts to religions that encourage hallucinatory experiences see their new life as the path of truth and their old as that of error. So-called ayahuasca churches in Brazil, which blend elements of Catholicism, native folk religion, and spiritualism, use ayahuasca, a vegetable brew containing a powerful psychoactive substance. The rest of the world may disagree, but devotees tell how the spirit of ayahuasca helped them overcome "a lifetime of self-delusion." The spirit of ayahuasca appears in the form of vivid hallucinations, and users of it are among the many people who claim to have found in "visions" induced by drugs the truth that was hidden from them in ordinary life.

The opposite of finding faith, falling away from it, is typically attended by the same sense of having found the truth after years of false belief. Former believers who lost their faith feel that they had been deluding themselves. John Rock, born in 1890 and one of the inventors of the Pill, was a devout Catholic for most of his life. When Paul VI's 1968 encyclical "Humanae Vitae" declared all "artificial" methods of contraception to be against the teaching of the Church, his faith was shattered. Asked in a 1983 interview whether he still believed in an afterlife, he answered: "Of course I don't." Rock's disenchantment was complete. "Heaven and Hell, Rome, all the Church stuff—that's for the solace of the multitude," he told the interviewer. "I was an ardent practicing Catholic for a long time, and I really believed it all then, you see."

Apostates looking back on a time when they believed feel that they saw the world through rose-colored glasses and that the fault was their own: they had wanted to believe in God and had worked on holding on to their belief. They had wanted the comfort of life everlasting, of transcendence, of a universe sacred and inspired. Now, free from delusion, they see the world as it really is and recognize religion as the opiate of the masses, who would rather continue deluded than face the dismal truth of an empty universe.

Apostasy is, of course, not restricted to religion. People have turned away from any number of beliefs. Ex-communists, ex-cult members, ex-hedonists, ex-career military officers, even ex-psychoanalysts are examples of the many who at some point concluded that they had been deceiving themselves about something of enormous importance in their lives. The ranks of the disenchanted also include lovers who see their onetime soul mate as the manipulative narcissist he or she really is and ask themselves how they could have been so blind, renegades from causes they now recognize as destructive, misanthropes who have learned from experience that people will always let you down and that they had been fools when they had convinced themselves of the decent motives of others.

So where does all this leave "the truth"? Nowhere in a great many instances. When it comes to matters of faith, for example, the truth is something that depends entirely on our own beliefs. We may be convinced that people who are hallucinating as a result of chemical experiments are deluding themselves and are quite possibly destroying their brains. If we ourselves "enhance our consciousness" by ingesting or inhaling psychoactive drugs, we may consider the practice as old as humanity and may believe it to be a way to rend the veil of the ordinary and catch a glimpse of the divine. We may look from a medical perspective at saints who mortified their flesh, or mutilated or starved themselves, in order to have visions, and we may call these events hallucinations induced by chemical imbalances in the brain or by self-hypnosis. Or we may look at them as, well, visions of the divine.

In a more mundane sphere, I perceive my own ideas on a large raft of issues, from the environment to politics, from ethics to society, from education to scientific theories as by and large correct, although I may, on occasion, concede doubt. One thing is certain, all those times when I concluded that I'd had the wrong idea about something, I quickly replaced the idea with the right one (and when that idea turned out to be wrong as well, with a righter one yet).

The obvious point is that we have a penchant for thinking of our current beliefs or opinions as representative of the truth and of conflicting beliefs or opinions—those of others or those we ourselves held at an earlier time—as erroneous. And how could it be otherwise? To state that my current earnest belief in something is wrong would be paradoxical. If I believe it, I believe it to be true. The statement "I once believed this but now believe (or know) that," far from describing a neutral stance regarding two opinions, suggests not only an enlargement of understanding and knowledge but the sense that an erroneous belief has been replaced by actual knowledge. Usually the earlier "error" is attributed not only to exterior forces—false doctrines, preachers, or information—but also to self-deception. The true answers were always there, and only by deceiving myself had I been able to continue believing what was false.

Outside the realm of faith, the truth is what informed people know, or rather what they agree on as an adequate representation of reality. The Copernican system was a better representation than the Ptolemaic; the various theories of extinction offered by paleontologists come closer to what actually happened in the history of the earth than the creationists' literal reading of the Bible. Modern protozoology, bacteriology, and virology give better explanations of diseases than earlier theories about bad air or the stars causing malaria or influenza. Science, theoretical and experimental, offers models of reality. When these models accurately predict observations they are useful representations of physical processes; when they do not, we discard them and look for other models. The truth about the physical world may be elusive but some answers come closer to it than others.

Other truths require information about notoriously ambiguous things such as personality or society. People who see all of their problems caused by others or by bad luck rather than by themselves may be diagnosed by psychiatrists as sufferers of one of the personality disorders. But suppose they are minorities in a society where discrimination is pervasive? All at once their perception seems much closer to reality. As the bumper sticker says: "It ain't paranoia if they're *really* after you."

When all is said, what most of us who acquire a new insight have in common is not only the feeling that we now know the truth, or at least are closer to knowing it, but unease at the suggestion that we may have traded one delusion for another. This time we got it right, we think and settle into some activity less strenuous than the search for an ultimate answer to some fragment of existence. Our moment-by-moment conviction that our beliefs coincide with reality may just be essential to keep us from being sucked into the maw of perpetual uncertainty.

What is truth? Possibly anything that gives us peace of mind.

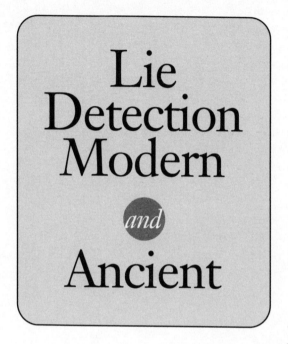

Lie
Detection
Modern
and
Ancient

The APEX Truth Meter®

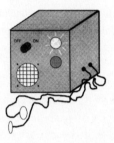

"Lie detection at a fraction of the cost"™

Are you tired of polygraph exams that take hours and require a trained opera-tor? Have you had enough of paying through the nose for exams that are AT BEST 90% accurate in detecting deception? Does a 1' × 1' × 1' box with one simple switch and no fancy dials or messy charts appeal to you?—a device that signals TRUTH or LIE unmistakably and with unsurpassed **100% accu-racy?**

Then you want the **APEX Truth Meter®**.

The **APEX Truth Meter®** features:

 • **100% accuracy**—no matter how good at deception the subject is.

 • **Simplicity**—a single measurement makes the **APEX** a monometer, not a complicated and confusing polygraph.

 • **No possible confusion**—a ringing bell and green light signal **TRUTH**, a blowing whistle and red light signal **LIE**. Nothing could be clearer!

- **Economy**—low initial price, no training costs, no expenses for paper or costly paraphernalia.

The **APEX** is simple to operate and comes with a **FREE** easy-to-read instruction manual and five-year warranty. It is the result of precision engineering and is **NUMBER ONE** in the field of deception detection. Convenient, portable, lightweight, and safe, it requires none of the complicated and confusing operations of "polygraph" lie detectors—no blood pressure, heartbeat, or breathing measurements are required. Two electrodes (included) connect the subject to the **APEX's** precision electronic psychometer, then the operator simply asks the relevant questions and the answer is **TRUTH** or **LIE**, *with no ifs or buts!*

The APEX Truth Meter® is, alas, not commercially available—although in 1977 the device it parodies could be ordered from its manufacturer and cost "as little as a good typewriter." A 100 percent accurate lie detector is an absolutist's pleasing fancy—Pinocchio's nose in a box—but the appeal of such a device in the area of criminal justice is indisputable. In the United States, where hundreds of millions of dollars and an untold amount of time, effort, and energy are devoted each year to trials whose purpose is to establish the innocence or guilt of suspects, an infallible lie detector test would greatly simplify the practice of criminal investigation and prosecution.

Suppose for a moment that the APEX exists and has been proven in rigorous, double-blind scientific studies to be perfectly accurate in ferreting out intentional deception. Suppose also that this is common knowledge, as widely accepted as the knowledge that the earth is round or that there are such things as viruses causing such things as the flu. In other words, the APEX's accuracy falls into the category of things that we know even if we have not necessarily experienced them in person or have a specialist's understanding of them. This being the case, the part of criminal investigation having to do with the interrogation of suspects becomes remarkably simple. If a suspect hooked up to the APEX answers "No" to the question "Did you rob X?" and the advertised bell rings, we know with as much certainty that this is the truth and that the suspect is innocent as we know that the earth is round, or that during the flu season an injudiciously touched nose can send us to bed. If, conversely, the whistle blows, then all that is left for a court to do is decide on the sentence—which may still be time-consuming, but is perforce far less so than the pre-APEX process for establishing guilt, or lack thereof, before the court. Similarly, the veracity of witnesses and police officers in charge of the investigation can be determined instantly: the witness who lies, the officer who has tampered with the evidence are quickly stripped of credibility.

The result is a number of things conspicuous for their absence: Gone is the two-, three-, or nine-month trial in which judge and jurors become catatonic listening to stultifying rounds of testimony needed to determine beyond a reasonable doubt the defendant's guilt. Gone also are lengthy police investigations in cases where there are several suspects. Anyone innocent will insist on being tested instantly, knowing that something as amazingly uncomplicated as a truthful answer will guarantee freedom and complete vindication.

But what about those among the guilty who refuse to answer? Clearly in post-APEX days the law will require anyone arrested to submit to being hooked up to this "truth meter" even before being fingerprinted. But suspects cannot be coerced to answer questions put to them. We shouldn't be surprised if an amazingly large fraction of them suddenly develop the moral equivalent of a disbelief in the earth's curvature, protesting that the reason they refuse to answer is that they *do not believe* in the contrivance. A psychiatric exam should cull the few true psychotics out of touch with objective reality from the herd of those who have a very good reason for not wanting to answer the question: "Did you, on the night of October 8 . . . ?"

Given the enormous simplification of criminal investigation and prosecution that would result if the APEX existed, it is small wonder that the quest for such a device is more than a hundred years old. In 1895, an Italian criminologist, Cesare Lombroso by name, was the first to report on a medical diagnostic device that could also be used to test a person's veracity. The device, a *hydrosphygmograph*, measured changes in the amount of blood in the arm of a suspect being interrogated. The changes were recorded on a chart, and after the interrogation Lombroso could correlate the questions with any recorded physiological changes. An Italian physiologist who worked closely with Lombroso found that breathing patterns changed in response to various stimuli, and two German psychologists proposed in 1904 that changes in respiratory patterns might be of use in criminal investigation. A few years later, in Austria, another researcher tested this suggestion and claimed to have found that the inspiration/expiration ratio changed when people lied.

The American pioneer in scientific (or, as skeptics put it, "scientific") lie detection was one Hugo Münsterberg at Harvard University. Münsterberg in 1908 published a book in which, while studiously avoiding giving credit to the European pioneers, he suggested that research be done on a variety of physiological measures to detect a suspect's knowledge of guilt. In 1915, one of Münsterberg's students, Harvard psychologist William Marston, claimed to have discovered a link between changes in systolic blood pressure and deception, and he devised a test in which the systolic blood pressure of someone being questioned was intermittently measured.

Marston became involved in the first attempt to introduce the results of a lie detection test in a court proceeding. In 1923 the U.S. Circuit Court of Appeals in Washington, D.C., ruled that the results of a "systolic blood pressure deception test" conducted by him were inadmissible as evidence on behalf of the defendant in a criminal trial (*Frye v. United States*, 1923). The ruling stated:

> while the courts will go a long way in admitting expert testimony deduced from a well-recognized scientific principle or discovery, the thing from which the deduction is made must have gained general acceptance in the particular field in which it belongs. We think that the systolic blood pressure deception test has not yet gained such standing and scientific recognition among physiological and psychological authorities as would justify the courts in admitting expert testimony deduced from the discovery, development, and experiments thus far made.

Marston's test used a single measurement; the first multimeasurement apparatus for lie detection was developed in 1921 by John Larson at the Berkeley, California, police department. This "polygraph" device measured and continuously recorded respiration, blood pressure, and pulse. Larson's protégé, Leonarde Keeler, refined and improved the device and made it portable. A man with a vision and a keen sense of the commercial possibilities in selling lie detection to American business, ever fearful of being defrauded by employees, Keeler became the most prominent practitioner of scientific lie detection.

Not surprisingly, both Keeler with his polygraph and William Marston with his systolic blood pressure device became peripherally involved in the then Trial of the Century (meanwhile superseded)—the Lindbergh Case. In 1936 both offered their services to clear Bruno Richard Hauptmann, by this time awaiting execution in the electric chair. Keeler, having promised the governor of New Jersey that he would keep mum about the governor's involvement in the case, promptly leaked to the press that he had examined Hauptmann's wife and would examine Hauptmann. As a result the governor, politically in hot water for having granted the condemned man a reprieve, failed to make the necessary arrangements for Keeler to get into the death house. With Keeler out of the running, Marston offered his services, but the governor's request to the trial judge to grant permission for him to visit Hauptmann was denied. Thus ended the quest to use scientific lie detection to determine the truth about the kidnapping and murder of the Lindbergh baby.

In 1938 Keeler opened the country's first private polygraph firm; in 1939 he added an electrodermal channel tracking galvanic skin response to the Keeler Polygraph; by 1941 he was a millionaire. The courts, who had found the results of Marston's "systolic blood pressure deception test" inadmissible as evidence in 1923, were gradually persuaded in the course of decades of empirical development of instruments and techniques by Keeler and others to admit the results of lie detector tests. By 1984 the results of stipulated lie detection tests were admitted as evidence in the courts of twenty-six states, provided both parties agreed to their introduction in the trial.

On the business and "human resources" side, lie detection proved to be a booming enterprise: in 1942 a two-week course on the use of the polygraph was available for police and military examiners; six years later, the course was six weeks long. By 1988 over thirty polygraph schools accredited by the 3,000-member American Polygraph Association existed. Private schools had at least a seven-week curriculum; U.S. and Canadian government courses lasted fourteen weeks. The polygraph was by then routinely used in criminal investigation, but as many as 90 percent of all polygraph examinations administered in the United States were employment-related. Most were intended to unmask prospective employees' past infractions and proclivities for future ones—say, embezzlement. The rules differed from state to state, with some states forbidding companies to force workers to submit to a polygraph test but allowing voluntary testing.

But the biggest single consumer was the federal government. A congressional mandate in the 1986 Defense Authorization Bill called for the expansion of the Department of Defense's polygraph capability to allow screening employees, to "effect a significant deterrent to spying." The bill authorized 10,000 plus "National Security" screening examinations annually for 1986 and 1987. (Before December 1984 the DoD polygraph directive did not authorize personnel screening; use of the polygraph was allowed only in criminal or counterintelligence investigations—even so, between June 1984 and June 1985 over 11,000 polygraph examinations were conducted in the course of such investigations.) These are sizable numbers, but they were tiny compared to the millions of people who were screened as employees or prospective employees of corporate America. Banks, retail chains, even fast-food restaurants used polygraph testing to vet job applicants or subject them to periodic honesty checks.

In addition to the polygraph, various single-graph devices like William Marston's systolic blood pressure recorder and even no-graph devices appeared on the market over the years. All were alleged by their manufacturers to yield the same information about deception with less fuss and bother. A device bearing an uncanny resemblance to the APEX Truth Meter was the B&W Lie Detector. With an alleged 95 percent accuracy and sporting three "simple knobs" and a dial (no bell and whistle, sadly), it was advertised as "the lie detector you can afford" and hailed as "unsurpassed for simplicity, low cost and high percentage of accuracy." The B&W made do with a single measurement of galvanic skin response, determined by monitoring the conductivity between two points on a finger, and it required no chart or graph. At a low initial cost and with no training required (the operator simply read the "free, easy-to-use" manual), the B&W, according to its manufacturer, removed instrumental lie detection from the "high-priced professional secret class."

In 1977 the company's president appeared before the California legislature during a hearing on the licensing of polygraph examiners and argued fervidly that single-measurement lie detectors such as the B&W should not be declared unlawful as a result of pressure from polygraph manufacturers, who hoped to drive competition offering low-cost alternatives out of the market. The committee ignored his request and stipulated in the licensing requirement that "each type of instrument shall record visually, permanently and simultaneously the cardiovascular pattern, the respiratory pattern, and the galvanic skin response." No instrument that was not "type-approved" by the director of the licensing board was lawful.

The proponents of the B&W Lie Detector no doubt smelled collusion, but objectively viewed, the decision is understandable. The B&W washed out because, for one, it used only one of the parameters of the polygraph; the hearing committee no doubt felt that a device measuring a single thing was inherently inferior to one measuring that thing plus several others. Worse, the B&W could, after thirty-three years of use, boast only one article touting its merit in a scientific journal, and that 1954 article was co-authored by the W of B&W—and hence was not exactly the stuff of unbiased research. Finally, the B&W was advertised in a brochure that sounded like it had been written by someone whose snake-oil business had just folded, someone whose pièce de résistance was a raft of glowing testimonials, one from its own operation manual (yes, its *own* operation manual), others from such unimpeachable sources as "Professional examiner, California," "Polygraph operator, Indiana," and, somewhat magnifying the challenge of pinpointing the accolade's origin, "Police Official, an Asian Nation."

The disreputable elements thus eliminated, licensed California polygraphers—just like certified DoD, FBI, CIA, and municipal police examiners—have been determining the truth and detecting deception ever since, to the universal applause of the scientific community.

Or have they?

As it turns out, the reputable, certified, licensed, widespread use of the polygraph ran against the opinion of a sizable number of people who make it their business to study the workings of the mind. In a 1982 poll asking members of the Society for Psychophysiological Research their opinion about the ability of trained polygraph operators to determine accurately whether a subject is or is not telling the truth, 34 percent of the respondents found polygraph tests "of questionable usefulness, entitled to little weight against other available information." True, 62 percent thought it "a useful diagnostic tool when considered with other available information," but only 1 percent thought it "a sufficiently reliable method to be the sole determinant." In other words, only 1 percent viewed the polygraph in the same rosy light in which its manufacturers and operators tend to view it. In a comparison of several well-designed and well-controlled studies of polygraphic lie detection, one critic determined that it was wrong a startling one-third of the time overall and was seriously biased against the truthful subject.

In 1984, in a mordant attack on the U.S. government's expansion of its polygraph activities, two University of Illinois psychologists published the results of studies on the reliability and validity of polygraphs. Their findings: lie detection is unscientific, its premise that suspects will experience more arousal to relevant questions if they are deceptive than if they are truthful is simplistic, and polygraph examiners have high rates of misclassification, the most damaging by-product of which is false positive results—truthful people who are judged to be lying.

Even skeptics by and large agree that false negative results—liars being judged truthful—occur less often than false positive ones—truthful subjects being judged liars (which, by the way, has to be a most disquieting piece of information for anyone blameless who is about to take a polygraph test). This is most likely because fear of detection of the lie *is* a powerful emotion that *will* show up on the polygraph much of the time (how large *much* is remains a matter of debate). Still, people have been successfully trained by researchers to foil polygraph tests with false negative results. How well laboratory experiments, based usually on the incentive of a reward if the liar is successful at duping the examiner, represent real situations is unknown, although there is anecdotal evidence that the spy services of various countries train their operators in how to pass the test, which, if true, suggests that screening people to deter spying may be futile with respect to those most likely to compromise security.

The arrest of Harold Nicholson, the most highly placed Russian spy in the CIA, in November 1996 was possibly the result of an investigation begun after a routine lie detector test administered a year earlier flagged him as deceptive when he answered the question "Are you working for a foreign intelligence service?" He failed two more tests, and during the third, the CIA polygraph examiner thought he noticed that Nicholson was trying to influence the test by taking deep breaths before certain questions. If true, then either Nicholson had not been trained at foiling the polygraph or the training did not sufficiently prepare him for reality. The horse's mouth, CIA Director John Deutch, claimed that the lie detector tests were merely part of a more comprehensive, periodic background check into bank accounts, travel records, etc., that tripped up Nicholson. In the typical mode of indirection that is second nature to government officials, Deutch told reporters: "So, I would not say that the polygraph was the initiating piece." (Meaning, I suppose, not quite that he *would* say that the polygraph was *not* the initiating piece.)

How one might go about hiding a lie from a lie detector is an old challenge. Of the various countermeasures that have been tested in laboratory experiments designed to foil the "control-question technique" (of which more soon), the most successful has been that of augmenting physiological responses to the control questions. Biting one's tongue or pressing one's toes against the floor has been shown to elicit an artificial physiological response indistinguishable from a genuine one—most effective seems to be to apply both measures at the same time. Several words of warning for the would-be foiler of the polygraph test, though: it is unclear

how well lab experiments, with their mock crimes and subjects paid
to lie, approximate real situations, and simply knowing about countermeasures seems to be ineffective even in the lab—some experts
claim that actual training hooked up to a polygraph is necessary.

Aldrich H. Ames, another notorious, if less illustrious, CIA rene-
gade, passed scores of polygraph tests. In prison, he told a reporter
that his Russian handlers had laughed at his worries about taking
the tests. They had told him to relax—lie detectors didn't work.
Ames may, of course, have been lying, uninterested in revealing advice or training he *had* received from his handlers.

Which brings us to a lucky man indeed, Floyd "Buzz" Fay, who
could easily furnish a chapter in the annals of lie detection. Fay's
hearty dislike of the polygraph made him become something of an
expert on it and a coach in how to beat it. His animosity against the
device was well founded, given that he served two and a half years
of a life sentence for a crime he did not commit because two lie
detector tests "proved" him deceptive. He was arrested after a
botched armed robbery at a convenience store in Perrysburg,
Ohio, in 1978. The clerk behind the counter was fatally wounded
by a blast from a sawed-off shotgun in the hands of a man in a ski
mask. Asked about the man who shot him, he answered: "It looked
like Buzz, but it couldn't have been." During the next five hours,
the dying man kept losing blood and received large doses of De-
merol—and he became more and more certain of his assailant's
identity, stating numerous times that "Buzz did it."

Buzz Fay was arrested. The prosecution's theory was that he had
suffered from a delayed reaction to some PCP he had allegedly
smoked several days before the shooting, which turned him into
some kind of a murdering zombie. When after two months of investigation not a single corroborative piece of evidence turned up,
the prosecution offered Fay a deal: If he was found to be truthful
in a polygraph exam administered by the Bureau of Criminal
Identification, the charges would be dismissed. If he was found
to be deceptive, a second, privately administered exam would be
conducted. If the results of the second exam were in conflict with
those of the first, both would be discarded and the case would proceed to trial without them. If both tests indicated deception, Fay
would plead guilty to the lesser charge of murder. If he refused to

do so, he would be tried on the aggravated murder charge and the polygraph results would be admitted as evidence.

Seeing in the polygraph chart his ticket to freedom, Fay submitted to Test One, was judged deceptive, submitted to Test Two, and failed it as well. He persisted in maintaining his innocence, was tried, and was convicted of aggravated murder and sentenced to life in prison. Bloodied but unbowed, he began contacting nationally known polygraph experts, sending them copies of the charts of his exams and asking for their evaluation. One of them told him that he would have interpreted the charts as "truthful"; two others read them as "inconclusive." Yet another called them, together with all other polygraph charts, "without probative value."

Despite the dedicated effort of a public defender, these expert opinions might not have resulted in the verdict being overturned because the trial court was hostile. The judge had made an independent ruling that Fay's polygraph examiners were qualified, and he was not interested in the dissenting opinions of experts. What did result in Fay's release was the fortuitous appearance of a man providing information about one of the three people who had staged the would-be robbery, a teenager who had acted as lookout (the third robber drove the getaway car). All three were arrested, and Fay was a free man.

Not only did Fay avoid becoming a lifelong victim of the polygraph, but he learned from a paper authored by one of the experts on the polygraph test whom he contacted how the control-question test was supposed to work and how it could be beaten. In his last year in prison, he used this knowledge to coach 27 fellow inmates scheduled to take polygraph tests (usually because they'd been charged with drug offenses, which if they failed the test could result in their being transferred to a maximum-security prison). All 27 admitted to him that they were guilty. Fay claimed that after fifteen to twenty minutes of instruction 23 of the 27 managed to pass.

If Fay's experience tells us one thing, it is that polygraph tests can destroy lives. Experts have known this all along, and one result of their vociferous skepticism was that in 1988 President Ronald Reagan signed the Employee Polygraph Protection Act, which prohibited the private sector from using polygraphs to screen employees. Federal employees were exempted. The wheels of justice ground more slowly, but in March 1998 the U.S. Supreme Court, too, paid heed to the experts. It ruled that a criminal defendant had no constitutional right to present evidence at a trial of having passed a lie detector test because there was "no consensus that polygraph evidence is reliable." The ruling echoes the one mentioned above made in 1923 by a U.S. Circuit Court of Appeals on William Marston's "systolic blood pressure deception test." The argument then was that for expert testimony deduced from a scientific principle to be valid, "the thing from which the deduction is made must have gained general acceptance in the particular field in which it belongs" and that the test in question had "not yet gained such standing and scientific recognition." Seventy-five years later, that "not yet" must have suggested an uncalled-for optimism to those Supreme Court justices writing the majority opinion.

The federal government remains committed to the polygraph, possibly because the powers that be assume that surely polygraph operators trained by the government have superior expertise. After the discovery in 1999 of a security breach of major proportions at Los Alamos National Laboratory, allegedly by a spy for the Chinese government, Energy Secretary Bill Richardson ordered polygraph tests for all of the laboratory's nuclear weapons scientists. Understandably, the prospect made most of them uneasy. A false positive result, the error most frequently committed by the examiners, can cast a shadow over anyone's career. However, the case also seemed for a while to provide fodder for proponents of the polygraph: Government officials alleged that it was a failed polygraph test in February 1999 that had sounded the alarm about Wen Ho Lee, the alleged spy. Then, in April 2000, an FBI agent testified that Lee *had* passed a private company's polygraph examination with flying colors but—hold on!—the test did not follow the protocols accepted by the FBI.

Those looking for 100 percent accurate lie detection through improved technology should note that the Supreme Court ruled against the polygraph despite the technological changes it had undergone in the mid-1990s. The systems used by the FBI and many police departments throughout the United States had by then been computerized. In the state-of-the-art polygraph, a computer program charts and scores a subject's physiological responses (the usual blood pressure, pulse and respiratory rate, and galvanic skin response) and renders an opinion about whether or not the subject is lying. And still there is no consensus that "new and improved" means reliable.

The lack of consensus regarding the polygraph is not over the question of whether devices that measure a subject's blood pressure, pulse rate and amplitude, respiration, or galvanic skin response can detect stress and emotional response to stimuli. No one doubts that they can—although the actual mechanisms connecting psyche and soma are still far from well understood. Disagreement arises over the claim that the stress and strong emotional responses picked up by the polygraph can be accurately and unambiguously identified as resulting from deception. Again, no one doubts that the attempt to deceive *can* induce stress and emotions, but opponents of the polygraph make the obvious point that so can other mental operations that have nothing to do with deception. Confusion begins, they argue, with the misleading term "lie detector"— invented by the popular press in its usual quest for the sexy tag—for what should mundanely be called a polygraph stress detector. Studies conducted in the laboratory and the field have shown that the polygraph "lie detector's" greatest weakness is in the number of false positive results it gives (where *positive* indicates deception). That false positive results—people who are telling the truth but appear, according to the test, to be lying—occur is hardly surprising: imagine yourself answering *any* question knowing that your truthful answer had better not be accompanied by any undue stress—or you may lose your job, go to jail, or find yourself strapped to an electric chair.

The proponents of the polygraph, while conceding that their wonderful machines are perfectly capable of recording strong emotional responses that are unconnected with lying, claim that the technique of questioning is such that a trained operator will be able to separate truth from lie up to 99 percent of the time. Popular techniques involve desensitizing the subject in a pretest interview to things emotionally connected with what is under investigation by repetition of key words in various contexts. The attempt is to invalidate, say, a murderer's predictable claim that, although innocent of the crime, he or she had a strong emotional reaction every time the victim's name was mentioned, and that that reaction rather than lying accounted for the polygraph's reading of high stress when the question was "Did you kill . . ."

Equally important in the most widely used technique is the use of "control questions" to which the examinee will probably answer with a lie. These questions are thematically related to the offense being investigated (or potential offense for which a prospective federal employee or an applicant for a security clearance is being screened). If, say, the subject is suspected of embezzlement, the control questions will have to do with theft. "Before the age of eighteen, did you ever steal anything?" "Have you ever in your life stolen anything?" are typical examples. Those not guilty of the embezzlement will, the theory has it, feel worried that some minor past infraction—maybe they once stole a ballpoint pen at a drugstore—will be considered evidence of their having committed the crime under investigation and will lie about the ballpoint pen episode. But this intention to deceive the polygraph examiner will induce stress, which will register on the graphs as a larger response than their later, honest, answers to the questions about the embezzlement. Ergo, the truth about the nonembezzlement will be crystal clear. An appealingly logical argument, compromised only by the fact that in situations of any complexity at all, human beings do not excel at reacting along universally shared, predictable lines.

Another approach, the Guilty Knowledge Technique, is limited to criminal investigations. It uses knowledge only the police and the perpetrator possess, a textbook case being the position of the body of a murdered man, in the quest to detect the guilty and exonerate the innocent. It does so by pairing the actual scenario with a possible one. "Was the body lying on its face?" "Was it lying on its back?" might be two questions asked of a suspect. Guilty or innocent, the suspect would answer: "I don't know." But the physiological response of someone innocent and therefore ignorant should, in theory, be the same for both questions, whereas the murderer, remembering, say, that the dead man was lying on his face, should have a stronger response when the examiner mentions that position. The technique was developed by David Lykken, at the time a professor of psychology and one of the foremost experts on the polygraph. A vehement critic of the lie detector, Lykken was looking for ways to improve its accuracy; ironically, some researchers found the Guilty Knowledge Technique to perform slightly worse than the usual polygraph test.

Lykken remained highly skeptical of the polygraph. In March 2000, by then an emeritus professor, he was a member of a chorus of prominent voices—professional author and skeptic Robert L. Park was another—who scorned the Department of Energy's order of polygraph tests for all of the nuclear weapons scientists at Los Alamos National Laboratory. "There is something about us Americans that makes us believe in the myth of the lie detector. It's as much of a myth as the tooth fairy," he complained.

Another American myth that deserves brief mention here is the "truth serum," the pharmaceutical version of a low-tech approach that has been alleged to work for at least two and a half millennia—namely, to get someone drunk. The proverb *In vino veritas* (In wine is truth) expresses the notion, and it was already old by the time Plato voiced it in his *Symposium*. What truth there is in wine comes out of its effect of reducing anxiety and inhibitions, which can make those under the influence inadvertently blurt out things they meant to keep hidden. The tongue-loosening feature of alcohol is duplicated by barbiturates, and the use of sodium amytal and sodium pentothal in psychotherapy to induce a state of relaxation and drowsiness or grogginess in patients has led to the popular belief that these drugs can force people to tell the truth against their will.

Hollywood loved the concept, and World War II movies featured the truth serum, usually in the form of sodium pentothal, as standard equipment in the kit bag of the interrogator of spies and saboteurs. In the 1961 movie *The Guns of Navarone* much is made of the leader of the team of saboteurs giving a captured comrade false information in the hope that the Germans will drug him and extract the wrong information. The SS, of course, has more primitive methods, and it takes the intervention of a humane Wehrmacht general to make them switch from tried-and-true torture to drugging. Whereupon the prisoner reveals the false information and sends the Germans off to set up defenses against an attack on the coast, buying the saboteurs time. Administered by Hollywood, the truth serum can allow the hero to advance the plot by revealing crucial information without tarnishing his heroism.

In psychotherapy, sodium amytal has been used in conjunction with hypnosis in "repressed memory therapy" (RMT). Mental health professionals remain deeply divided over the treatment. Proponents claim that it can help force into consciousness repressed memories, usually of sexual abuse in childhood. Opponents argue that people under the influence of sodium amytal and hypnosis "remember" suggestions planted by the therapist. The 1990s saw some highly publicized legal cases coming out of RMT. In some of these, people went to prison as a result of charges brought against them by patients convinced they were remembering abuse, in one case even murder, while undergoing RMT. In others, therapists were successfully sued by the accused, who filed malpractice suits against them.

The problem with sodium amytal and sodium pentothal as truth (or lie) detectors is that the semi-sleep they induce makes people prone to mix fact and fantasy. Although these drugs have been used by investigators to find leads, they are not accepted in courts of law for this reason. The popular imagination is, as usual, another matter. When in 2000 Paul Fray accused Hillary Clinton of having hurled an ethnic slur at him twenty-six years earlier, he said he was willing to take "a lie detector test or a truth serum" to prove his claim.

The Achilles' heel of the polygraph has always been that its results are unverifiable by scientific standards. The question of how often the objective truth is reflected in the device's findings is impossible to answer even in criminal cases, where there is at least some opportunity for cross-checking. Cases in which the polygraph found deception and a subsequent confession proved that the suspect had indeed been lying or cases in which the polygraph found no deception and the suspect was cleared because the actual perpetrator confessed are not uncommon, but they tell us nothing about how often the results are wrong. In pre-employment screening the possibility of independent verification becomes minuscule. A deceptive applicant for a job at the U.S. Mint who fails a polygraph exam is unlikely to break down and confess to a history of embezzlement. And suppose the powers that be run a routine background check on someone who passed and indeed find no evidence of past malfeasance. Does this prove the polygraph accurate? Of course not. The prospective employee may have foiled the polygraph now and may have been good at hiding the evidence in the past.

The continued controversy about the accuracy of lie detectors makes it tempting to say that when it comes to the detection of lies we know only that we know nothing. But in the words of universal pessimism: we should be so lucky! In fact, we all know something about lie detection and have on occasion assumed the role of lie detector. Very few of us would disagree with the statement "*Some* people while lying *sometimes* signal the act in *some* way that can *somehow* be detected." The qualifying pussyfooting is necessary since without it we enter that dangerous world where fragments of experience are mistaken for the whole picture and anecdotal evidence is served up as universal truth.

Let's for a moment put aside the question of physiological changes induced by lying and go to an area in which each of us has some empirical familiarity and where the tools of observation are our own eyes and ears. We all have some common-knowledge notion of body language and other signs that tell us (we think) whether someone is lying. The avoidance of eye contact is one of the things we associate with lying (which is why dishonest salesmen and con artists have learned to look us straight in the eye while they shake our hand firmly and get ready to fleece us). Other behavior we tend to see as a sign of lying in progress is throat clearing, protest that is too loud or emotional, a pause before the answer to a simple question, and half a dozen other actions akin to "tells"—the poker expression for behavior giving away a player's bluff or attempt to hide a great hand. The reason we think we can recognize clues to deception is that we have seen bad liars in action, hemming and hawing their way through some bogus explanation—and we may even have told a lie or two before our conversion to scrupulous honesty and may have observed ourselves behaving awkwardly in the process.

Yet already a warning is in order: In our personal lives, we are far more likely to detect a lie when we are suspicious—in other words, when our observation is accompanied by the question of whether or not we are being told the truth. Unless we are paranoid, our suspicion tends to be based on physical evidence (liquor on the breath, a ringing phone that was not picked up by someone claiming to have been at home, the stranger's earring or cuff link under the bed), and this evidence predates the clues we are picking up from the suspected liar. Plus, we may know that we're dealing with someone who has lied to us in the past. So one obvious problem is that we're by no means unbiased observers listening without prejudice but (a) have our detector on high sensitivity and (b) are more often than not observing someone who not only knows that we are suspicious but also knows that we have every right to be. To sound convincing under those circumstances is not an easy thing. (But, of course, someone who senses suspicion may sound unconvincing even when telling the truth—the old weakness of the polygraph holds for lie detection in domestic life as well.) Being ultra-observant only in those cases where there is an excellent chance that suspicion is justified is an unimpressive way to establish that we are good at detecting lies. Imagine any scientific tool touted at being excellent at detecting the presence of one substance that is mixed in with another. Except you find out that the claim is based exclusively on the tool having sniffed a prefiltered system in which there was an overabundance of the substance to be detected—but, lo, it's been a wizard at detecting that substance! You may be tempted to tell the inventors of the device to delay sending their paper on it to the *Review of Scientific Instruments*.

As it turns out, lacking other evidence we are poor at detecting lies by looking for the kinds of behavior we associate with the act. In scientifically conducted experiments, the success rate of people being asked to sort out lies from truths, say by watching people on videotape either lying or telling the truth, has been shown to be poor. Clues do exist, but they tend to be more subtle than shifty eyes or fidgeting. Psychology professor Paul Ekman (he at whose cavalier view of "natural liars" I took umbrage earlier) has determined that when people lie about something they consider important, an expression of the emotion they are hiding may flit across their faces for a fraction of a second. Ekman claims he can teach people to become better lie detectors by showing them how to recognize such "micro expressions," fleeting facial clues to deception. But he warns that even after such training lie detection is a tricky thing.

Which brings us back to the question of physiological changes that signal a lie in progress more subtly than facial clues do. That the attempt to deceive can induce such changes has probably been empirically known since the first liar noticed a suddenly dry mouth or wet palms when claiming he (or she) had or hadn't done something, and it was in fact not so. Bedouins until quite recently made conflicting witnesses lick a hot iron—the one whose tongue was burned was assumed to be lying. The ancient Chinese are alleged to have forced suspected liars to chew rice powder and then to spit it out—if what was spat out was dry, the suspect was judged to have been lying. Unfortunately the Bible does not record the state of Cain's salivary output while he answered God's question about the whereabouts of his brother Abel with the prototypical answer of murderers regarding all things concerning their victims: "I know not."

Of the various reasons the act of lying may produce a physiological response in the liar—a guilty conscience about the act of lying in general, unease at deceiving, say a spouse or friend, and violating trust, fear of the lie's discovery—the latter is the one held responsible by the proponents of the polygraph for the physiological changes the device records and the examiner interprets. In the case of criminal investigations this intuitively makes sense. A perpetrator hooked up to a lie detector has no personal ties to the examiner and is more likely worried about being discovered lying than perturbed by a guilty conscience awakened by the act of lying. This worry may well show up in a change in breathing, blood pressure, pulse rate and amplitude, and skin conductivity. The only problem—back to square one—is that the lie detector does not, in fact, detect lies but detects changes in breathing, blood pressure, etc. Which *may* be induced by fear of a lie being detected, but may also be induced by fear of a truth being disbelieved or even by stress totally unrelated to what is being investigated.

In the final analysis, what matters is whether or not the polygraph is effective as a lie detector. The U.S. government believes it to be so and invests millions of dollars yearly in polygraph operator training schools and the salaries of polygraph operators. By comparison, the two most monstrously repressive schemes of the twentieth century—Stalin's and Hitler's—did not use the polygraph—certainly not because they excelled at respecting the rights of their citizens but for the chilling reason that the people in charge of the torture rooms of the Lubyanka prison and Gestapo headquarters had more effective ways of wrenching the truth from their victims. Post–World War II Germany, in what amounts to a resounding vote of confidence for the polygraph, outlawed it on grounds that any device compelling a person to tell the truth despite a conscious decision to lie violates "freedom of the will."

What emerges from all of this is a collection of partial truths, which I randomly list here to illustrate how confusing things remain even after the experts have been consulted:

- A sizable number of people judged to be intentionally deceptive by a polygraph examiner *are* intentionally deceptive, and their bodies signal the deception.
- A sizable number judged to be intentionally deceptive are *not*, but their bodies send signals indistinguishable from those sent by intentional deception.
- Some large number judged to be truthful *are*, while some smaller number judged to be truthful are *not*.
- The same polygraph chart may be scored "deceptive," "nondeceptive," or "inconclusive" by different evaluators.
- Expert opinion finds the polygraph highly useful, somewhat useful, and of no use at all.
- How often in terms of percentages the polygraph is accurate remains unknown because scientifically conducted laboratory studies may not be representative of what goes on in the field and the results of tests conducted in the field are most of the time unverifiable.
- False results of polygraph exams have occasionally done great harm.

Can the polygraph be useful? Yes, sometimes, under some circumstances. Can it be misused? Yes, if it is assumed to be infallible and if decisions affecting people's lives are based on that assumption. Is the polygraph with us too much? No doubt. Consider the amazing fact that for decades the lie detector test has been a standard refuge (although not always a safe one) of those in the public eye in connection with one scandal or another. Headlines announcing that X "Is Willing to Take Polygraph" or "Passed Polygraph" or "Failed Polygraph" are so common that by now we'd be surprised if they didn't pop up the moment contradictory claims or accusations become issues for anyone scrutinized by the media. What this frequent encounter with the polygraph in newspapers and magazines and on TV invites is a sense of lie detection as common practice, and we can only guess the extent to which this sense convinces people of the polygraph's validity. Consider the statement made in 1996 by a spokesman for the Bass Anglers Sportsman Society of Montgomery, Alabama, which used lie detectors whenever there was suspicion of misconduct by participants in one of the lucrative tournaments the society held each year: "If they are innocent, I don't know why they would worry about taking a polygraph test."

All of which still leaves unanswered the final, tricky question we've already furled brows over: can a lie be turned into a truth in the mind of the liar, making its detection a moot point? Our sally into the psychology of lying suggests the answer is yes, and so does an expert witness from sitcom land. The lie detector episode of *Seinfeld* posits how such transmogrification might work: Jerry Seinfeld lies to a policewoman he is dating about the number of times he has watched *Melrose Place*—never once, Jerry claims. Unconvinced, she makes him take a lie detector test. George Costanza, Jerry's friend, who lies with a flair and aplomb that should make the garden-variety liar green with envy, sends Jerry on his way with a single piece of advice: "It's not a lie if you believe it." Jerry, incapable of this leap of the imagination, fails miserably, producing accusatory spikes to every profession of ignorance ("Did Billy sleep with Alison's best friend?" "I don't know." "Did Jane's fiancé kidnap Sydney and take her to Las Vegas, and, if so, did she enjoy it?" "I don't know!")

Again, George's suggestion enters the realm of Method acting, in which the actor strives to believe on some emotional level the character's motives and actions, and it also touches on our ability to rationalize about our actions by casting things in a different light. With respect to the latter, polygraph operators in training are taught, for instance, not to ask a suspect: "Did you murder X?" since the murderer may already have decided that the killing was self-defense or justifiable homicide—certainly not murder! Obviously even a 100 percent accurate lie detector like the APEX Truth Meter would be utterly foiled if the lying examinee *believed* he or she was telling the truth.

We have encountered the lie manipulated into truth in the liar's own mind earlier. Once the possibility of self-deception is introduced, THE TRUTH in cleanly chiseled letters promised by "scientific" lie detection fizzles into nothingness. It is not the Holy Grail of Certainty but a mirage floating over the Bog of Ambiguity (due west of the Slough of Despond). Which means that some of us would be well advised to let go of the cherished notion that any lie can be exposed, provided only we work at it hard enough. Still, when all is said, a stubborn feeling remains that a lie is a lie, the truth the truth, and that the difference, dammit, matters! The feeling is as ancient as the quest for knowledge, and people have acted on the basis of it since time immemorial. Often with painful consequences.

The Ordeal

Pain forces even the innocent to lie.

Publilius Syrus, *Sententiae*, no. 171

The scene: A well-heeled swim, tennis, and health club. Administration consists of the director, Annette Praetor, her assistant, Candy Cohort, and three staff members, Harriet Dogsbody, Jim Fetches, and Sally Ne'er-Dowell. An assortment of tennis pros, swim coaches, and aerobics instructors are in and out of the administrative offices all hours of the day, and some of the members, too, are in the habit of popping in. Most notorious among them are Alan Huff and Marla Peeve. Huff finds the slovenly habits of other members an unending source of irritation, and he forever urges Praetor to draft memos stating in the strongest terms that failure to wipe apparatus after use constitutes a health hazard and is in violation of Section 3, Subsection 9 of the Rules. Peeve complains that Huff is "mental" because he examines every square inch of gym equipment for traces of sweat before using it.

One day Praetor returns from lunch to find that the petty-cash box, which she inadvertently left unlocked on her desk, has been rifled of $283.35. She calls a meeting in order to establish opportunity. (The motive is held to be self-evident, although there are cries of dismay about anyone sinking so low as to commit theft for such a piddling sum.) As it turns out, Cohort, Fetches, and Ne'er-

Dowell were in or around the office at the right time, as was one of the tennis pros, Bob Ace, and one of the swim coaches, Mary Laps. In addition, members Huff and Peeve had been seen knocking on the director's door. Praetor asks each of the suspects directly whether he or she took the money. One and all protest vehemently that they did not. Whereupon she enlists half a dozen impartial club members and summons them to the pool after hours. There, the members perform the following procedure: They take the suspects, one at a time, tie their hands to their knees, fasten a rope around their waists, and lower them into the pool. Then they record whether the immersed party sinks or floats. In either case, the wet examinee is pulled from the water once buoyancy or lack thereof has been determined.

The reason behind the procedure is obvious: the water in the pool is ultra-clean since it is being continuously filtered and chlorinated; it will repulse anyone who has become besmirched by committing theft. Those innocent of the crime, conversely, will sink because the water recognizes them as clean and accepts them. Director Praetor, incidentally, is also subjected to the test, since she could, after all, have been lying about finding the cash box empty. The results are as follows: Cohort floats, Ne'er-Dowell sinks, Fetches sinks, Ace sinks, Laps floats, both Huff and Peeve float. Praetor herself floats. The conclusion: Praetor with her accomplices Cohort, Laps, Huff, and Peeve stole the money.

This exercise in absurdity will have been recognized by students of the Middle Ages as a modern-day version of the *ordeal by cold water*, one of the more benign of the extraordinary means people have devised in the dogged and unending quest to separate truth from lie. Hincmar, archbishop of Rheims from 845 to 882, set forth the rationale for *iudicium aquae frigidae* in days innocent of knowledge about the relationship between body fat and buoyancy:

> He who seeks to conceal the truth by a lie is unable to sink into the waters over which the voice of the majesty of the Lord has thundered, because the pure nature of the water does not receive a human nature which has been cleansed of all deceit by the water of baptism but has subsequently been reinfected by lies.

This marvelous means to separate the liars guilty of the crime with which they were charged from the blameless truth-tellers was architecturally incorporated in many a medieval church. The eleventh-century church at Canterbury, for instance, had a basin large enough to allow the accused to be entirely immersed in sanctified water. So did the cathedral at Laon, an episcopal see in northern France with a cathedral school dedicated to educating ambitious youth of Northern Europe and England. An anecdote probably too good to be true concerns the theft of the sacred vessels from the cathedral. At a council called to consider what measures to take to discover the culprit, one Anselm proposed that the ordeal should be resorted to. He was apparently a methodical soul. In the words of a suspect but witty source:

> Anselm suggested the following procedure: A young child should be taken from each parish of the town and tried by immersion in consecrated water. From each house of the parish which should be found guilty a child should be chosen to undergo the same process. When the house of the criminal should thus be discovered, all its inmates should be sent to the ordeal, and in the end Achan [a Judahite who kept some of the spoil from the city of Jericho] would be taken. This plan was voted excellent, so far as the immersion was concerned. Nothing could be better; but the good people of Laon suggested an amendment, that those whose access to the church gave them the best opportunities of tampering with the sacred vessels should go to the ordeal first. Accordingly six of these were selected. They were in the meantime placed in prison to await the day of the ordeal. No. 6, overcome with anxiety brought on by the confinement, had himself placed in a tub full of water, and being bound hand and foot sank satisfactorily to the bottom. He came out feeling thoroughly reassured. The day of the trial, *dies illa*, came at last. The cathedral itself was chosen as the place of judgment, and an immense concourse of people foregathered to watch the proceedings. All was ready and the ordeal began. No. 1 sank. No. 2 floated. No. 3 sank, so did No. 5. No. 4 floated. No. 6, notwithstanding his experiment, obstinately floated, and was condemned with his accomplices in spite of his protestations of innocence. No. 6 was—Anselm.

The episode is representative of how the ordeal by cold water was conducted, but its specifics would be more convincing if the

1923 source quoted weren't a textbook example of how history in the wrong hands turns into a pack of lies. The writer does not document where he purportedly got his material and he claims that the Anselm in question, the one who proposes the ordeal—and who, in a manner of speaking, is hoist by his own petard—is "the great Anselm, surely the greatest intellectual light of his time." In vain do we trot to the first biography of St. Anselm, written by his close friend, the monk Eadmer, for a (possibly more favorable) account of the event. In vain do we peruse a thoroughly researched 1963 biography. A look at St. Anselm's theological writings makes it seem unlikely that a man who devotes a chapter to the rational proof that God cannot be coerced in any way would support the ordeal, with its implied assumption that God can be forced to interfere in the affairs of the world to separate truth from lie and reveal who is innocent and who guilty.

With St. Anselm out of the picture as one of the condemned thieves, another Anselm, one of his contemporaries, becomes a possible candidate. Anselm of Laon, master of the cathedral school, a lesser light and, according to one unkind commentator, "an illustration of the fact that great academic reputations can be made, and great academic influence exerted, without a spark of genius." But a detailed history of Laon that includes a thumbnail sketch of Anselm of Laon's life makes no mention of his participation in any ordeal, let alone his condemnation, nor does it mention the surely eyebrows-raising event of the theft of the cathedral's sacred vessels. Scratch one juicy anecdote.

The ordeal by cold water was an innocuous enough procedure, painless and mercifully quick, preferable—if its truth-determining ability had been less suspect—to the modern weeks- or months-long trial.* True, the outcome for floaters could be death by hanging or fire, and the crowd occasionally lynched on the spot accused

---

*Re the great health club cash box caper tried by ordeal: Although she sank like a stone and was therefore judged blameless, the thief was Sally Ne'er-Dowell, a lifelong victim of her parents' modish decision to go for the compound name when they were tying the knot.

heretics who failed the test, but the process of ascertaining guilt or innocence was not in itself punishing except on cold days. If immersion had been the only means of trial used, the word *ordeal* probably would never have entered the language as a harrowing, painful, and dangerous thing. The word itself, from the Middle English *ordal*, is akin to the German *Urteil*, meaning judgment, and the various ordeals in the official Latin of the day are simply called *iudicia*—that is, judgments. Unfortunately *iudicium aquae frigidae* was complemented by an assortment of other, more taxing judgments, among them *iudicium aquae ferventis* and *iudicium ferri caldi*. In the ordeal by boiling water and the ordeal by hot iron, we shake hands with the modern meaning, or would if our hand were in a condition to shake anything after we used it to retrieve a ring from the bottom of a cauldron of boiling water or to carry a rod of red-hot iron a designated distance, this in order to convince the authorities that we spoke the truth when we claimed that we did not commit the robbery or adultery or murder we stand accused of.

The idea is far older than the Middle Ages and predates Christianity. It appears in the tradition of curses directed against oneself, according to which a higher power will inflict punishment if one should fail to keep a promise or tell the truth. When Phaëthon is taunted about his alleged father, the sun god, and asks his mother whether he truly is the son of Apollo, she swears: "I call to witness the Sun which looks down upon us, that I have told you the truth. If I speak falsely, let this be the last time I behold his light." "Cross my heart and hope to die" is a childish leftover of the practice, and the oath sworn in court in the name of God is based on the one-time pious hope that fear of divine punishment for using God's name to support a lie will deter perjury.

Versions of the ordeal by fire or water (or poison or battle) to determine innocence or guilt appear in ancient Greece, pre-Christian Norway and Iceland, Polynesia, Japan, and Africa. The theory was that when someone who is suspected of a crime is placed in peril, an omniscient higher power will rescue the innocent. Sophocles' *Antigone* provides a classical example. The men guarding the corpse of Polyneices following Creon's decree that he be left unburied find that someone has sprinkled earth over the corpse. Fearing death or worse, one of the guards protests before

Creon that he and his fellow guards are innocent of the crime. He tries to draw a convincing picture of their turmoil when they discovered that someone had performed the hallowed rite:

> *. . . Rough talk flew thick and fast,*
> *guard grilling guard—we'd have come to blows*
> *at last, nothing to stop it; each man for himself*
> *and each the culprit, no one caught red-handed,*
> *all of us pleading ignorance, dodging the charges,*
> *ready to take up red-hot iron in our fists,*
> *go through fire, swear oaths to the gods—*
> *"I didn't do it, I had no hand in it either,*
> *not in the plotting, not the work itself!"*

Red-hot iron and fire will prove that the swearer of the oath is telling the truth, so help him the gods!

The medieval ordeal by hot iron reflects the same concern: you deny the charge—the implied claim being that you are telling the truth—or you swear a formal oath proclaiming your innocence. In either case God proves that you are telling the truth either by outright protecting from injury the hand holding the hot iron, or the bare feet walking on hot plowshares, or by making the wounds heal quickly and cleanly, which is apparent when the bandaged limb or limbs are unwrapped and inspected three days after the ordeal. The same is true for the *ordeal of the cauldron*: the hand and arm immersed in the boiling water either emerge unscalded or the scalded limb is found to heal quickly.

Legend, of course, favors the more clearly miraculous of the two possibilities. Virtuous queens accused of adultery walk barefoot over red-hot plowshares and pluck rings or gems from seething water without dismay. Cunigunda, wife of the emperor Henry II, was alleged to have vindicated her innocence by the ordeal of the plowshares. The boiling cauldron as test of the status of a wife's fidelity is described in *The Elder Edda*, a Viking poem dating to the Norse culture of the tenth century, as yet barely touched by Christianity. Queen Gudrun, falsely accused of adultery, first says to her husband: "I will give you my solemn oath, swear on the white holy stones, that never did I sleep with Thjordmar's son, we two have done no shameful deed." She then goes to a cauldron in the great hall, where seven hundred men gather to witness the ordeal:

> *She put her white hand into the water*
> *and gathered up the glittering gems:*
> *"My lords, you have seen the sacred trial*
> *prove me guiltless—and still the water boils."*

Her accuser (her husband's mistress, incidentally, but unilateral monogamy was of course the norm) is then made to put her hand into the boiling water and is horribly scalded.

Neither here nor in *Antigone* is the solemn oath alone held sufficient to establish innocence. It was as clear to an Athenian audience in 442 B.C. as to a Norse one in the thirteenth century A.D., the time when *The Elder Edda* first appeared in writing, that liars were capable of appealing to a divine power in the very process of lying and that more "evidence" than an oath might be needed to establish proof.

In the God-fearing Middle Ages an uncorroborated oath alone *could* clear suspects (invariably those of higher social standing) of many crimes, and the oath was a cornerstone of medieval judicial procedure. But there were also dire warnings about the oath's inefficacy in revealing the truth: In 967 Otto I gave a ruling for Italy according to which pleas of land could not be decided by oath if the case relied on the authenticity of documents. The objection was that "a detestable and wicked custom, which should not be imitated, has grown up in Italy, whereby those who do not fear God and are not afraid to perjure themselves make acquisitions by their oaths with the appearance of legality." Otto instead ordered the judicial duel, ordeal by battle with shields and clubs—known as "the judgment of God"—to decide the issues. (Otto apparently felt that God was willing to make the weaker of two combatants win a brutal fight in which bones were broken and heads bashed in, provided his cause was just, but was not willing to expose a perjurer by simply making him drop dead.) In many other instances, the oath alone was seen as insufficient and required the corroborating force of the ordeal. In Anjou in the 1070s, for instance, a witness was ordered "to swear on holy objects as to what he said he had seen and then confirm the oath by the ordeal of hot water, as is the custom of our region."

Although the Middle Ages inherited the concept of the ordeal, they did not find their rationale for it in Sophocles or other pagan sources. In the years 800–1200, roughly the period of the ordeal's heyday as part of the judicial system, those in favor of it found an analogy of sorts in the Book of Daniel, in the story of Shadrach, Meshach, and Abednego surviving Nebuchadnezzar's fiery furnace. The three youths, who refuse to worship the golden image the king made, are saved by an angel from fire in a furnace seven times hotter than it normally is—so hot, the point is made, that it kills the men who cast them into the furnace.

Note that the reason they are saved has nothing to do with their being proven by God's intervention to be telling the truth, only with their being righteous. An often-used invocation in the ordeal of hot iron shifted the focus from the detection of the truth to the protection of the innocent: "If you are innocent of this charge . . . you may confidently receive this iron in your hand and the Lord, the just judge, will free you, just as he snatched the three children from the burning fire." Obviously, there was a direct analogy between determining that a suspect's claim of innocence was true and determining innocence itself: if the suspected thief was not hurt by fire, this proved that (a) he told the truth when he protested his innocence and (b) he was innocent. The suspected thief hurt by fire, conversely, was thereby shown to be (a) lying and (b) guilty.

Setting the medieval interpretation of the Bible story aside for a moment and going on a blasphemous hunt for intention, we find that the miraculous delivery of the "Three Holy Children"—not a hair singed on their heads—closely parallels that of Daniel himself, untouched by the lions when King Darius is forced to lock him in their den. The moral of both stories is that those who honor the one true God are saved and promoted to positions of wealth and power, and both stories drive home the point of the clout of the God of Israel by showing the rulers of the world awed and swayed. After Daniel has escaped the lions unharmed and the lions have— possibly for the benefit of those readers who do not find this delivery quite as miraculous as that from a fiery furnace—broken "all in pieces" the bones of Daniel's enemies (and for good measure those of their wives and children as well), King Darius writes "unto all people, nations, and languages, that dwell in all the earth." Darius' letter is an accomplished promo piece for the god with a capital G:

> I make a decree, That in every dominion of my kingdom men tremble and fear before the God of Daniel: for he *is* the living God, and steadfast for ever, and his kingdom *that* which shall not be destroyed, and his kingdom *shall be even* unto the end. He delivereth and rescueth, and he worketh signs and wonders in heaven and in earth, who hath delivered Daniel from the power of the lions (Daniel 6:26–27).

The ordeal has pagan and pre-Christian roots, but in the Middle Ages bureaucracy went to work and encoded it in law, subject to rules and Christian rituals. Under what circumstances which ordeal was to be used, and on whom and how, became a matter of local law codes. The first recension of the Salic Law (ca. 510) mentions the ordeal of the cauldron. In the same century, additions made to the law contain provisions for both slaves and free men going to the cauldron on charges of theft and bearing false witness. Already the how is specified as well: "Whoever has to justify himself at the cauldron shall hold the staff [the court official's staff of office] with his left hand and draw out with his right." Southpaws as usual got a raw deal since their lack of dexterity must have made it harder to grab the object at the bottom of the boiling cauldron. Around 802, Franco-Chamavian law prescribes: "If a thief is proved guilty of seven thefts, let him go to the ordeal. If he is burnt, let them deliver him for execution. If he is not burned after he has gone to the ordeal, then his lord may go surety for him and make amends on his behalf and free him from death."

Interestingly, not being burned does not clear the thief "proved guilty of seven thefts" and only opens up the possibility of his escaping death by the intervention of someone willing to pay up. A measure of skepticism about the efficacy of the ordeal in establishing innocence in such a case seems to have had a hand in the drafting of this paragraph, and skeptical grumbling must have prompted no less a figure than Charlemagne to put down his imperial, thought-policing foot in the matter. In 809 he ordered: "Let all believe in the ordeal without any doubting." With or without doubting, the ordeal had staying power: Four centuries later, a Scandinavian code specified: "If a woman's husband accuses her of adultery, she must clear herself with the iron." The hot iron, it turns out, was a perennial favorite in charges of sexual misconduct, and men, too, could be subjected to it. However, in their case the charge brought against them had to be "carnal dealings with cattle of any sort" or sodomy or sexual relations with close kin.

All of this sounds like so much coercion to practice self-torture, but, as the scenes from Sophocles and *The Elder Edda* adumbrate, there were times when people asked for the ordeal to clear themselves of a charge. Obviously this is easier to understand if the ordeal was immersion in cold water rather than grasping and carrying a hot iron. Only if we remember the Middle Ages' ready acceptance of the supernatural, which made miracles a part of most people's unquestioned belief, can we begin to see how some poor wretch falsely accused of a crime punishable by death may ask to be tried by the ordeal by fire. A devout believer convinced that God will deliver the innocent from harm by miraculously changing the properties of a hot iron may well see in the ordeal the way to instant vindication and freedom. The formula pronounced by the priest (after much preparatory ado on the part of the accused, including fasting, confession, vigil in a church, communion, procession-cum-litany to the place of the ordeal, kissing of a cross, drinking of holy water) is clear enough, although most of the probands would have needed a translation from the original Latin to understand it:

> O God, the just judge, who are the author of peace and give fair judgment, we humbly pray you to deign to bless and sanctify this fiery iron, which is used in the just examination of doubtful issues. If this man is innocent of the charge from which he seeks to clear himself, he will take this fiery iron in his hand and appear unharmed; if he is guilty, let your most just power declare that truth in him, so that wickedness may not conquer justice but falsehood always be overcome by the truth. Through Christ.

In other words, the ordeal was a lie detector test, and the innocent believer was liable to ask for trial by ordeal just as a naive suspect nowadays may ask for a lie detector test. In fact, the ordeal by water, noninjurious and yielding quick results, parallels the polygraph exam as it is used in criminal investigations. In both cases a transgression is being investigated and someone claiming not to be guilty may or may not be lying. Hence the need for a means to determine if the claim of innocence is truth or lie. Detection (or make that "detection") of a lie establishes guilt, detection of truth innocence. In both cases a higher authority—God or science—is held responsible for revealing the truth. In both cases, people trusting in that higher authority have been victimized. How many innocent people have spent years in jail courtesy of the "scientific" lie detector test is unknown—we met one of them in the previous chapter—as is how many innocent people were hanged or burned in the Middle Ages because they floated, or not only did their hands or feet *not* escape unhurt the effect of hot iron on flesh but the wounds were found to be suppurating after three days. One twelfth-century manuscript illustration of the trial by fire shows a man about to grasp the hot iron bar offered to him straight from the fire. Teeth bared, eyes upturned, he is a study in fearful apprehension.

As for cleanly healing wounds, given the age's knowledge about antisepsis, which could have been inscribed on the head of a pin, infection must have been not uncommon. Still, the fact that not only the miracle of escaping the ordeal by fire unharmed but also the wound's proper healing was accepted as evidence of innocence shows what happens when an age believing in miracles runs smackdab into physical reality. Hearsay and pious anecdotes illustrating the miraculous salvation of the virtuous will go only so far in estranging people from personal experience, and personal experience tells all but the most gullible that *everybody* who handles a hot iron is hurt. Ergo either everybody undergoing the ordeal is guilty because everybody exhibits distressing signs of pain or another way has to be found to separate the guilty from the innocent. Enter the "cleanly healing" wound indicating that at least *some* of the accused were innocent.

Yet another similarity between medieval and modern lie detection is found in the not infrequent disputes about how to interpret the results of the ordeal or the polygraph test. Is the wound healing cleanly? Is a small blister or slight discharge acceptable for a not-guilty verdict? If so, how small a blister, how slight a discharge? Does the immersed suspect have to touch the bottom of the ordeal basin to be judged innocent? If she is fully submerged but her hair floats, does this mean she passed the test? *Was* her hair above the water? Compare this with the ordeal by polygraph: Were the control questions properly asked? Was the subject in a condition to be tested rather than too fatigued or high on drugs? Do the chart readings of blood pressure, galvanic skin response, etc., clearly indicate deception or no deception, or are they ambiguous?

Finally, in both cases, guilty suspects have insisted on taking the test from the conviction that they could foil it. According to one ecclesiastical critic of the ordeal, a man tested his sons in water and sent the one who sank to the bottom to undergo the ordeal for him as his proxy. And just as a suspect may seek to gain credibility when calling for a polygraph test, people involved in disputes have used the ordeal to up the ante, with no intention of actually submitting to it. In cases where one faction charged the other with murder or treason, the expressed willingness to carry a hot iron to prove the justness of one's cause could give force to the claim. A probably apocryphal account tells how an eleventh-century Norman historian envisaged the ordeal as a means to buttress deception. In 943, the tale goes, the count of Flanders, who had arranged the killing of the duke of Normandy, worried that their common ruler, the king of France, might seek revenge. The count sent messengers to the king to dispel the "false rumor that our lord condoned the death of the duke." Nothing could be further from the truth. In fact, the count "wishes to clear himself before you by the ordeal of the fire." The result? The king's counselors advised him, "You should not prejudge any man who seeks so hard to justify himself to you." Thus, Norman tradition holds, the king was "deceived and blinded" by this brazen move—which instantly promoted the murderer to the position of aggrieved victim of a false accusation—and the duke's death remained unavenged. Although it was an age in which most people believed in miracles, it was clearly not an age ignorant of human guile.

Even in the case of people going to the ordeal, there was the worry that some of the accused might resort to trickery physical or magical in nature in attempting to pass. The hand was washed and carefully inspected to assure it hadn't somehow been prepared to lessen the effect of the hot iron, and the suspect was stripped of amulets and charms. This awareness of the possibility of fraud suggests that there were people who tried to pass the ordeal by means that had nothing to do with awe of the judgment of God and who were more concerned about saving their worldly skin than their immortal soul. All of which may be used as evidence supporting the argument that some aspects of human nature are immutable and that the desire to foil attempts at detecting deception is as old as the urge to detect deception.

One difference between the ordeal and its modern version is that we have not, as far as I know, hanged people for failing a polygraph test. Another is that the ordeal was used as a last resort, when no other ways of determining the truth were available. Only when reliable oaths, material evidence, or eyewitnesses were lacking did the ordeal come into play. The "reliable" oath had the effect of acting as a filter protecting some from the ordeal. In many cases, the wellborn could get off by swearing an oath that they had not committed the crime of which they were accused and by getting others to swear for them as well. Compurgation, in which co-jurors attested to the accused's good reputation, was the medieval equivalent of character references, and the law might stipulate sevenfold, tenfold, or twelvefold compurgation, the number of people needed for exculpation depending on the vagary of local ordinance or severity of the crime. Bondsmen, of course, were not oath-worthy since those of low birth could not be trusted to be as aware of what it meant to swear an oath as men of honor. They were subjected to the ordeal when neither witnesses nor evidence established their innocence or guilt. The belief that the well-to-do are more likely to be morally upright has a long history and clings to us even in the age of the S&L scandals, and the CEOs of tobacco companies, and ethics violations committed by politicians of all stripes etc., ad nauseam. Thus the underprivileged were then as now more likely to be punished for crimes committed or not committed.

Even the wellborn, however, were subjected to the ordeal if they had in the past been proven to have perjured themselves or if the charge was treason. The reason for both is obvious: since someone who has once lied under oath may do so again, and since committing treason is already an act of deception and the violation of an explicit or implicit oath of loyalty, any man guilty of these crimes would have no compunction about swearing a false oath to save himself.

Another group of people not deemed oath-worthy were those accused of being witches or heretics. Witchery involved a pact with the devil, hence an oath to God would be meaningless to those practicing that crime. Heresy meant doubt in received religion; again, an oath would be meaningless to the doubter. Both were crimes of stealth and secrecy. People grew sick and died, or their livestock did, because their neighbor, who was a witch, had cast a spell over them. Of course, there was no material evidence in the form of a bloody cleaver and no witness placing the culprit at the scene of the crime. The witch may have been observed mumbling to herself (that is, casting a spell), and perhaps suspicious herbs had been found in her cottage, but though damning, this evidence was not sufficient to burn the suspect at the stake. Similarly, proof might be hard to come by in the case of the suspected heretic, whose wrong-thinking was locked inside his head or who might even claim that he was a true prophet of God. At a glance, both seem ideal candidates for the ordeal, but those who pondered weightily on the subject disagreed, and by the time the persecution of witches became widespread, in the late fifteenth century, the ordeal was no longer a legal form of proof in ecclesiastical courts. Powerful opponents objected to it on the grounds that Satan would help witches pass the test. Especially suspect were accused witches who *asked* to be tried by ordeal: they obviously counted on their dark master to come to their aid. In fact, the witch who passed the ordeal of the red-hot iron was thereby *proven* to be a witch!

The *Malleus Maleficarum*, the standard reference work consulted by ecclesiastical courts for a hundred years of witchcraft trials, excelled in illogical thinking in this area as in every other. If an accused witch will not confess, the judge is advised to ask her "whether, to prove her innocence, she is ready to undergo the ordeal by red-hot iron. And they all desire this, knowing that the devil will prevent them from being hurt. Therefore a true witch is exposed in this manner." Never mind the hapless defendant who, believing in God and believing that God will protect the innocent from harm in the ordeal, wishes to undergo it to prove her inno- cence. Never mind also that someone innocent and ignorant of the learned jurists' cogitations on the subject will assume that if she re- fuses the ordeal, the judge will consider it evidence of her guilt. What does the *Malleus* recommend to get the confession needed before the witch can properly be burned alive? Torture and long stays in prison under the most squalid conditions to wear her down, and duplicity—false promises, lies, and spies to trap her. The upshot was that anyone accused of witchcraft was well advised to abandon hope. As one of the modern commentators on this evil book put it: "The judicial process advocated in the *Malleus* is inex- orable."

Heretics did on occasion undergo the ordeal, with dire conse- quences. Volunteering to pass through fire to prove their divine mission, some burned to death. The notion of demonstrating God's approval by surviving fire was still around in the late fif- teenth century. In 1489, one of Savonarola's disciples accepted an ordeal by fire to prove the "prophet's" holiness. The event was rained out and Savonarola hanged and burned.

The waning of the ordeal had a great deal to do with the growing protest of the educated clergy, many of whose members worried about the procedure on theological grounds and saw it as a "tempt- ing" ("testing" in modern parlance) of God, sacrilegious and more closely allied with a superstitious belief in magical control over the supernatural than with religion. Aquinas, its most prestigious critic, argued that the "ordeal by hot iron or water is illicit because a miraculous effect is required of God." Nevertheless, local vestiges of the ordeal remained for centuries and suspected witches were sporadically tried by it.

Puritan colonial America used the trial by cold water, known as "the swimming of witches," as late as the 1690s even though au- thoritative clergy opposed the procedure. On September 15, 1692, near Fairfield, Connecticut, two women, Mercy Disborough and Elizabeth Clawson, were swum. They were tied hand and foot in a manner in which the right thumb touched a toe on the left foot and the left thumb a toe on the right foot. In this position they were tossed into a pond. According to report, both women "swam like a cork," and when one spectator tried to push them below the surface, they bobbed back up. The consequences might have been dire, but in a formal court trial conducted a month later, Clawson was acquitted of witchcraft despite her failure to sink. Disborough came closer to meeting her maker on short notice: she was found guilty and sentenced to hang, and she escaped that fate only because a higher court found a technical error in the composition of the jury.

The most notorious of the trials, the Salem witchcraft trials of 1692, did not use this means of detection—called a "superstitious experiment" and "diabolical invention" by Increase Mather (the father of Cotton Mather)—but, in the spirit of enlightened justice, based the verdict on the accusers' testimony about the defendants having appeared to them in spectral form with the devil in tow.

That the ordeal was no longer widely used in court proceedings by the end of the thirteenth century may be construed as a sign of a less superstitious legal system. Jubilation at a more enlightened way of doing business was, however, premature. The ordeal was replaced by judicial torture, and that abomination, with its assumption that only a confession of guilt constituted the truth, increased the amount of suffering immeasurably—especially for those belonging to the lower social order, who bore the brunt of this innovation. But surely wrenching the truth from the mouth of someone in excruciating pain was worth all the fiery tongs and thumbscrews and racks and people crippled by them in the world. If occasionally a mistake was made in who was tortured, and a false confession and wrongful execution resulted—well, God was sure to put things right in the next life. Plus the powers that be were no doubt as capable as those of later centuries at adopting the view of the omelet made at the expense of a few broken eggs.

Conclusion? Human beings have devoted inordinate effort to exposing lies and determining the truth. This being the case, we shouldn't be surprised to find that there has been a great deal of effort in the opposite direction as well. As we'll see, the quest to keep the truth hidden has been as doggedly pursued as that to bring it to light, and the care and feeding of lies has been of deep and abiding interest.

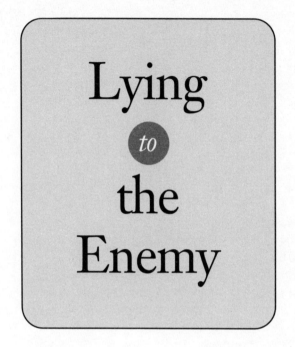

Lying _to_ the Enemy

Generals, Greeks, and Other Liars

In wartime, truth is so precious that she should always be attended by a body-guard of lies.

Winston Churchill

1

On the morning of April 30, 1943, three years and eight months into World War II, a local fisherman near Huelva, Spain, caught sight of something floating in the sea. He alerted a nearby launch. The object the sailors hauled on board turned out to be a grisly find—the body of a man. The somewhat decomposed corpse had been kept afloat by an inflated Mae West and carried close to shore by the wind. It wore the battle dress of a British officer, a major in the Royal Marines. The major had been on official business. Attached to the body by a leather-clad chain that was looped around the belt of its trench coat was a black briefcase, and the corpse's hand was clenched around the case's handle as if the courier had not wished to be separated from this piece of baggage even while dying of exposure and drowning.

The launch landed the body on the nearest beach, where a Spanish officer was exercising a detachment of infantry, and Spanish authorities impounded it for investigation. After a medical examination, the corpse was buried with full military honors in the graveyard of Huelva. The gravestone's epitaph expressed that ancient state-approved sentiment for fallen soldiers: *Dulce et decorum est pro patria mori.*

As soon as news of the dead courier got out, an urgent request came from the British naval attaché in Madrid that the corpse's effects immediately be turned over to British hands. The request was satisfied—after a brief delay during which Spanish officials friendly to the Germans opened the briefcase and took from it two confidential letters in sealed envelopes. They extracted the letters without breaking the seals, photocopied them, and then returned them to the envelopes and the envelopes to the briefcase. The copies they passed on to the German intelligence service. The Germans had been eagerly awaiting them ever since one of their agents, operating out of Huelva, had passed along details about the dead officer.

Those details had enabled them to draw a composite picture of the dead man's identity, personality, and final days. According to the identity card he carried, his name was William Martin. Acting Major William Martin had been born in Cardiff in 1907, and personal letters he carried showed him to have been the somewhat profligate, fun-loving, and impetuous son of an Edwardian gentleman. His life had been full and promising when he had met his end. Among other personal effects, he carried a letter alerting him to being overdrawn at his bank, two love letters from his fiancée, a young woman named Pam, to whom he had gotten engaged two weeks earlier, and a receipt for an engagement ring that had set him back 53£/6s. He had been in London a week before the discovery of his body and had during his stay found time to meet his father for lunch on April 21 and to go to the theater with Pam on the evening of April 22. A receipt from the officers' club where he had stayed, a letter from his father, and the stubs of two tickets to the Prince of Wales Theatre chronicled his moves.

And now he was dead, cut down in the prime of life by an accident. The shortness of the span between his presence in London and his death, estimated by the Spanish doctor who examined the body to have taken place about a week before the body's recovery, suggested he had been en route from England to Allied Headquarters in North Africa in an airplane when the plane had crashed at sea.

Of more interest to the Germans than young William Martin's poignant fate were the documents in his briefcase. They consisted of three separate items. Item one was a letter from Lord Louis Mountbatten, the Chief of Combined Operations, to Admiral Sir Andrew Cunningham introducing the "quiet and shy at first" major as an expert on landing craft, who "really knows his stuff." Item two was the proofs of a Manual on Combined Operations sponsored by Mountbatten, with a foreword by General Eisenhower. Item three was a personal letter, dated April 23, from the Vice-Chief of the Imperial General Staff, Lieutenant General Sir Archibald Nye, to General the Honourable Sir Harold R. L. G. Alexander.

Nye's letter to Alexander was the sort of find intelligence services dream about. The general informed his friend that Sicily, which General Maitland Wilson, Commander-in-Chief of Persia and Iraq, had proposed to use as cover target for the invasion of Greece, had already been chosen as cover for Operation Brimstone, the invasion of Sardinia. As Nye explained:

> The C.O.S. Committee went into the whole question exhaustively again and came to the conclusion that in view of the preparations in Algeria, the amphibious training which will be taking place on the Tunisian coast and the heavy bombardment which will be put down to neutralise the Sicilian airfields, we should stick to our plan of making it cover for "BRIMSTONE"—indeed, we stand a very good chance of making him think we will go for Sicily—it is an obvious objective and one about which he must be nervous. On the other hand, they felt there wasn't much hope of persuading the Boche that the extensive preparations in the Eastern Mediterranean were also directed at SICILY. For this reason they have told Wilson his cover plan should be something nearer the spot, e.g. the Dodecanese.

What did the German high command learn from this stupendous find? That Sicily, an obvious objective for the Allies, was used by them instead as a cover for an invasion elsewhere and that there were internal quibbles over *which* planned invasion Sicily should be made to cover, the one in Sardinia or the one in Greece. The final conclusion reached by the Allied Chiefs of Staff was that the Germans could hardly be persuaded that Sicily was the target for preparations made in the Eastern Mediterranean for a landing in Greece; better stick to making them believe it was the intended target for the forces amassing in Tunisia for a landing in Sardinia. The point of all this deception being, of course, to make the German high command commit troops to Sicily in anticipation of an invasion that would *not* take place, which would mean fewer German troops in Sardinia, where the Allies *would* attack.

The fortuitous interception of Nye's letter—a triumph for German intelligence—strengthened the German high command's suspicion that the Balkans and Greece in the east and Sardinia in the west were the Allies' primary objectives, and it was partly responsible for only two German divisions, neither up to full strength after having been weakened in Africa, being available to assist the Italians when an Allied landing took place on July 9—in Sicily! For despite the assurance of German intelligence to its high command that the intercepted documents were highly credible, Major William Martin of the Royal Marines had never existed. He was an invention of British naval intelligence, a concoction from first to last whose sole purpose was to deceive the enemy.

Who was "Major Martin"? The corpse was that of a man in his early thirties who had died of pneumonia after exposure (which meant he had some water in his lungs, easily mistaken for seawater by a medical examiner who assumed he had under his knife a victim of drowning). The body had been procured from a hospital in the late autumn of 1942 and had been kept in cold storage until the elaborate preparations for its launch had been made. Then it had been dressed in a major's uniform, equipped with bogus personal effects, letters from a fabricated fiancée and father, a bill of sale for a diamond ring, theater stubs, etc., and a briefcase containing two letters loaded with false information. Packed in dry ice in a sealed container, it had been transported to the Spanish coast by submarine, to be removed in the early hours of the morning of April 30 and allowed to float inshore near Huelva.

Operation Mincemeat was devised by Lieutenant Commander Ewen Montagu, a member of British naval intelligence—who indulged in a macabre sense of humor in picking that code name from a list of possible ones. He persuaded his higher-ups of the plan and managed to get splendid cooperation from the two men, Mountbatten and Nye, whose purported confidential letters Major Martin was carrying. Nye's letter to Alexander, in particular, was a masterpiece in tone, and it bracketed the bogus information about Sicily with high-level chat about the need for reinforcements here and there, the general's regret that an officer sponsored by Alexander had not gotten a command, and the general's impatience with their American Allies' ill-conceived proposal to give wounded British troops fighting with the Americans the Purple Heart (when British soldiers fighting alone would receive no such decoration).

The ruse is a textbook case of how a successful lie is fabricated so as to maximize its chance of being accepted as the truth. Its simple aim was to convince the enemy that Sicily was *not* the Allies' objective, but there was nothing simple about the game that was being played. The Germans were made to think that the Allies were *trying to make them think* that Sicily was the intended target when in fact it was not. The primary goal of the deception was to keep German troops away from Sicily; a secondary effect was the cherry on top: any preparations for the invasion of Sicily that the Germans spotted through aerial reconnaissance or learned about from agents could be attributed by them to the attempt to make them *think* preparations were underway to invade Sicily. Ingenious? Yes.

And splendidly successful. After the war, Montagu had the thrill of finding in a German archive the translation of the two letters and an intelligence appreciation attached to the one by General Nye. The document had been initialed by Admiral Karl Doenitz, the commander-in-chief of the German naval staff, meaning that Doenitz had read not only Nye's letter but the opinion of German intelligence concerning the credibility of the "*Kurierfund*." That opinion was heartening: "The genuineness of the captured documents is above suspicion," the report stated at the beginning. The claim is a reminder that anyone who hopes to get away with lying to someone who is alert to that possibility had better be very good at it. People in the spying business know that their opposites in the enemy camp are forever trying to mislead them. Any information, however acquired, may be fact or may be fabrication intended to make them reach the wrong conclusion. The Germans who were working on the case were well aware that the letters in the courier's briefcase might be false and planted in order to misinform. They also knew that they might be genuine—accidents and lucky finds did happen—in which case learning of their contents was a major coup. "Above suspicion" seems a bit strong in this context, and in the next sentence the writer of the report stated that the investigation into the possibility that the document might have been planted in German hands is continuing but that "the probability is low." (Apparently the CYA memo was not entirely unknown in German military circles.) One of Ewen Montagu's tasks had been to anticipate skepticism and provide evidence that would persuade someone worried about a possible plant that the information was genuine. Clearly he had done his job well.

After the war, Montagu wrote a book, titled *The Man Who Never Was*, about Operation Mincemeat. The book is a fascinating read and illustrates the imaginative effort required to pass off invention as genuine in the face of suspicion. The task was daunting. The story of the unfortunate major had to reveal itself to the German investigators all by itself: there was no possibility of correcting problems with it down the road. The verifiable facts had to fit—the body had to be that of a young man, had to wear the right uniform, be in the right state of decay, carry the right kind of identification with the right stamps and a photo that looked sufficiently like the dead man's face. The personal effects had to fit the character Montagu and his colleagues invented and had to form a plausible, convincing picture—a young officer on leave in London would stay at such a place, go to such a theater, have this kind of minor banking problem. Major Martin also had to have a personal life—everybody did. It was a stroke of genius to give the dead man a history: His death following his recent engagement to the charming young woman whose photos and letters he carried gave the story a special emotional gravity in addition to making it fit the familiar tableau of wartime losses.

A conundrum faced by Montagu and his colleagues was the briefcase, and his rumination on it shows the subtlety of the thinking that went into this all-important part of the deception—all-important because, for one, the briefcase needed to remain with the body in the water and, for another, the fact that it remained with the body had to make sense and not look rigged. Montagu inquired about rigor mortis: would it be safe to place the handle in the body's hand? He found that the risk of the handle slipping out was too high. A permanent attachment was needed. Although it was the only possible solution, nobody on the team liked the idea because it was, in Montagu's words, "the only point in the 'set-up' which did not ring true." To feel comfortable with it required a bit of reasoning:

> We decided to assume that an officer who carried really secret and important papers might attach his briefcase to one of the leather-covered chains which some bank messengers use, wearing them down their sleeves so they are not visible to the normal glance, but prevent their bag of valuables being snatched out of their hands. Such an arrangement seemed horribly phoney to us, but then *we* knew that this method was not one used by British officers. We decided that we would have to take a chance and rely on our opposite numbers in Berlin swallowing this feature. After all, *they* could not be sure that in no circumstances would a British officer adopt this method of safeguarding such documents.

Since the worrisome chain did not appear in the intelligence report, it either was not mentioned by the Spanish agents informing the Germans or, if it was, raised no suspicious German eyebrows.

Montagu's book also touches on the extent to which successful deception depends on the clues planted by the fabricator of false information being read by the enemy the way they are intended to be read. Clever and complicated clues require clever and competent victims to decipher them "correctly." The intelligence report showed that the Germans committed two mistakes in pondering Operation Mincemeat. The first was their misreading the date on Major Martin's theater stubs and concluding from the mistaken reading that he had died no more than two days before he was found. Ironically, the second mistake compensated for the first: they ignored that if the major had indeed died only two days before his body was found, this contradicted the finding of the doctor who had done the autopsy and who had judged that death had occurred five to seven days before the body's recovery—exactly what Montagu had planned for. Apparently the Germans wanted to believe in this gift from the sea and were blind to the contradiction.

Montagu's book recounted a thrilling real-life adventure, but when it was turned into a movie by the same name in 1955 the writers of the screenplay ratcheted up the suspense by a few notches. The movie introduced a fictitious German spy in London, sent there to determine whether the dead courier was real or a plant. He is about to discover the truth when an ironic coincidence of mistaken identity, which convinces him he has located and talked to the dead major's bereaved fiancée, saves the day. Not exactly the way it was, but how to convey to an audience the suspense and elation felt by the men who had orchestrated the ruse and who were monitoring its progress by reading intercepted and deciphered cables? Montagu et al. had to wait until the invasion of Sicily to see evidence of their success and until the end of the war to find proof positive in the form of the translated letters and report on Major Martin; the movie could close on the spy (played by Teutonic-looking Stephen Boyd) well and truly duped.

Operation Mincemeat was one of countless strategic deceptions carried out by the Allies and the Axis in World War II. All participants had their own intelligence services and within them "dirty tricks" departments. Services like MI6, the Deuxième Bureau, the Abwehr, and Japanese intelligence dedicated considerable personnel (called "deception staff" by the British) and resources to misleading and confusing the enemy. On the British side alone, staff and agents engaged in flurries of deceptive actions in scores of often whimsically named operations. Thus Operation Purple Whales was a series of red herrings presented to the Japanese high command. Operation Cloak successfully hid from the Japanese the British attack on Meiktila by making the enemy believe Mandalay, seventy miles to the north, was the intended target. Operations Ferdinand and Barclay were triumphs of deception in the Mediterranean. The former masked the Allied intention of landing in the South of France, the latter was the central operation for all deceptions aimed at hiding the landing in Sicily; Operation Mincemeat was one of its offshoots, as was Operation Waterfall, which involved the creation in North Africa of a bogus "8th Armoured Division" and of an impressive display of dummy airplanes and dummy landing craft for providing false information to aerial reconnaissance. And so it went from Operation Avenger, a stillborn plan meant to confuse the Germans about the movement of Allied forces inside Germany, to Operation Zeppelin, a comprehensive stratagem employed to keep the German high command from identifying the Normandy landings as the main thrust of the Allies.

Double agents from Apprentice to Zigzag were important elements in much of this, bombarding the enemy with bogus information. Brutus and Puppet, Biscuit and Balloon, Gelatine and Meteor, and the flamboyant Garbo and Tricycle—all were run by their British handlers with varying degrees of success. Garbo and Tricycle, in particular, were variable sluice gates of misinformation about massive troop concentrations and preparations in the United Kingdom and about landing craft, airplanes, and amphibious vessels being readied and hospitals prepared for receiving casualties in planned attacks on Norway and on the beaches around Calais. Both were masters at deception: Tricycle indignantly blamed any lack of success on not being given the necessary resources; Garbo not only created a network of fictitious agents but excelled in the tone in which he transmitted his "findings." His radioed messages mixed excited burbling about the intelligence he had gathered with conscientious advice to be cautious and not leap to the wrong conclusions: he might be misinterpreting the data he had amassed on his spying trips to Scotland and the South of England—the troops he observed might be training for invasions that would not occur for another year.

2

As we'll see, double agents have a long history. And the idea of regaling an enemy with the body of a courier carrying misleading information is probably as old as that of allowing an agent to fall into enemy hands so he can pass on wrong information. In literature, the prototype for the latter is Sinon. "Perjured" Sinon is the Greek warrior who convinced the Trojans that they ought to wheel the giant wooden horse left behind by the Greeks into the city, and he remains one of the greatest liars of our storied past.

As Aeneas tells it in Virgil's *Aeneid*, after ten years of unsuccessfully laying siege to Troy, the Greeks burn their tents and sail off, leaving on the shore of windy Troy a large, hollow wooden horse, its belly crammed with Greek warriors in hiding. While the Trojans are arguing about what to do with the strange beast—hack it to pieces? burn it? throw it down a cliff? take it into the city?—a Greek by the name of Sinon is captured by shepherds in the countryside, put in fetters, and dragged to the city. The Trojans assemble to taunt the captive, and Sinon bewails his unhappy fate: he has no place among the Greeks, who tried to murder him, and now the Trojans will surely kill him. The Trojans are intrigued and ask him to tell his story. He consents to do so and to "hide nothing of the truth," for "fortune made of Sinon a miserable man but not a man of faithlessness and falsehoods." (Beware of Greeks, or anyone else, professing their honesty—or speaking of themselves in the third person.)

This is miserable Sinon's story: A short while ago he escaped death at the hands of his fellow Greeks. They had prepared to sacrifice him to the gods for a safe journey across the sea. The rites were being readied for him and garlands had been wrapped around his temples when he slipped his bonds, and he hid in a muddy pond among the rushes all night long, waiting for the Greeks to sail away. The treachery of Ulysses (Odysseus in Homer) was to blame for his plight. Their mutual hatred was of long standing. Sinon hated Ulysses for having had Sinon's kinsman Palamedes killed. Motivated by envy, Ulysses had used "lying evidence" and false charges to destroy Palamedes. Sinon does not flesh out that story, but Virgil's audience knew it well: Ulysses planted a fake letter from Priam, king of Troy, in the tent of Palamedes and accused him of treachery. When the tent was searched, the incriminating letter was found and blameless Palamedes was stoned to death by his fellow warriors. As Sinon tells it, he had vowed to avenge Palamedes and kill Ulysses after their return from the war, and ever-guileful Ulysses, in order to eliminate the threat, had conspired with a seer to pick him as the sacrificial victim favored by the gods.

Sinon is a crafty liar, who could have served as a sterling example in our how-to chapter. He tailors his lie to confirm his Trojan dupes' preconceived notions about the treachery of Ulysses and appeals to their hatred of him. He is a superb actor, putting feeling into his role. He sticks as much as possible to the facts and alters them only here and there for the desired effect: fact is, he *is* a kinsman of one of the two antagonists, but his relative is Ulysses rather than the late, framed Palamedes. (And while we're on the subject of cross and double cross: Ulysses hated Palamedes because Palamedes exposed one of his ruses. Not wanting to join the punitive expedition to Troy because a prophecy had predicted twenty years of hardship if he did, Ulysses feigned madness when the other Greek chiefs came calling. He yoked a young ass and an ox to the same plow and sowed his field with salt. Palamedes, who saw through the performance, put Ulysses' infant son on the ground ahead of the plow. The mad plowman reined in the animals to keep the child from being trampled to death, thereby giving himself away as a sane man fit for war.)

Sinon ends his tale of Ulysses' treachery by expressing his great anguish that the Greeks will make his own tender sons and his father pay with their deaths for his escape—he is surely the most wretched of mortals. Choked with tears, he begs of his captors:

> . . . *by the High Ones, by*
> *the powers that know the truth, and by whatever*
> *still uncontaminated trust is left*
> *to mortals, pity my hard trials, pity*
> *a soul that carries undeserved sorrows.*

(Again there is a lesson here: people from whose lips the words "truth" and "trust" flow too freely are probably playing fast and loose with both.)

The Trojans are moved by Sinon's eloquent plea. King Priam himself takes the fetters off the captive and tells him to forget the Greeks—from this time on he will be considered a fellow Trojan. And now that that has been settled, what about the massive horse the Greeks have left? Why did they build it? Is it an offering to one of the gods or an engine of war? "Answer truthfully!" Priam urges the newest Trojan.

Sinon, apparently deeply touched by the Trojans' generosity but in reality "schooled in Grecian guile and wiles," lifts his hands to heaven. He cries:

You everlasting fires, and your
inviolable power, be my witness;
you altars, savage swords that I escaped,
you garlands of the gods I wore as victim,
it is now right for me to break the holy
oath of my loyalty and right for me
to hate the Greeks, to bring all things to light,
whatever they conceal.

The horse, he tells them, is an offering to Minerva (Pallas Athena in Homer's idiom), built by the Greeks to assure a safe return to their homeland. If the Trojans manage to drag it into the city, the Greeks will perish and the Trojans thrive. The reason the builder made it so massive was to ensure that it could not pass through the gate and could never protect the people with its sanctity. If the Trojans destroy it, as the Greeks hope they will, ruin will fall on Troy; if they bring it into the city, their war against the Greeks will be successful. Sinon feels no remorse about giving away the secret, he claims; the Trojans have promised him safety and they will not regret it: "I tell the truth and so repay you fully."

The Trojans believe him. Aeneas puts the blame for this colossal gullibility squarely on the shoulders of Sinon:

> *Such was the art of perjured Sinon,*
> *so insidious, we trusted what he told.*
> *So we were taken in by snares, forced tears.*

Eager to get the horse inside the city so Minerva will begin her destruction of the enemy, the Trojans put wheels under it and break down a wall and, using ropes, haul the trophy inside the city, to the temple of the goddess. During the night the Greeks, led by Ulysses, come out of the horse's belly and massacre the inhabitants. Their comrades, allegedly far away, return from the nearby shore where they had anchored and complete the destruction of mighty Ilion.

The Trojan Horse is not mentioned in the *Iliad*, which ends before the fall of Troy. It is touched on in the *Odyssey*, but without any mention of Sinon. According to Homer's version of the events, the stratagem of the wooden horse was planted in the head of one Epeios by Athena, and Epeios built the giant statue with her help. Odysseus' contribution to the effort was to fill the horse with warriors, himself included. The first known version fleshed out with Sinon appears in the *Aeneid*.

The *Aeneid* occupied Virgil for the last eleven years of his life, and he was planning to revise it one final time when he died in 19 B.C. The first full texts of the *Iliad* and the *Odyssey*, by comparison, were available from at least the end of the sixth century B.C. and probably from long before that. In the *Aeneid*, much is made of those Trojans who do not trust the Greeks even if they "bring gifts" and who suspect that the Trojan Horse is, well, a Greek Horse replete with warriors armed to the teeth. Presented by Virgil, a Roman who like all Romans traced the mythical founding of Rome and his ancestry to the Trojan prince Aeneas, Sinon's guile is spectacular. As it should be from Aeneas' point of view. The Greeks' view of this perjurer and breaker of vows may have been featured in one of the six other epics about the war against Troy narrated by early bards, but, if so, all that is left of it is circumstantial evidence. Virgil drew on accounts of the Trojan War that were still current in the first century B.C. but of which now only fragments of a few lines and summaries of the contents made around A.D. 140 remain.

For the Greek take on Sinon, one has to go to the middle of the fourth century A.D. Quintus Smyrnaeus, or Quintus of Smyrna, tells the story of the wileful captive quite differently. His sources are a matter of conjecture—he departs from all known ones, and many of the episodes he describes in his *Fall of Troy* may be his own invention based on sketchy knowledge of original texts and Virgil's cast of characters. What is certain is that his Sinon is seen from the Greek point of view and that he is a man of extraordinary courage and resolve. "Some brave man, unknown of any in Troy, with a stout heart" is what the "cunning stratagem" of the wooden horse requires, according to Odysseus. Sinon is that man. "Loyal of heart," infused with "high courage," he volunteers his services and promises to Odysseus and the other Greek chiefs that he will tell the false story of the horse unwaveringly, "yea, though they torture me, though into fire living they thrust me." Which is exactly what the Trojans do "long time unceasing," finally cutting off Sinon's ears and nose and torturing him with fire.

Sinon perseveres under extreme duress, telling the Trojans over and over "the same guileful tale" of how the Greeks built the wooden horse to appease Athena and meant to sacrifice Sinon for a safe journey, and how, fleeing from them, he flung himself down at its feet, making them afraid to kill a man who sought the protection of the goddess. "In subtlety so he spake, his soul untamed by pain; for a brave man's part is to endure to the uttermost." Enter Laocoön, who here, as in the *Aeneid*, calls the wooden horse a fraud (and is not mentioned anywhere in Homer). He is blinded by Athena, which the Trojans take to be evidence corroborating their captive's story. They draw the "Horse of Doom" into the city.* Worried about "the outrage done to hapless Sinon's flesh, whereby they hoped to wring the truth from him," they release him. During the night, he softly calls to the warriors inside the horse that they may safely come out since the Trojans are in a drunken slumber after celebrating. And so begin the great massacre and conflagration that mean the ruin of Troy.

When the slaughter is done, the Greeks celebrate and make sacrifices to the gods to give thanks for the victory. They also sing the praise of Sinon, that "resolved soul who endured dire torment." Sinon is glad the foe has been vanquished and thinks nothing of having lost ears and nose. To "the wise and prudent man" renown is far better than handsomeness or any other good thing, the narrator concludes. (Ewen Montagu might disagree, but he too was rewarded for guile above and beyond the call of duty. In 1944 he received the Military Order of the British Empire for devising Operation Mincemeat.)

So much for guileful, perjured, insidious Sinon, or stouthearted, loyal, courageous Sinon. That wily Greek is obviously useful in fleshing out the story and lending it verisimilitude, but the pivotal

---

*Quintus postpones the strangeness of Laocoön's fate as it is described in the *Aeneid*, where Laocoön and his two small sons are strangled by two giant serpents coming out of the sea. Not until the blinded priest warns the Trojans one more time, after they have already begun dragging the horse toward the city, does Athena summon the monsters to destroy father and sons in Quintus' version of the tale.

element of Troy's destruction is unaffected by his presence or absence, and it is what will most impress any military strategist studying the Trojan War and its great heroes and battles. What counts in the end is not that a woman's face launched a thousand ships, nor that Achilles was angry enough to keep stewing in his tent while his fellow warriors suffered one bloody defeat after another. The most amazing thing for anyone interested in how to win (as opposed to how to start or unsuccessfully wage) a war is that *this* war, after ten years of fighting and untold losses on both sides, was won by a single, successful act of deception.

3

"There is no new thing under the sun" is one of the great pessimistic insights of Ecclesiastes. (Others are that "all is vanity and vexation of spirit" and that "of making many books there is no end.") There is certainly nothing new about strategic deception in war. Operation Mincemeat would not have surprised in the least Sun Tzu, or rather the Chinese strategist who wrote under that name the first of all military classics, *The Art of War*.

Written sometime between 400 and 320 B.C., *The Art of War* is a systematic treatise on all aspects of warfare. Sun Tzu is knowledgeable and astute. He gives advice on concerns ranging from weather and terrain to the chain of command, the qualifications of a good commander, provisioning, equipment and its transportation, and the economic costs of war. Throughout this, he continually returns to one topic: the advantage gained by deceiving the enemy. "All warfare is based on deception," he categorically states. "Therefore, when capable, feign incapacity; when active, inactivity. When near, make it appear that you are far away; when far away, that you are near." He elaborates: "The enemy must not know where I intend to give battle. For if he does not know where I intend to give battle, he must prepare in a great many places. And when he prepares in a great many places, those I have to fight in any one place will be few."

The instructions given by Sun Tzu have proven timeless. China's Taiping Rebellion (1851–64) was led by men who had studied *The Art of War*, and Mao Zedong's military thinking was strongly influenced by Sun Tzu. So what would Sun Tzu make of a modern Western deception like Operation Mincemeat? He would most likely conclude that Ewen Montagu, too, had simply followed instructions. Similarly, the method employed would strike him as no more than an adaptation of methods he outlined in his final chapter, which is on the use of secret agents. The chapter lists five types of secret agents: *native agents* (country people whom one can employ to work against their own side—"fifth columnists" in modern parlance), *inside agents* (members of the official class who have been dismissed or otherwise disenfranchised, or officials who can be bought with gold and silk), *double agents* (enemy spies discovered and turned by lavish bribes), *expendable agents* (agents given fabricated details or plans in the hope that they will be caught and will reveal the false information and confuse the enemy), and *living agents* (agents who infiltrate enemy territory and report back the enemy's movements, doings, and plans).

Operation Mincemeat was clearly a clever variant of the expendable agent method of deception. A precursor was described in the eleventh century. One of Sun Tzu's interpreters furnished the following example of wars won and lost because rulers did or did not conduct them according to Sun Tzu's advice:

> In our dynasty Chief of Staff Ts'ao once pardoned a condemned man whom he then disguised as a monk, and caused to swallow a ball of wax and enter Tangut. When the false monk arrived he was imprisoned. The monk told his captors about the ball of wax and soon discharged it in a stool. When the ball was opened, the Tanguts read a letter transmitted by Chief of Staff Ts'ao to their Director of Strategic Planning. The chieftain of the barbarians was enraged, put his minister to death, and executed the spy monk.

Chief of Staff Ts'ao's ruse has elements of Ulysses destroying Palamedes by falsely implicating him in correspondence with the enemy. It also has elements of Operation Mincemeat in using a condemned-to-death (and therefore legally dead) agent as the vehicle to convey false information into an enemy's camp.

So what would Sun Tzu have made of Operation Gift Horse? He would no doubt have approved, if only in principle. (In principle because, being a realist and disbelieving the influence of the supernatural on the conduct of war, he would have doubted that such a massive construction project could have been completed in three days.) "Offer the enemy a bait to lure him" is another of his recommendations, and has there ever been a juicier bait than an object guaranteed to destroy one's enemies provided only one makes the effort of getting it inside a city?

Writing in the fourth century B.C., Sun Tzu could not have heard the story of the Trojan Horse as Virgil tells it in the *Aeneid*, and it is unlikely he had ever heard of the *Odyssey*, or, for that matter, the Trojan War, even though the former preceded him by at least a few centuries and the latter by close to a thousand years. But the Greeks' trick horse would make sense to anyone who advises deception in the conduct of war. The idea of warriors entering an enemy city concealed inside a container is older than the Trojan War. An Egyptian text from the fifteenth century B.C. tells of the taking of Joppa (modern Tel Aviv). Egyptian soldiers, smuggled into the city in baskets, fling open the gates, allowing their comrades to pour in.

As for Sun Tzu's "living agents," who infiltrate enemy territory and report back what they find, the Old Testament anticipates them. The Book of Joshua, estimated to have been written in the late seventh or early sixth century B.C., tells of Joshua sending "two men to spy secretly" across the Jordan. Their mission is to "view the land, even Jericho" (Joshua 2:1). When the king of Jericho learns of the spies and sends men to arrest them, the harlot Rahab hides them on the roof of her house, and she protects them by lying to the king's men, telling them that the visitors had come and gone. The spies return safely to Joshua and tell him of all they have learned—including that the inhabitants of the land are faint with fear of the Israelites.

What all of this shows is that deception has in all cultures and ages been used to get the better of someone in hostile circumstances, especially by those who were weaker than the enemy they were fighting. Only those who know themselves to be vastly superior in strength may see no point in deception and opt for direct attack. In doing so they may incur unnecessary costs. In the latter part of the twentieth century, the commanders of modern armies were increasingly tempted to think in terms of high-tech, high-cost matériel to throw at an enemy. This attitude led to an alarm being sounded at U.S. Army headquarters in Washington, D.C. The fear of an important element of warfare being ignored prompted the publication in 1988 of a field manual titled *Battlefield Deception*. The manual calls for a revitalizing of the "lost art" of deception, and it warns that "many deception-related skills that have served the Army well in the past have been forgotten, and where remembered, have not been made part of our war-fighting capabilities Armywide."

Although Sun Tzu is not mentioned among the manual's cited authors, its list of deceptive measures might just as well have been copied from *The Art of War*. Which suggests that anyone thinking intelligently about warfare will intuit that it is useful to "create the illusion of strength where weakness exists or of weakness where strength exists," and to "confuse enemy expectations with regard to size, activity, location, unit, time, equipment, intent or style of mission execution—to effect surprise in these areas." (The acronym SALUTE may help the reader contemplating warfare remember the first six items "enemy expectations" need to be confused with regard to.) The manual gives examples of successful deception in wars ranging from the American Revolutionary to the 1973 Middle East war (World War II looms large, as it should), and it provides a rich assortment of possible ploys and nuts-and-bolts details on how to convince an enemy that, say, a decoy installation is genuine— one way is to provide an ever-growing number of tire tracks; other ways are to move personnel in and out, increase the amount of trash, send electronic messages that can be monitored by the enemy. All of this, of course, has to look as if serious effort is being made to disguise it—that is, the enemy has to believe that discovery of the installation was due to a poor job at camouflage or some other oversight and that information obtained about it is the result of hard work and diligence. In other words, the fancier armaments notwithstanding, there is once again nothing new under the planet Mars.

4

Claims about the universality of ideas irrespective of cultural cross-pollination are difficult to prove, but anything that is found throughout the mythology, literature, and recorded history of the world is more than likely hardwired in the brains of *Homo sapiens*. One more literary example, this one from India, not only suggests that lying as a weapon is universal but shows how uncannily the way it is practiced and perceived echoes through the ages.

One of the high points in the *Mahābhārata*—the longest epic poem in any language (about seven times the length of the *Iliad* and the *Odyssey* combined)—is the final of a series of battles between the Pāṇḍavas and the Kauravas on the historic plain of Kurukṣetra. The battle is won by a false report Krishna advises the Pāṇḍavas to make.

As in most epics, conflict and strife propel the narrative. The *Mahābhārata*'s main theme is the rivalry between royal cousins—the five Pāṇḍavas and the hundred Kauravas—which culminates in war.* The genealogy is more complicated than any found in the Bible because it is ramified by characters dying and being reincarnated and/or being the sons of gods or goddesses. Vishnu appears as his eighth avatar, Lord Krishna. We've met Krishna as the mischievous infant who delights in stealing butter and ingeniously lying about the theft, but in the *Mahābhārata* he is a figure of high seriousness and dignity. Siding with the Pāṇḍavas and their forces, he plays a pivotal role. The story is rich in marvels and incidents—gambling matches leading to exile from their kingdom for the Pāṇḍavas, visits to the gods, a duel in which an invincible warrior is slain by a blow to his only weak spot, his thighs, ninety-nine brothers, all sons of a single mother, killed in the course of eighteen days, a drunken orgy and massacre, magical weapons, armor that confers immortality, and much, much more.

The crucial battle occurs when the Pāṇḍavas—exiled for thirteen years because they were the stakes in a game of dice lost by the eld-

---

*The date for the historical war on which the epic is based is traditionally given as 1302 B.C., but most historians hold that this is too early. The *Mahābhārata* reached its present form around A.D. 400.

est brother, Yudhiṣṭhira—return to reclaim their kingdom. Their cousins, the hundred Kauravas, refuse to give it up and war results. The fighting takes place on the field of Kurukṣetra. For nine days the forces clash indecisively. On the tenth day, the Kauravas' supreme commander allows himself to be mortally wounded, and for the next five days the preceptor Droṇa becomes supreme commander. Droṇa wreaks havoc among the forces of the Pāṇḍavas and Krishna, the Pāṇḍavas' counselor, grows afraid that they will be defeated. In addition to his role as counselor, Krishna is the charioteer of Arjuna, the third brother. He tells Arjuna that Droṇa cannot be vanquished in battle. "Hence you must put aside fair means, and adopt some contrivance for gaining victory, so that Droṇa may not slay us all in battle." The contrivance Krishna suggests is keyed to his opponent's psychology and could come out of the bag of tricks of a Ulysses or Iago. He is sure that Droṇa will cease to fight if his son, Aśvatthāmā, is killed. "Let some man, therefore, tell him that Aśvatthāmā has been slain in battle," he advises Arjuna.

Though others approve of it, Arjuna does not relish the suggestion. His brother King Yudhiṣṭhira is just as reluctant to accept it. Another of the brothers, Bhīma, overcomes his scruples. He approaches Droṇa on the battlefield and shouts: "Aśvatthāmā has been slain!" Still, he too feels unease at what he is doing and manages to speak the lie only because he has slain a huge elephant named Aśvatthāmā: he is therefore not outright lying but rather equivocating—in this case by counting on Droṇa's assuming that if a warrior tells him about the death of someone bearing his son's name, he is telling him about his son's death. Omitting the minor detail that *this* slain Aśvatthāmā was an elephant also helps. The Jesuits at the time of the Gunpowder Plot would at once have recognized a kindred spirit. The narrator shows Bhīma well aware of his own underhandedness and uncomfortable with it—he makes the announcement of Aśvatthāmā's death "not without embarrassment."

But Krishna is still worried "because Droṇa, foremost of warriors, was capable of sweeping all the Pāṇḍavas off the face of the earth." He tells Yudhiṣṭhira that if Droṇa is roused to anger and fights for even half a day the Pāṇḍavas' army will be annihilated. "Save us then from Droṇa! Under such circumstances, falsehood is preferable to truth," Krishna implores, and he announces a maxim which, as becomes shortly apparent, is not borne out by the ensuing events: "By telling a lie to save a life, one is not touched by sin." Bhīma, less squeamish now that he has done the lying, supports Krishna's argument. He tells Yudhiṣṭhira that Droṇa did not believe him, and he urges his brother, "To ensure our victory, accept Krishna's advice. Tell Droṇa that his son is no more. If you say so, Droṇa will believe you and will never fight thereafter, since you are famed for your truthfulness in the three worlds."

So what will sell this lie will be that the one who speaks it is renowned for his honesty. The narrator, clearly aware of how seriously Yudhiṣṭhira's honor will be tarnished in the process, reminds the reader of mitigating circumstances: "Urged thus by Bhīma and induced by the counsels of Krishna, and also because of the inevitability of destiny, Yudhiṣṭhira gave in." Giving in takes the form of Yudhiṣṭhira repeating his brother's ruse and telling Droṇa about the death of "Aśvatthāmā." He does not follow his brother's suggestion of saying to Droṇa: "Your son is no more," and, unlike his brother, he is a man so loath to relinquish his integrity that he cannot even lie by omission—"Fearing to tell a downright lie . . . Yudhiṣṭhira added indistinctly that the elephant was slain." Again, Jesuitical equivocation comes to mind: a statement is not a lie (or a "downright lie") provided it is somehow truthful—even if the part that makes it truthful is not heard by the person to whom it is addressed, and who therefore reaches the wrong conclusion.

If included as an example in a "Why Lie, and How To" manual this one should come with an asterisk. At first glance, the lie is unremarkable: its aim is to win the battle and the war; it is designed to feed the worst fear of the one lied to; it is carried out by equivocation. The asterisk is needed because this is the first time we've encountered anyone whose lie succeeded because he *was* an honest man—as opposed to someone like Iago, whose reputed honesty was a sham from beginning to end. It would be bizarre to advise anyone to be honest at all times in order to get a reputation for truthfulness, a reputation that can be used at some point to get someone to believe a single monstrous lie.

The wrong conclusion reached by Droṇa has the desired effect. He is afflicted with grief and loses all desire to live. Despondent and filled with anxiety, he is almost deprived of his senses by his grief. Still, when one of the heroes fighting for the Pāṇḍavas rushes at him, the still invincible Droṇa takes away all his weapons but his mace and sword. Bhīma, furious at the continued resistance, approaches Droṇa and accuses him of being a Brahmana who has forsaken the highest virtue of the caste, nonviolence to all creatures. "You, Droṇa, are supposed to be the best of the Brahmanas. And yet you fight while your son lies dead on the field of battle, unknown to you and behind your back. Yudhiṣṭhira the Just has told you this. It behooves you not to doubt this fact." The effect of Bhīma's words is that Droṇa lays aside his bow and no longer defends himself when he is attacked by the Pāṇḍavas' great hero. He dies as a result of having believed the lie told by "Yudhiṣṭhira the Just."

The lie about the death of Droṇa's son is one of several deceptions Krishna either suggests to the Pāṇḍavas or carries out in order to help them. After the death of Droṇa, he eliminates another of the Kauravas' heroes, King Duryodhana, when the king fights Bhīma in a duel with maces. He tells Bhīma's brother Arjuna that Bhīma will never win if he fights fairly but will kill his opponent if he fights unfairly, and he reminds Arjuna of Duryodhana's weak point, his thighs. Arjuna signals Krishna's advice to his brother, and Bhīma fells his foe with a mighty blow to his thighs.

The Kauravas are incensed at this foul blow below the navel, which is in violation of the rules of mace fighting, and before the mortally wounded king dies, he has harsh words for Krishna. He enumerates Krishna's deceptions. These include the use of illusory powers to cause other great heroes of the Kauravas to be killed by various means in battle. "If your side had fought me by fair means, victory would not have been yours," he complains. The Pāṇḍavas are stricken with remorse at the dying king's remonstrance, but one can almost hear Krishna's response along the lines of "Your point being?" He explains to the Pāṇḍavas that his use of deception stands to reason: "If I had not adopted such deceitful ways, you would never have been victorious, nor would you have regained your kingdom or your wealth." He gently chides them, "You should not mind that your enemy has been killed deceitfully," then pronounces the verdict for all times: "When one is outnumbered by his enemies, then destruction should be brought about by strat-agem."

Krishna's notion that deception is necessary when the enemy is stronger is universally acknowledged. It fits hand in glove with his precept that "by telling a lie to save a life, one is not touched by sin": to be victorious by destroying an enemy means to save one's life, and in order to save one's life, one is allowed to lie. Despite this matter-of-fact attitude, the *Mahābhārata* shows consider-able unease at lies ostensibly justified by the circumstances. The Pāṇḍavas' remorse is one example, but a more amazing one appears after the lie about the death of Droṇa's son. Before Yudhiṣṭhira told this lie he, "famed for his truthfulness in the three worlds," moved about magically—his chariot stayed at a height of four fingers above the surface of the earth. Not so afterward: "after he had ut-tered that lie, his vehicle and animals touched the earth." General Sun Tzu would have lauded him, Greek warriors would have heaped spoils on him, but the narrator of the battle of Kurukṣetra demotes him by literally lowering him. Yudhiṣṭhira is shown to achieve victory, which is a warrior's noble aim, but the means he uses decrease the esteem in which the gods held him.

The *Mahābhārata*'s unease about deception in warfare arises from the tension between two of its ideas that are guaranteed to be in conflict under certain circumstances. The first is that the warrior is an honorable, courageous figure who wages war regardless of the consequences because to do so is his role in life. The second is that to strive for victory is a warrior's duty. Conflict arises when he can-not win fairly because he is overmatched by his enemy. To do his duty, he has to resort to deception, but being deceptive is not the mark of an honorable man. We've seen this tension between moral imperative and realistic necessity before. Here, the fact that Krishna promotes deception ill agrees with his role as Arjuna's philosopher guide, who before the great battle on the field of Kurukṣetra sits down with his disciple to enlighten him about the world. In that philosophical aside, known as the *Bhagavad-Gita* (the Lord's Song), Krishna discourses about the permanence of the eternal, indestructible soul, the physical world and the metaphysi-cal one, proper conduct, the characteristics of the good and the bad. The good, unsurprisingly, are patient, strong, modest, moral, gentle, and loving, and they live without lies, devoted to truth about the world and themselves. The bad, just as unsurprisingly, are immodest, lustful, malicious, greedy, deceived about the world, hypocritical, and deceitful. In a lengthy description of what constitutes the warrior, Krishna makes no mention of deception being one of his weapons but rather prescribes indifference to the outcome of battles: if the warrior is defeated, he goes to heaven; if he is victorious, he continues enjoying life on earth. Either way, what matters is that he has fulfilled his role.

The discrepancies between the ideas on deception that Krishna expresses in the *Bhagavad-Gita* and those found in the rest of the *Mahābhārata* stem from differences in intent. Krishna is the pivot around whom all of the *Mahābhārata* revolves and Krishna is both God speaking through one of his incarnations and Arjuna's charioteer. As the former, he speaks as a philosopher and teacher who bases his view of the world on a religion in which the gods (the Devas) chose the light and truth and the demons (the Asuras) chose darkness and lies. As Arjuna's charioteer and friend, he speaks as a warrior and realist, who knows that wars are won by deception.

And while we're on the subject: recollecting Krishna the infant Butter Thief and liar, we may be tempted to see the pragmatic charioteer as the adult version of that larcenous fibber, but scholars have made a point that the dignified Krishna of the *Mahābhārata* is a creation of Sanskrit literature, invented and read by the educated, whereas the mischievous purloiner of butter belongs to popular imagination and to the other languages of the people of India. The Krishna of literature is a part of the serious, official side of Hindu religion, the Butter Thief a part of ordinary piety, and there is no evidence that Krishna the rascally child and Krishna the charioteer were linked by the notion of an evolution from butter stealing, lying infant to deception-counseling charioteer.

The explanation for Krishna's inconsistency as Arjuna's charioteer on the one hand and the wise teacher who sings the *Bhagavad-Gita* on the other can be found in the process of composition of the *Mahābhārata*. Although reputedly written by the sage Vyasa, the epic took shape in the course of centuries. Small wonder that different sections of it express contradictory concerns and beliefs. Still, whoever wrote about Krishna's deceptions in war seems to have been sensitive to the contradiction between Krishna's philosophical and religious teachings and his practical advice to friends threatened by a superior enemy. The writer's unease about a teacher of the moral life recommending deception may appear in the opportunities he creates for the divine charioteer to justify stratagem and trickery and in Yudhiṣṭhira's lowering after he uttered the lie about Droṇa's slain son. All warfare may be based on deception (except that of invincible heroes unmatched in prowess), but whenever pragmatists have pointed out the necessity and inevitability of deception, some philosopher prescribing ethical conduct has winced.

The Briar Patch Revisited

Krishna's maxim—"By telling a lie to save a life, one is not touched by sin"—defines deception in war in terms of self-defense. Moving troops under cover of darkness, camouflaging armament, setting off fires and smoke bombs to convince an enemy that an installation has suffered heavy damage and that the bombing raid can be stopped—deceptions of this kind are obvious measures of self-defense in war. And since one of the basic premises of war is that any enemy who is not killed or captured, or whose resources are left intact, can do harm to one's side, even aggressive deceptions like ambushes or booby traps can be seen as forms of self-defense.

War is the most large-scale expression of human hostility. But hostility in any arena makes us use deception reflexively to defend ourselves when we are too weak to do so by direct means or when the truth would endanger us. Mass murderers have forever been deceived by people who have feigned death to keep from becoming one of their victims. The larger the carnage, the more likely that someone will fool the killers. Thus, in an instance of ethnic cleansing a villager falls down while his neighbors around him are riddled with bullets. He pretends to be dead when the killers throw straw on the pile of corpses, douse it with gasoline, and set it on fire. He crawls out of the blaze badly burned but survives.

Deception used for self-defense can come out of exceedingly grim circumstances, but an amusing instance of it is alleged to have occurred during—of all times!—the Reign of Terror. If true, a whopping big lie saved the life of the American minister in Paris, Gouverneur Morris. At one point, Morris found himself surrounded by an angry mob suspecting him of being an Englishman and a spy. The good citizens were ready to hang him from the nearest lamppost, when Morris unfastened his wooden leg, held it above his head, and protested that, far from it, he was an American and a kindred spirit, having lost his limb fighting for liberty. The mob turned from belligerent to enthusiastic and gave him a rousing cheer. Actually, this honorably wounded champion of liberty had never in his life fought for anything, and, although he had espoused the cause of the colonists in the American War of Independence, he, according to one student of the time, "retained a cynically aristocratic view of life and a profound contempt for democratic theories." Morris had lost the leg replaced by the wooden one not in the fight for liberty but in a carriage accident in 1780.

In general, the threat of violence by someone stronger invites deception as a countermeasure. And when the weaker party in a conflict is perceived as unfairly at a disadvantage, we tend to see deception as a justifiable means to right the imbalance of power. Which is one reason the heroes in fairy tales and folk tales so often resort to deception. Told from the point of view of the underdog, many of these tales glory in the triumph of those who are weak but tricky over those who are strong but gullible. The tricksters of mythology are the archetypes, but the heroes who live in the world of once-upon-a-time have no magical, shape-shifting, illusion-making powers. Pitted against those who are stronger, they survive and thrive by common wiliness, albeit an uncommon amount of it.

Hansel and Gretel are famous examples. Children threatened by a wicked witch—an adult possessing supernatural powers—they would be lost were it not for their skills at deception. They also exemplify the triumph of clever liars over clumsy ones within the framework of a moral tale. The siblings use deception in the service of good—they save themselves and free the gingerbread children. The witch has used deception for evil ends—she has lured her victims to her hut by making it of gingerbread. But the witch utterly fails when she catches the siblings, who are more wily by far. She believes for a month that the boy she is fattening remains thin, simply because whenever she asks to feel one of Hansel's fingers, he sticks a small bone through the bars of his cage. Then, when she tries to trick Gretel into the oven by telling her to check the fire, Gretel easily gets the better of her by pretending not to know how.

In Humperdinck's opera, this ploy is suspenseful and Gretel feigns ignorance adroitly. First the witch turns on the charm:

> *Come, Gretel dearie,*
> *sweetie pie.*
> *Peer in the oven,*
> *check on the gingersnaps.*
> *Carefully look*
> *to see if they're cooked*
> *or if it's too early.*
> *It's easy to do.*

Gretel doesn't get it: How can it be done? She doesn't know the first thing about looking inside an oven. The witch is helpful: Gretel has to lift herself up a little, then duck her head. It's child's play. But poor Gretel remains baffled and is abashed at her confusion:

> *I'm so stupid,*
> *please bear with me.*
> *Show me how to do it.*

The witch impatiently obliges by demonstrating, and when she is halfway in the oven, Gretel and her brother shove her inside and slam the door shut.

Someone encountering Hansel and Gretel for the first time in

Humperdinck's opera may be puzzled at innocent children being such old hands at trickery. In the Grimm tale, however, their trickery is an organic part of their surroundings. Whereas in the opera the mother simply sends the children into the woods to gather strawberries, in the Grimm tale they've witnessed the most appalling deception before they ever set foot in the woods. During a famine, their stepmother persuades their father to get rid of them so more food will be available for the parents. The parents then tell the children that tomorrow they are all going into the forest to fetch some firewood. But the children, who have overheard the evil scheme, know that this is a lie, and Hansel puts shiny pebbles in his pocket. On the way to the forest, he keeps dropping them on the ground so he and Gretel can find their way back to the house in the night. When his father asks him why he so frequently stops, he lies that he is looking back at his little cat on the roof of the house.

Parents and children make their way to the middle of the forest. There, the parents tell Hansel and Gretel to gather wood and rest while they go off to chop wood. Actually, the father ties a branch to a dead tree so that the wind will bang it back and forth and the children will think the banging is the sound of him chopping wood nearby. That done, he and his wife go home. The heartless trick keeps the children waiting until they fall asleep. When they wake up, it is night, but soon the full moon rises and they follow the path of shiny pebbles back to the house.

One paragraph later, another famine strikes, and again the stepmother persuades the father to get rid of the children with the same ruse. This time Hansel drops bread crumbs on the way, but birds eat them and the children truly are lost when the parents abandon them. If Humperdinck's Hansel and Gretel are innocents when they arrive at the witch's house, the Grimm brothers' siblings have had a persuasive course on deception by that time, and their getting the better of the witch is all in a day's work.

One reason folk tales are popular is that they allow the audience to identify with and vicariously participate in the adventures of someone ordinary—say the son of a poor widow forced to set out and make his way in the wide world because he cannot feed himself at home. Often his assets are a good heart, courage, and a nimble mind. On his journey, he encounters pitfalls and villains, but after a series of trials, he overcomes adversity, attains wealth, marries the king's daughter, lives happily ever after. Sometimes magic helps him: he refrains from killing an animal, and out of gratitude it shows him a hidden treasure, or he acquires a magical object that has useful features. Sometimes he is naive to a fault but stumbles upon his good luck precisely because of his ignorance or stupidity.

But folk tales also have another kind of hero, a shiftier one, who uses deception to triumph over those more powerful by duping them. He may defraud a king, bishop, or lord mayor, a genie or witch, even the devil himself. Just as in the case of the trickster figures of mythology, the sense that deception is justified to right an imbalance of power is often at the heart of the tales, and just as in mythology, the tales can feature an antihero—amoral, ruthless, oblivious to the harm he does in the process of getting by trickery what he wants.

A prime example is Till Eulenspiegel, the German folk hero whose "merry pranks" range from inspired to brutal. Till may have been an actual vagabond and professional buffoon living in the first half of the fourteenth century. Stories about him circulated in the fourteenth and fifteenth centuries, and in 1515 a collection narrating ninety-five of his *Historien* came out in Strasbourg. The book was followed by a large number of editions and versions of Till's adventures put out by adapters and translators. "Till Owlmirror" has been part of popular and literary imagination for at least five centuries—dozens of works based upon or influenced by him have appeared in addition to Richard Strauss's famed symphonic poem—and although he has been sanitized and abridged for children's books, his anarchistic spark has rarely been entirely quenched.

The unregenerate Till lives by his wits and wiles in surroundings that do not tolerate the kind of idle, lazy fellow he freely confesses himself to be. His world is one in which a greedy tailor, baker, blacksmith, or shoemaker will hire a poor lad for starving wages or inedible fare, work him hard, and kick him out on a whim in the winter. Till is not interested, and he gleefully victimizes those who would victimize him by hiring himself out to them and then tricking them out of money or goods, ruining their wares and establishments, publicly embarrassing them. At other times he exposes the hypocrisy, pomposity, and stupidity of priests, doctors, professors, officials. He can be the innocent abroad, making a mess of things by following instructions to the letter and upsetting the applecart by his stupidity—although his is a peculiar stupidity, which unerringly exposes the sloppy or pretentious use of language: he relieves himself, for instance, of a large pile of excrement in a bathhouse because the place is billed as a "House of Cleansing" by its supercilious owner. Till claims that his insides were as much in need of cleansing as his outside. In general, excrement is a weapon or calling card he never tires of using for revenge or practical jokes. It features in more than a dozen of his adventures. Other famous personages may have slept here or there; in the case of Till, plaques all over Germany might well commemorate that "Till Eulenspiegel Shat Here."

Till's special vexations are arrogance, pomposity, and hypocrisy, but he also scorns gullibility and naiveté, qualities he finds offensive in a thinking creature, and he mercilessly takes advantage of gulls. His more sophisticated victims, members of the aristocracy, are not far from this view. They admit to having been gotten the better of by the lying rogue, but rather than being furious they laugh, and admire and forgive him—shades of Apollo and Zeus admiring Hermes, the newborn cattle thief and liar. They chalk up to experience having been tricked. People who boast that the famous Eulenspiegel could never trick them, on the other hand, pose a challenge to which he rises with alacrity.

To get what he wants, Till lies, steals, poses as someone he is not—a scholar, doctor, painter, craftsman, priest traveling through the land with a sacred relic, the skull of St. Brendan. But if he is a hero of sorts in many of his adventures, wreaking havoc for morally justifiable reasons, in a large number of them he is not. He can behave with a cavalier brutality toward people who have neither meant nor done him harm, and any pleasure the reader derives from those episodes has to do with Till's limitless ability to get away with outrages that should at the very least have earned him a sound thrashing. If there is a lesson in all this, it is that anyone who finds that the rules of society don't serve him will have little compunction about breaking them—and once he starts breaking them, watch out! Although lacking their supernatural powers, Till Eulenspiegel shares with the tricksters of mythology—a Loki or Hermes; an infant Krishna or Coyote—a penchant for upsetting the world to have things his way, for creating anarchy when law and order obstruct him. His peculiar charm comes out of his will to thrive by hook, crook, or grand larceny no matter what cards he has been dealt and to have fun in the process.

Till Eulenspiegel is by no means unique. A descendant of his is Hanswurst—later Kasperle or, in England, Punch—a peasant or servant character in puppet shows since the seventeenth century. Hanswurst opposes authority with a vengeance, sneaks up on the constable and whacks him, cheats the devil himself, runs riot in a society that tries to stifle him. But the servant who can pull the wool over his master's eyes faster than His Grace can say Jack Robinson is ubiquitous on the stage and in literature. He is a stock figure in comedy, a crafty rogue dedicated above all to doing well for himself, the devil take his master—although he may on occasion employ his guile for the benefit of that dullard or some other higher-up who crosses his palm with silver. Figaro, a.k.a. the Barber of Seville, is a sterling specimen, brilliant in the trickery he uses against his foils, Count Almaviva and Dr. Bartolo, but the type is much older than the Beaumarchais comedies on which Mozart's and Rossini's operas are based.

The Roman playwright Plautus (250–184 B.C.) lovingly portrayed him in *Pseudolus* (*The Liar*). Pseudolus is a slave who is far smarter than his master and who delights in deceiving him and other well-to-do citizens. Entreated by his master's lovelorn son, he devises a swindle to free the girl of the young fool's dreams from the clutches of a pimp who is about to sell her. In the process, he dupes his master out of a tidy sum. (A recent master-friendly variant of Pseudolus is Jeeves, the butler without whose craftiness the Bertie Woosters of this world would forever fall victim to their own spectacular incompetence.)

Plautus inherited the idea of Pseudolus from the Greek "New Comedy," which derived its amusement from ordinary people in upper-middle-class households—the irascible, hidebound father and his formidable wife, their lazy son, dull-witted cooks or other servants, eternally ravenous freeloader "friends," and a man who needs no introduction—the scheming slave. The Greeks, of course, were interested in the lower echelon trying to get the better of the upper ever since they started telling stories about Prometheus and Hermes trying to bamboozle the ultimate master, Zeus himself.

Works of the imagination that feature scheming slaves or servants or other characters who trick those higher up on the social ladder are intrinsically subversive. In illustrating the impermissible, they exert pressure on society. If masters can be duped by slaves and counts by valets, what does this say about the innate superiority of the former over the latter? Maybe that this superiority is nothing but a fiction promoted by those in power at the expense of those not. Beaumarchais' 1784 comedy *La Folle Journée, ou Le Mariage de Figaro* was banned as subversive in Vienna because of its political sting. Mozart's librettist took out the sting, but not the egalitarian gist of a tale in which a servant plots to repay his master for the advances he is making to the servant's fiancée. When Figaro muses to himself: "If the little count wants to dance, I'll play the guitar for him," he puts Almaviva on equal footing as a rival in love, and the trouncing the count receives shows him to be less gifted at intrigue than his servant.

That comedy is the vehicle for the revolutionary notion of servants or slaves triumphing over their masters by use of their wits is not surprising. Humor is a time-honored way to deal with what would otherwise be too threatening. A Pseudolus can behave outrageously and to outrageous effects, given his role in society, and can get away with it because his role is comic, as are the roles of those around him. The masters he cheats are fools or buffoons and are laughable even by the standards of the masters in the audience who—a fortunate thing for satirists of all ages—recognize all others but themselves in the unflattering mirror. Archconservatives may worry about the message sent to the hoi polloi by a play in which a slave successfully dupes his master, but most members of the audience will laugh and leave the question of whether or not comedy can promote social revolution to professional thinkers. That the archconservatives are right, that the subversive message is there, loud and clear, is ironic. The effect may be subtle—a very small nail in a very large coffin—but still, empires have fallen and the blood of kings has been shed when thinking along certain lines has reached a flash point.

The extent to which the comedy of a Plautus reflected his actual world can only be guessed. Satire and comedy are by design distorting mirrors that exaggerate and crop the image they return in order to stress certain laughable features. No doubt slaves as devious as Pseudolus existed in the third century B.C. Did they dupe their masters? Probably. But if they did and were caught, we can be quite sure that the ending was not the happy one of Pseudolus and his master nipping off for a drink. In the Roman Empire, the owner's control over his slaves was total. Slaves could legally be killed or coerced to do any kind of work, fight in a war or arena, satisfy their masters' carnal appetites as mistresses or catamites. They could be flogged with whatever type of flagellum promised to inflict the maximum pain while doing the least damage to the master's property. Roman comedy was not squeamish about providing "hilarity" by showing a rascally slave get his just deserts with a whipping. "I've decided not to spring on Pseudolus what they always do in comedies. No whips, no canes," Pseudolus' master decides (setting the stage for a shelf of essays on "Roman Comedy as a Self-Conscious Genre"). But the master's admiration of his slave—"There's a fellow who's really smart, really tricky, a real scoundrel. He did better than Ulysses and the Trojan Horse"—was not something widely found along the Appian Way.

Human beings have handled the pressure of being property in a variety of ways. In the ancient world, some of those who had been enslaved in wars redefined themselves in their new roles and derived a sense of self-worth from their loyalty to their masters, hoping for manumission after a number of years. *Pseudolus* has such a character, the slave orderly of the major who bought the girl Pseudolus is trying to pry from the pimp's claws. He is a model of officiousness and self-importance who prides himself on doing his master's bidding, and Pseudolus double-crosses him as slickly as he double-crosses the pimp and his own master. The majority of slaves, though, never lost sight of what they were even when they were playing the roles their masters had assigned to them:

Thucydides records the desertion of tens of thousands of them—from skilled workmen to the baggage carriers of heavily armored infantry and cavalry—during the Peloponnesian War. After the Athenian army's disastrous defeat in Sicily in 413 B.C., the 40,000 soldiers who were fleeing toward illusionary safety (most of them were killed within the next few days) lost all faith in their slaves. They chose to carry their own gear rather than entrust it to those who had not yet run away. This suggests that on foreign soil, and under conditions in which there was little chance of an escaped slave being recaptured, the loyalty of chattel to its owner was non-existent.

Greek and Roman plays were not written by slaves but by middle-class dramatists, who drew on their surroundings and imaginatively extrapolated a potentially funny situation—tricky slave, tricked master—to absurd heights. Slaves in the New World, their status as outsiders made more extreme by racial difference, had no one within society who rendered a sympathetic portrait of a wily scoundrel of a slave. But they had brought along their own subversive character in the form of the African trickster hare and had adapted him as Brer Rabbit, a consummate rascal who tricks more powerful but less nimble-witted beasts like Brer Fox or Brer B'ar. In Africa, the trickster hare was an exceedingly clever animal, superb at surviving in hostile surroundings, an obvious hero for people living where large predators roamed and where the ability to deceive was useful in the daily struggle not to be eaten. He is one of a large number of animal characters smuggled into the New World in slave ships; African animal and folk tales, transformed and adapted, were one of the ways in which the African element survived in African-American culture.

Brer Rabbit served in a slave culture as a symbol for the potential of the powerless to turn the hierarchy topsy-turvy and come out triumphant despite overwhelming odds against them. Slaves could live vicariously through a creature so superbly suited for survival by guile in a world of brutality and hostility. The rabbit's exploits granted the wishful fantasy that oppressors would become the butt of the oppressed, just like Brer Fox, Brer Rabbit's most persistent enemy. Not that Brer Rabbit is a model of moral uprightness. Like Till Eulenspiegel, he can be amoral or even malicious. He can harm innocuous beings to satisfy his appetite or his delight in mischief; he can lie up a blue streak to shift the blame for a crime he committed onto someone else. One can imagine him summarizing such an episode with the words of his descendant, Bugs Bunny: "Ain't I a stinker?" He is yet another reminder that there is no such thing anywhere in the world as a habitual liar who can be counted on to do the morally right thing.

Joel Chandler Harris popularized for a white readership many of the Brer Rabbit and other animal tales told by slaves. His frame was Uncle Remus, the serene, kindly old "darky," and the little white boy who listened entranced to story after story—the stories of how Brer Rabbit framed Brer B'ar and by trickery caused the demise of Mr. Possum, both to cover his own thievery, and of how the Rabbit fooled Brer Wolf and Mr. Buzzard and Miss Cow, and that most famous of the Rabbit's episodes, in which Brer Fox set a trap for Brer Rabbit with that wonderfully sticky contraption, the Tar Baby, and almost ate Brer Rabbit. The Rabbit engineers his getaway by a masterstroke of reverse psychology: he begs Brer Fox to kill him in any way imaginable, no matter how heinous, but please, please not to throw him in the briar patch. Brer Fox, who "wanter hurt Brer Rabbit bad ez he kin" (a grim note in the tale), flings him into the briar patch and waits around to learn the dire consequences to the Rabbit. Brer Rabbit's mocking cry from the top of a hill to which he repairs to leisurely comb the pitch out of his hair is "Bred en bawn in a briar-patch, Brer Fox—bred en bawn in a briar-patch!" It is the triumphant laugh of all those who by trickery escape from the clutches of powerful enemies and come out on top.

Uncle Remus was Harris's fiction, an alter ego through whom he, a pathologically shy man, found a way to shed his inhibitions, but the tales Uncle Remus tells are authentic. Harris, a white Southerner who had heard them told by slaves in his adolescence, recognized their wit and vitality and frequently laugh-out-loud humor. He had an ear for the dialect in which they were told, and it was his largely successful aim to present the stories in such a way that they came "fresh and direct" from their source.

Slaves of the American South also invented tales more obviously subversive than the Brer Rabbit tales. The Rabbit's exploits, no matter how obvious their coded revolutionary message was to the astute observer, could always be chalked up to the "Negroes' childishness" by their masters. Not so tales about John, a slave who usually got the best of his old master.

"John-Massa" anecdotes were collected after the Civil War in many of the former slave states. Although Ole Massa occasionally turns the tables on John, the anecdotes' theme overwhelmingly is the ability of wily John to dupe his master. John is reminiscent of Pseudolus, and John's master, just like Pseudolus', is no match for his slave's stratagems. Yes, Ole Massa in one tale tells John that he is God and has come to answer John's nightly prayer to be taken away from this vale of tears (the ensuing chase of God under a bed-sheet tearing after John, who didn't want his prayer answered, is a hilarious image), but John more than gets even in another tale. He tells his master, who is about to hang him for killing his hogs and carousing in his house, that God is making lightning and that the flashes of light are his sign that the master and his family will die. Actually, the lightning is John's friend Jack hiding at the top of the hanging tree and lighting matches at John's cues. The upshot? Ole Massa runs away so fast it takes an express train going ninety miles an hour six months to catch him. After which he gives John his freedom, and land and stock.

John was a figure custom-made by slaves in the battle to maintain a sense of self-worth and autonomy under conditions in which systematic effort was expended to deprive them of both. Locked in a position of weakness, he nevertheless triumphed, and he did so by deception. The narratives of slaves, both those who escaped and those who told their stories after emancipation, stressed the need for deception to survive in a climate of extreme hostility. Henry Bibb, who documented in his autobiography the long odyssey of escapes and recaptures and more desperate escapes by which he finally found freedom in Canada, wrote that "the only weapon of self defense that I could use successfully, was that of deception." Early on, when he ran away for days or weeks and hid out in the woods to escape abuse by his masters he "learned the art of running away to perfection." He, for instance, would always take a bridle with him. Then, when someone saw him in the woods and asked him whether he was a runaway, he'd lie: "No, sir, I am looking for our old mare" or "looking for our cows."

To those who were on the run for freedom, deception was essential, and fugitives used a gamut of deceptive devices to throw off pursuers and people who made a living capturing escaped slaves and returning them for the reward. Women disguised themselves as men; men made wigs of horses' manes to disguise themselves as women or wore false beards. Light-skinned slaves passed for whites. Those who planned to flee had to pretend that to do so was the thing furthest from their minds. William Wells Brown, presented with an opportunity for escape when his master decided to visit Cincinnati on a Mississippi River boat, found himself in this position. Worried about bringing his slave to a free state, where he might try to run away and gain his liberty, his master asked Brown whether he had ever been in a free state. "Oh yes," Brown lied, "I have been in Ohio; my master carried me into that state once, but I never like a free State." His mistress, practicing her own brand of subtle interrogation, asked him whether he thought as highly of the woman she intended for him to "marry" as ever? Again, he lied. Yes, Eliza was very dear to him indeed, and nothing but death would part them. The desired result was that Brown accompanied his master's family up the river and escaped at the first opportunity. Describing an earlier instance, in which he had managed by deception to shift a whipping intended for him onto another man's back, Brown asked for understanding:

> This incident shows how it is that slavery makes its victims lying and mean; for which vices it afterwards reproaches them, and uses them as arguments to prove that they deserve no better fate. I have often, since my escape, deeply regretted the deception I practiced upon this poor fellow; and I heartily desire that it may be, at some time or other, in my power to make him amends for his vicarious suffering in my behalf.

Note that no regret accompanied Brown's later deception of his master and mistress. As the abolitionist who edited Henry Bibb's narrative in 1849 wrote in his Introduction: "Deceit in a slave is only a slight reflex of the stupendous fraud practiced by his master."

A coda: slave owners, ever worried that their property might steal itself away by taking to its heels, were prone to do their own bit of deceiving. Some told their slaves about the awful fate awaiting the fugitive in the North or Canada: Yankees were cannibals who looked upon slaves as tasty morsels; Canadians ate young slaves and skinned the heads of older ones to make collars for their coats out of the "wool," and they blinded them and put them to work in lead mines.

The world being what it is, people have found themselves in a large variety of hostile situations. Slave states, inflexible bureaucracies, witch-hunts (inquisitorial or congressional), fanatical religious majorities, genocidal regimes, homophobic authorities, abusive spouses or parents, and so forth and so on—countless are the things that are intrinsically hostile to some members of the population, all of them inviting deception in the service of self-defense. One example among myriad: The National Origins Act of 1924 barred wives of Chinese immigrants from entering the United States. The husbands were grudgingly admitted because their cheap labor was of use, but the authorities knew what would happen if their wives were allowed to join: yellow children. In response, Chinese immigrants bought false identity papers. A wife would join her husband as his sister, and the two, and any children they had, learned to live with the secret, lying when they had to to keep the authorities from finding out. (The 1882 Chinese Exclusion Law, whose name unapologetically announces its purpose, had begun the thriving trade in false papers.)

With so many situations inviting deception, an obvious question is once again under what circumstances deception is justified. As before, the answer depends on our subjective view of the world. Human beings have been accused of seeing the world through a glass, darkly, or through rose-colored glasses, or blinkered. The fact is that what we see is inseparably tied to our own imagination, our sense of self and the world, our wishes and fears. "Reality," as Nabokov insisted, should always be in quotation marks. Except under extreme circumstances like the threat of physical violence, the things I encounter in the world are defined as friendly, neutral, or hostile not by their intrinsic nature or by universal fiat but by me. Friendly, in this vocabulary, means conducive to what I need or want; hostile means determined to hurt or harm me. So what happens when I find myself in what I believe to be hostile circumstances and encounter a situation in which telling the truth promises to hurt me? Most likely, I lie to protect myself. So far so good, and quite a few of my fellow citizens—although by no means all of them—will see nothing wrong with my lying.

But what happens if I relax my definition of what constitutes hostile circumstances to include anything that is antagonistic toward my wants. What happens is that I've now given myself carte blanche to deceive anyone opposing me, since, after all, all is fair in war. Aldous Huxley, as usual, was right: "For a clever man, nothing is easier than to find arguments that will convince him that he is doing right when he is doing what he wants to do." We're back in the land where the self is free to play with smoke and mirrors until what we see allows us to act whichever way we wish. A bit of rationalizing and finding excuses and—presto!

Anyone who uses subjective judgment to identify the world or a part of it as an arena of intense and unfair competition will be tempted to use any means to fight hostile circumstances, and deception is one of those means. (Note how quickly *unfair* became *hostile* here.) Your classmates were born with a silver spoon in their mouths and had the benefit of prep schools and tutors? Small wonder they get A's and their chances of admission to a prestigious law school are higher than yours. That is unless you level the playing field by buying term papers from a paper mill and cheating on exams. The bank will not give you a loan if it finds out about your credit-card debts and bankruptcy? (which were the result of your legitimate desire to live as well as your neighbors who happen to have better-paying jobs). You fight the system's unfairness by lying on the loan application. Your state will not approve a proposed hate-crime law? To generate publicity, you hire someone to beat you up and claim your bruises were inflicted by homophobic rednecks. Your school's security is too lax? You plant on school premises a bogus note threatening students.

The excuse of hostility justifying deception has been used by a motley assortment of sinners and saints. Police officers have planted false evidence to incriminate people they "knew" were guilty in order to ensure they would not get away with it and have lied in court for the same reason. The military/industrial complex used to lie with panache for that most urgent of causes: national security. Erstwhile Senator Joseph McCarthy announced in 1950 that 205 communists had infiltrated the State Department—a figure that had the virtues of being alarmingly large and convincingly precise. Although McCarthy was a demagogue and certainly knew that he had picked the figure out of a hat, he may also have believed the lie was justified by the need to awaken a complacent nation to the Red Peril.

Even the Fathers of the Church practiced what acquired its own term—pious fraud—in the battle to bring heathens and heretics into the fold of revealed religion. For this good cause they richly embellished episodes in the history of the Church and invented martyrs and their miracles. St. Augustine objected in the strongest terms, calling a lie uttered in the service of religion a deadly one, to be shunned from afar, but the practice continued. At the time of the Reformation, some Catholic clergymen in England orchestrated miracles. In one case, a crucified Christ was made to move his eyes and lips by means of hidden strings of hair; in another, a priest surreptitiously pricked his finger during mass to make drops of blood appear on the altar and the host. Elsewhere statues were rigged to move or weep or bleed at the appropriate moment. Much of this "fayninge and counterfeyting," as one chronicler put it, may have had the purely mercenary motive of filling coffers and lining clerical pockets, but some of it may also have come out of the perceived need to strengthen the faith of Catholics and convince Protestants of the reality of miracles and make them return to Rome. In an age of unbelief, extraordinary measures were needed to save souls—and surely divine authorization was certain where the motive was pure.

Unless we're absolutists and disapprove of dishonesty for any purpose, the degree of sympathy we have for people lying for what they think of as self-defense or defense of a good cause has a great deal to do with whether or not we accept their version of reality in the matter. In the case of a repressive government, we may wholeheartedly agree with the claim of Alexander Yakovlev, Gorbachev's closest advisor. Asked why lies snowballed in the Soviet Union during the last years of Brezhnev's government, he answered: "To succeed in anything one had to be sly, to lie, to violate rules and laws." And the hero of Antoni Libera's charming novel *Madame* is on target when he applies the rhetoric of proletarian revolt tongue in cheek to a rebellion against ticket inspectors on a Polish streetcar in the 1960s:

> Inequality before the law relieves us of the obligation to stick to the rules of fair play: isn't that what the history books and most of our schoolbooks teach us? The struggle against the exploiter is a noble and progressive one. Breaking the laws of bloodsuckers is a virtuous act, not a sin. In a world of violence and oppression it's permissible to seek justice in any way one can . . .

The plague of lies during the reign of Stalin is another matter: the regime lied incessantly for propaganda purposes; people lied to save their lives.

Obviously, when people's actions are illegal, our view of the law as something that either must be obeyed or can be broken for any of a number of reasons enters. Consider deception practiced by the users of illegal drugs in the face of institutions committed to detecting, arresting, and imprisoning them. Anyone who sees, say, ecstasy as no more or less potentially harmful than alcohol, and the drug laws as arbitrary, may not be perturbed by people lying to get and use it. And a far larger number of people will condone the action of cancer patients who surreptitiously bought marijuana as pain and nausea relief.

But what about the following "hostile" circumstances? In 1997, a sixty-three-year-old woman gave birth to a baby girl after undergoing the "donor egg" fertility treatment. She received the treatment despite the fact that the age limit for admission to it was fifty-five by claiming she was fifty when she was sixty. Since she had lied on previous occasions to other doctors, she was able to present medical records supporting her claim. Only in the thirteenth week of her pregnancy did she reveal her actual age. Fertility specialists were sanguine: apparently, when news got out that the donor-egg procedure could be successful not only during a woman's normal reproductive years but later in life, more and more women began lying about their age in order to get into programs. Doctors also admitted that the cutoff age of fifty-five was arbitrary—a round number and about ten years (another round number) beyond the age at which reproduction most of the time happens without medical intervention. The moral? A woman desperate to have a child late in life may lie about her age to counter what she perceives as unfair discrimination.

This leaves us once again in a complicated world in which we're forced to judge lies case by case. Do we agree that in lying to doctors to qualify for fertility treatment, a woman does something that is "legitimate," "permissible," or whatever else we may substitute for Krishna's "not touched by sin"? And if so, do we also approve of lies coming out of judgment calls backed by expertise—say those of doctors who exaggerate the severity of a patient's illness because they know that an HMO would not authorize treatment that *is* necessary according to their own professional opinion? In a 1999 nationwide survey of United States physicians, 98 out of 169 doctors who responded said they would be willing to submit "deliberately deceptive" documentation to ensure that a patient got needed bypass surgery or other treatment for a life-threatening condition. Where, in other words, do we draw the line?

The last example seems to bring us back full circle to Krishna—the lie told in order to save a life is not a sin. But it and other "well-intentioned" lies have one thing in common: the liar assumes that he or she is in possession of knowledge that those lied to do not possess and that the lie is necessary to make them do what they would do anyway if they had access to the facts or the bigger picture or weren't confused by conflicting or mistaken claims. In other words, if they knew what was what, they would convict the criminal, authorize the treatment, convert to the One True Church, allocate resources to combat communism, etc., etc. The assumption made by all liars for a just cause is that they are right and that the hostile conditions they are battling arise because others, who have power or influence, are not recognizing this. Of course, this is dangerous territory for a number of reasons. One is that the liar may simply be wrong, in which case the well-intentioned lie in the service of the "larger truth" can persuade people to believe in something that is wrong. McCarthy's 205 communists in the State Department did not "misrepresent" by a dozen the number that had infiltrated government posts; it grossly exaggerated it. The alleged severe threat to the United States did not exist. The police officer who managed to put someone behind bars by framing him may have framed the wrong suspect. A physician who exaggerates symptoms to guarantee a bypass operation for a patient may be overestimating the need for a dangerous surgery. The likelihood that a church whose leading lights see the need to fabricate martyrs and miracles is the One True Path to Salvation is small.

Add to these complications the ever-present possibility of a lie being exposed and thereby contributing to the amount of distrust in the world. Add, finally, the fact that deception can very easily turn into a lazy way of taking care of business—a quick and dirty solution where more effort and honesty might produce the same or better results—and it becomes very obvious that the notion of deception in hostile circumstances can be a tricky thing. We've returned to the question of the cost of lies and the harm they may do. What is certain is that people who use the excuse of hostility to lie in response to anything that poses difficulties have moved away from those conditions under which Krishna's maxim applies and have substituted their own: "It's fine to lie to get what one might otherwise be denied." The world is their oyster, and we recognize them by the crowbars they wield.

Even Educated Flies Do It

Thecla togarna

We've traveled far on our journey through the Land of Lying, and if we've discovered one thing, it must be that this exotic place is home. We may not like what we see, we may chafe at it or gnash our teeth, but the truth—if you will—is that we are natives here and remember the topography.

Much of what we've encountered has had to do with lying in the narrow sense of the word—language used with the intent to deceive. But we've also seen many instances in which the "lie" took on another form—say the body of a man who had *not* drowned, notwithstanding the water in his lungs, and had *not* been an officer in the Royal Marines, notwithstanding the uniform he was wearing. We use language to communicate, and, strictly speaking, we can lie only to someone who understands our language. But lying is merely one weapon, albeit the most important one, in our arsenal of deception. We can deceive someone whose language we do not speak by acting pleased, or uninterested, or any of a large number of other things—when in fact we aren't—or by heading in one direction and, the moment we're out of sight, changing course for our true destination . . . The possibilities are endless.

Much has been made of the human animal's unique possession of language. More recent consensus holds that other animals, too, "talk" to each other and that we simply haven't decoded what they say. While language is enormously important in shaping our thinking and determining who we are, the fact remains that we *do* deceive without it, and deceive not only members of our own species, whether or not we speak their language, but animals whose language we may never learn. Our final destination is their world, a world where in addition to gorgeous plumage and other finery some spectacular deception is to be found.

Franz Schubert's song "Die Forelle," the germ of his *Trout Quintet*, features a nefarious fisherman. Unable to catch a gaily swimming trout by the usual means—that is, by getting it to bite the lure he cast into the clear brook—he resorts to trickery: he muddies the water. Unable to see, the poor trout bites and becomes his victim, to the chagrin of the wanderer who observed the vile betrayal.

The poet of the poem Schubert set to music probably had in mind a metaphor—the young maiden who can fend off the seducer only if she recognizes his true motive—but a fisherman friend of mine doubts a trout will sizzle anytime soon in the skillet of someone who uses the muddy-the-water trick. Fish tend not to snap at what they cannot see. At any rate, Izaak Walton, arguably the world's most famous fisherman, would have scoffed at Schubert's amateurish scoundrel. In *The Compleat Angler* he boasted: "I have an artificial minnow . . . so curiously wrought, and so exactly dissembled that it would beguile any sharp-sighted trout in a swift stream." In other words, Schubert's *Forelle*, sharp eyes and clear brook notwithstanding, would have succumbed to Walton's wiles.

Nature's own compleat angler is the anglerfish, some of whose species carry affixed to the tips of their snouts a dorsal fin spine resembling a worm, crustacean, or small fish. Shallow-water species usually have bumpy bodies and look remarkably like rocks covered by sponges and algae. They rest inert on the bottom and wiggle their lures near their mouths. The predator who chooses the tasty morsel quickly becomes prey, when the "rock" the lure seems to swim above comes to life and has a large enough mouth to make a meal out of the would-be diner.

The difference between Izaak Walton carefully crafting an "exactly dissembled" minnow and the anglerfish growing a lure is obvious. Walton, a highly evolved animal with a large brain and opposable thumbs, studied minnows in nature and selected proper materials, putting them together in such a way that the finished product resembled a minnow well enough to fool a trout. The anglerfish, a lower-order critter, makes do without all that bother by simply growing her lure. She does so because natural selection smiled upon those of her ancestors who by random chance grew earlier versions of such things, and thereby gained a slight edge in what Darwin alternately called "the struggle for life" and "the struggle for existence."

Aggressive disguise is the name of the game the anglerfish plays, and other animals have perfected their own versions of it. Brazil has the matamata, a turtle that lives on the bottom of rivers and lakes. The matamata bears beneath its lower jaw red filaments that closely resemble small worms. When a fish or frog approaches one of these, the matamata sucks it into its mouth. North America has the alligator snapper, a mud-colored turtle that has gone even further in optimizing efficiency. It rests motionless on the bottom of the brown waters of the Mississippi and lures prey *inside* its mouth with a growth on the interior of its lower jaw, close to the tongue. The bait in this death trap looks like a large white grub crawling about in the mud.

Predators using aggressive deception are relatively rare. Far larger is the number of animals whose evolutionary path involved modifications in structure, appearance, and behavior for the sake of defense. Darwin, addressing the question of how the evolutionary process could be responsible for animals uncannily resembling things in their surroundings, listed a variety of such pretenders:

> Insects often resemble for the sake of protection various objects, such as green or decayed leaves, dead twigs, bits of lichen, flowers, spines, excrement of birds, and living insects . . . . The resemblance is often wonderfully close, and is not confined to colour, but extends to form, and even to the manner in which the insects hold themselves. The caterpillars which project motionless like dead twigs from the bushes on which they feed, offer an excellent instance of a resemblance of this kind.

Darwin's explanation of the evolution of such defenses is that any "rude and accidental resemblance" to an object commonly found where an insect lives can be the first start.

> Assuming that an insect originally happened to resemble in some degree a dead twig or a decayed leaf, and that it varied slightly in many ways, then all the variations which rendered the insect at all more like any such object, and thus favoured its escape, would be preserved, whilst other variations would be neglected and ultimately lost; or, if they rendered the insect at all less like the imitated object, they would be eliminated.

Protective resemblance is a widespread defensive device among insects. What Darwin describes—animals looking like objects that are found in their surroundings—is known in zoology as *mimicry*, not to be confused with *crypsis*, which refers to the infinite permutations of camouflage used by animals to blend in with their larger surroundings, such as the white fur of polar hares, reflective scales of fishes, mottled plumage of ptarmigans—grouse who live on high mountain slopes among lichen-covered rocks (and turn white in winter).

Fauna masquerading as flora to keep from being eaten by other fauna is only one type of mimicry. My personal favorites among animal pretenders are those who masquerade as themselves, only "arse up'ards." *Thecla togarna*, this chapter's epigraphic butterfly, is an example. A fake head painted on the tip of its rear wing, which is complemented by false antennae, is only the beginning of an amazingly integrated defense system. Like many of its fellow lycaenid butterflies, *Thecla togarna* rests on vertical surfaces with the head downward; most other butterflies rest head up. A predator anticipating evasive action will do the standard thing: compensate for the butterfly's takeoff by aiming the attack at its head or even slightly in front of where it is resting. And may, in the case of lycaenids, grab thin air, since the butterfly takes off in the opposite direction. But *Thecla togarna* is even better at faking out the opposition. When it lands, it quickly turns 180° so that its rear rather than its front points in the direction of its flight. It also moves the false antennae on the tips of its hind wings up and down for a few seconds while holding its true antennae motionless. Any bird that sees the incoming butterfly had better not blink. If it does and misses the quick turnabout, it will see an entirely plausible picture of what it should see if all were aboveboard—a butterfly that has just landed and is pointed in the direction of its previous flight, the same direction in which it will, naturally, take off if threatened. A swift attacker going for the false front may still get a piece of butterfly, but since the false front is the hind wings, the butterfly may nevertheless escape, albeit slightly tattered.

Thecla togarna is a mimicker with relatively modest ambition. Brasher contenders are harmless or tasty animals who mimic non-harmless or ill-tasting ones and survive by pretending to be bad, as it were. More than forty years before the first edition of Darwin's *The Origin of Species* (1859), the naturalists W. Kirby and W. Spence noted the odd fact that certain drone flies bore a striking resemblance to bumblebees. But the first clear account of mimicry was published by H. W. Bates in 1862, buttressing Darwin's theory of evolution.

Bates, one of those indefatigable Victorians who went to the ends of the earth in the pursuit of knowledge, had spent eleven years exploring the valley of the Amazon, collecting almost 15,000 insect species, 8,000 of which had been unknown. When he began to study his collection, he found what he described as "resemblances in external appearance, shapes, and colours between members of widely distinct families . . ." (A reminder for those who no longer have the lore of Biology 1 at their fingertips: a *family* is taxonomically below an *order* and above a *genus*, which, in turn, is above a *species*.)

While out exploring, Bates had noticed that certain common butterflies of the tropical family Heliconiidae were never eaten by birds or lizards even though their brilliant coloration and slow, conspicuous flight seemed to make them prime candidates as food for these predators. He also noticed other butterflies, belonging to an unrelated family, who seemed by appearance identical to the Heliconiidae. To explain this odd coincidence, Bates proposed what became known as "Batesian mimicry," which, if we use the heliconiids as an example, works as follows: The heliconiids are unpalatable to insect-eating vertebrates. A bird or lizard trying one will find it too distasteful to be eaten, will reject it, and will re-member not only its bad taste but also its conspicuous coloration. When it again comes across a heliconiid, it will ignore it. A palat-able butterfly can, therefore, escape being eaten by mimicking a heliconiid (or, in the language of evolutionary adaptation, forebears of the heliconiid look-alikes who bore a slight resemblance to the forebears of the heliconiids were eaten less often than members of the same species who did not bear this slight resemblance; they therefore had an edge in terms of propagation). Bates realized that since the predator could not learn to ignore the unpalatable butter-flies except by sampling one of them, they had to be much more common than their palatable mimics for the deception to work; otherwise a predator would be likely to sample an edible butterfly and learn that at least some of these colorful slowpokes made good eating. The preponderance of the unpalatable "model" made it rel-atively rare for a predator to learn the wrong lesson.

Batesian mimicry not only is found in widely different families or in different members of the same species (examples of which are harmless snakes or moths mimicking poisonous ones—the mimics of poisonous coral snakes being famous examples) but also makes the jump from animals of one order to those of another—harmless flies mimic poisonous wasps, bees, and ants, grasshoppers mimic bombardier beetles, spiders mimic ants. And animals even more dissimilar in terms of taxonomy can have anatomical features and behavior that allow one to mimic another: The caterpillar of one large tropical American sphinx moth (*Leucorampha*) lives upside down among vines and creepers. If the vine it clings to is shaken, the larva lets go with all except its hind legs and swells up in front to reveal a pair of highly convincing dummy eyes that seem to be menacingly glaring in a triangular head. It also immediately begins to sway in a sinuous manner. When touched, it even lashes its head back and forth like a viper striking. Its appearance and behavior are guaranteed to be disconcerting to caterpillar-eating predators not in the least keen on tangling with a viper.

Batesian mimicry is often connected with *aposematism*: conspicu-ous coloration meant to signal to a predator the fact that the potential prey is dangerous or unpalatable. The aposematic ani-mal—the black and white skunk, or red, white, and black coral snake, or black and yellow bumblebee—is protected against attack because one of its kind has paid the price, in terms of injury or death, of being conspicuous—not without teaching the predator a lesson by giving it a snoutful of fetid secretion or other surprise. The sprayed, stung, or bitten aggressor, or the one trying to get that nasty taste out of its mouth, will remember the unpleasant experience and will stay away from such noxious prey. In addition, social animals who have observed a member of their group coming out of an unfriendly encounter the worse for wear probably caution their young against varmints wearing flashy livery. The Batesian mimic of the aposematic animal takes advantage of the latter's evil reputation. Dressing the part, it is protected by its own gaudiness, which misinforms the knowledgeable predator by sending the same signal of danger.

All of this shows nature to be remarkably inventive when it comes to deception for the sake of self-protection, but there is more. According to Müllerian mimicry (after F. Müller, who suggested the mechanism in 1878), aposematic species, too, mimic one another because if one or more species of noxious animals look alike, the number of members sacrificed in teaching predators not to attack is reduced. The reason is that a predator that attacked a member of one species learns to avoid members of all similar-looking species, not just of the one that stung, or bit, or tasted horrible. In this case, the deception becomes a curious thing, a lie that is of no consequence to the one lied to but that tells a truth of considerable consequence—the lie being that all of these look-alike species are identical, the truth being that they are all equally noxious. Enter that one in the category "White Lies in the Non-Hominid Animal Kingdom" since it minimizes the number of unpleasant encounters a predator has.

Then, there is (possibly) Mertensian mimicry, named after R. Mertens, who carried out research on coral snakes in the 1960s. Still debated, it argues that a highly poisonous species may mimic a mildly poisonous one because only the mildly poisonous one can maintain what one zoologist has called "an educated population of predators" in a given territory. The reason is that a highly poisonous animal will kill an attacking predator (while, most likely, being killed itself in the attack). The problem is the power vacuum this creates. Predators tend to be territorial. If one dies, a new, inexperienced one will move in—bad news for all potential prey in the territory, whether dangerous or harmless.

Most mimicry is defensive, but some aggressive mimicry exists that beggars that of the anglerfish et al. One character that has taken the lure-your-supper skulduggery to an outrageous height is the African water mongoose. Its favorite diet is bird, and according to the lore of many tribes, the animal resorts to a startling trick to procure this delicacy. It conceals itself in vegetation but raises its rear end to view. Not just its rear end, however. In this position, it distends its anus to make it resemble a ripe fruit. Any bird who approaches to sample the offering is seized in a flash by the nimble beast.

A more sinister character in the book on aggressive mimicry is the European parasitic cuckoo. This notorious offender pushes out eggs from the nests of other birds and plants eggs that look like those of the hosts. The fledgling cuckoo continues the foul play, expelling its nest mates. In some species the mimicry goes even further. They resemble a bird-eating hawk and behave accordingly, zooming in and frightening away the host birds until the cuckoo's egg is in place.

But nature, relentlessly opportunistic, has long ago also filled the opposite niche, that of the predator mimicking a harmless animal to get close to prey. The rare American zone-tailed hawk, for instance, resembles a vulture. It is nearly black and its wings are long and narrow like those of a vulture. Looks are one thing, but this impostor also acts the part. Unlike other hawks, it does not use a lookout perch and it does not hover. It glides like the vultures it mimics, and it does so in their company. Why? Because vultures pose no threat to small animals and are therefore ignored by them. Which means an ideal cover for a zone-tailed hawk hiding among a group of vultures. The hawk will suddenly dive from the group and swoop down on its unsuspecting prey.

"Glides with Vultures" must be a cruel surprise to many small furry or feathered creatures, but a possibly even ruder surprise awaits male fireflies who fall into the trap of certain females of another firefly species. All fireflies attract members of the opposite sex by specific signals of flashing lights. But the female of one species, *Photuris*, attracts the males of different species by mimicking the flash signals of *their* females. Alas, an interspecies amour is not her intent. The male approaching this femme fatale will promptly be eaten.

A quick detour into another kingdom shows that even plants can contribute to the world's bag of trickery. What Richard Dawkins calls "deceptive advertising" in his compulsively readable *Climbing Mount Improbable* allows some plants to "duck out of the expense" of manufacturing nectar to bribe insects into doing the work of pollination. Bee, fly, and wasp orchids, for instance, mimic the females of the respective insects in order to attract their males. The ardent males get saddled with pollen in the process of extracting themselves from encounters that are surely disappointing. The effect of the trap set by the aptly named hammer orchid on a suitor's libido is unknown, but we're free to guess. The orchid has a dummy female wasp on the end of a hinged and spring-loaded stalk. In Dawkins' words:

> When the male wasp lands on the female dummy the spring is released. The male wasp is slammed, violently and repeatedly, against the anvil where the pollen sacs are kept. By the time the male wasp shakes himself free, his back is loaded with two pollen sacs.

If there is an effort to please, it is not apparent.

But back to animals and self-defense. Mimicking other animals is only one category of self-protective deceptions. Darwin used the example of the hen who ruffles her feathers and spreads her wings when a dog approaches her chicks as one of "the many ways by which animals endeavor to frighten away their enemies." This kind of bluffing by pretending to be larger and more formidable than they actually are is in the repertoire of a great many animals. When threatened, vipers swell up and hiss, cats erect their hair and raise their tails, the chameleon expands its body, puffs out its throat, and raises its head flap. (Whether the chameleon changes its color to match that of its background is still debated. Some zoologists argue that light, temperature, and emotions are responsible for the color change.) Known as *deimatic* (from the Greek *deimos*, panic), the behavior is intended to intimidate a potential attacker into retreating. It announces, on the one hand, that the animal poses a danger and, on the other, strives to make that danger seem as alarmingly massive as the animal can make it seem. Predators prefer to keep their weapons for hunting and are, in the argot of sociology, "risk-averse." They would rather scare a potential attacker into retreat by puffing or fluffing themselves up, hissing, rattling, screeching, or otherwise alarming the enemy than fight and invite injury or death.

Bluff in terms of faking bulk is part of the equation even in the case of dangerous animals who *can* hurt an attacker. But it should come as no surprise that again mimicry abounds among harmless animals whose own deimatic behavior is a false threat intended to bluff the enemy into thinking that they are dangerous, when in fact they are not. The harmless green snake imitates a poisonous adder—when threatened, it raises itself up and hisses like an adder ready to strike. We've already met a more outrageous fraud in that arena: the caterpillar who plays viper and whose makeup includes dummy eyes and a puffed-up triangular head. Eye spots are part of the arsenal of many species. The Brazilian toad *Physalaemus nattereri* sports a dramatic pair on its rump. Threatened by an approaching predator, it turns said rump toward the would-be attacker, who is suddenly, alarmingly, presented with what looks like a large face with shiny eyes.

Naturally, all of these actions aimed at intimidating an enemy are the result of instinct, of which more shortly. A snippet of a snake who pretends to be an adder has never been told by a parent, friend, or teacher that this is the proper way to behave in a life-threatening situation. Compare the lowly snake with human beings, poor in instinct and often clueless when it comes to survival but smart enough to understand instructions. We have to be told by the forest service that, should we meet a bear or mountain lion out in the wilderness, it behooves us to face the animal, stand up straight, and spread our arms and parkas to appear as large as possible. Deimatic behavior and a bluff to boot.

Quite the opposite strategy in the game of not being eaten is *thanatosis*, also known as "playing possum." Feigning death can save the life of animals whose predators will only strike to kill prey that moves. Faced with what looks to all the world like dead meat, the predator may relax its attention, allowing the animal to escape, or may lose interest altogether and move away. Some beetles, bugs, grasshoppers, and other insects become inert when they are attacked, as do some small birds, the African ground squirrel, and, of course, the American opossum.

Then there is feigning injury. To draw a predator away from their eggs or chicks, some birds who nest on the ground or in bushes stage an elaborate diversion. They flap about as if they had an injured wing, or they limp or tumble. While giving this "distraction display," they keep moving away from the nest. Then, when the pursuing predator comes a little too close for comfort, they miraculously recover and fly off. Other birds, regular Academy Award contenders, will creep along on the ground uttering squeaks resembling those of a small mammal. A predator giving chase will be startled to find the alleged rodent suddenly taking to the sky. (An avian pretender of literary fame is the wife of Darzee the tailorbird in Rudyard Kipling's "Rikki-Tikki-Tavi." She flutters desperately on the ground feigning a broken wing in order to lure the cobra Nagaina away from the melon patch where the cobra's eggs are hidden and give Rikki-tikki the opportunity to destroy them. It goes without saying that RTT, although a mongoose, would never stick his rear in the air to lure birds by displaying his distended anus. Not only is he a friend to all animals except snakes but so uncouth an act would be beneath him.)

The many ways by which animals deceive one another in the quest to survive and thrive resemble remarkably the deceptions of human beings in hostile surroundings. Small wonder people who study them have to beware of the temptation to ascribe thought and intention to animal behavior. Consider this statement by J. L. Cloudsley-Thompson, a zoologist with impeccable credentials: "The chief difficulty in resembling a leaf, in so far as an animal is concerned, lies in achieving the appearance of being very thin." Cloudsley-Thompson is not for a moment confused about the origin of the leaf-shaped insect—or the stick-shaped one, or the snake-mimicking caterpillar. He simply finds it here and elsewhere more economical to use language that inadvertently suggests intentionality.

It is impossible to learn about animals—even about the lowly bug crawling in the dirt—without time and again finding oneself thinking: How ingenious! What inventiveness! How clever! But, no, the leaf insect did not assume its ingenious shape after having surmised that such mimicry might do it a world of good when the next foraging bird or snake appeared in the neighborhood. And the probability is zero that a digger wasp, whose contribution to the catalog of animal deceptions is to dig false nesting burrows next to its true ones, ever cogitated as follows: "Let's see, if I build a false burrow next to my real one, there is a fifty-fifty chance that one of those infernal parasites—those pestilential bee flies, velvet ants, and cuckoo wasps—will deposit its eggs in the false burrow and leave my nest uninfested. Come to think of it, digging two or three false burrows is the way to go. Improving my offspring's chance of survival is well worth the additional effort."

The digger wasp who did not have these thoughts is *Sphex argentatus*. Industrious insect, it builds two or three false burrows as soon as the true burrow is in good enough condition to be temporarily closed while the wasp moonlights. *Bembix sayi*, another species, builds only a single false burrow—again without having given the matter the careful thought it deserves—after it has completed and blocked up the true one for the last time. Laziness does not seem to be the issue: the false burrow of *Bembix sayi* is deeper than the several false burrows of *Sphex argentatus*. Yet another species, *Sphex flammitrichus*, has arrived at a radically different solution. It opts for building more nesting burrows and laying more eggs rather than wasting time on building false burrows. (Or perhaps *S. flammitrichus* is an absolutist in addition to being a moralist and holds that deception under any and all circumstances is wrong?)

Evolutionary adaptation driven by natural selection accounts for the shape and color of the leaf insect and of the countless other animal mimickers and pretenders; instinct, again honed by natural selection, accounts for striking like an asp, and turning around after landing, and false-tunnel digging, and so forth. No matter how humanlike the deceptive behavior of certain tropical spiders is—not only do they mimic ants in running about in a jerky manner but they carry over their backs the empty dried skeletons of ants so as to hide their own bodies completely from view and create the impression of just another ant carrying a fallen comrade—decision making based on observation is not involved. Instinctive behavior is by definition an involuntary, reflexive response to an external stimulus and is characterized by a fixed pattern of behavior. It is not learned but is genetically "hardwired" and cannot be modified to adjust for changing conditions. As we go up the evolutionary ladder in terms of brain capacity, we find instinct more and more supplemented or replaced by intelligence.

The long and short of all this? The ability to deceive confers a reproductive advantage to organisms that by virtue of being deceptive avoid being killed and live to a reproductive age. It also confers the advantage of longevity, which living things seem to appreciate even though it is not obvious that nature cares as long as the adult animal lives long enough to nurture and teach its young. The innate hostility of surroundings in which a large part of life is spent struggling not to become food or, conversely, is spent struggling to catch food that is reluctant to be eaten, makes deception a useful item in any organism's kit. The ability to deceive is one of the many abilities or characteristics that have made some animals better equipped to survive than others. It therefore falls into the same category as long necks in giraffes, keen eyesight in birds, fleet-footedness in cheetahs and gazelles, and the sharp tooth and claw nature is famously red in. The struggle for life has favored the better mimickers and bluffers just as it has favored, depending on the pressure exerted by the environment, the faster, stronger, thicker-furred, sharper-sighted, spinier, nimbler, smarter. Instinct does the job for the lower animals; intelligence does it for the higher ones.

Exactly where instinct leaves off and intelligence starts continues to be a much-debated issue. People insecure about humanity's lofty position in the natural world's pecking order have traditionally attributed all behavior in animals to instinct alone, but anyone who has spent time with animals, domestic or wild, will find it hard to believe that their responses to what the world throws their way are entirely involuntary and reflexive. Careful observers of animals have long noted that instinct is only part of the equation. Darwin himself stated that even "animals low in the scale of nature" cannot be said to function by instinct alone and that "a little dose of judgment or reason . . . often comes into play." Still, deciding what behavior is instinctive and what comes out of an intelligent appraisal of a situation is not easy.

Regarding deceptive animals, the question of intentionality can help clarify several things. Richard Byrne, a researcher and engaging writer on intelligence in apes and monkeys, has closely studied deception in primates. He finds the philosopher Daniel Dennett's view of deception useful. Dennett distinguishes among "zero-order," "first-order," and "second-order intentionality." In his book *The Thinking Ape*, Byrne uses these concepts to differentiate between the purely instinctive behavior of an eyed hawkmoth in response to a threat and the intelligence-driven behavior of a house cat in response to the challenge of a favored easy chair being unavailable because occupied. A Batesian mimic par excellence, the hawkmoth when approached by a bird flicks open its wings, which bear a pair of painted eyes, and, presto, it resembles the face of a hawk. The moth shows zero-order intentionality because it behaves this way in response to any looming shape, be it a bird or a sheet of cardboard held up by an experimenter. The act is akin to our throwing up an arm to deflect any object flying at our face, be it a brick or foam-rubber ball. The moth does not open its wings with the intention of saving itself (although that may be the outcome of its action) but does so instinctively. Given that it cannot even conceive why it is doing what it is doing, it is obviously incapable of higher-order mental perception. It cannot know, far less understand, that if it flicks open its wings, a bird about to seize it will be duped into mistaking it for the face of a hawk and will abort the attack because it is frightened.

Compare this behavior with that of the cat whose wish to curl up on the easy chair by the fireplace is frustrated by the fact that its owner is sitting in it. Rain is pelting the house, but suddenly the cat is meowing in the hallway by the front door. The owner gets up, unlocks the door, and opens it to let the cat out. And finds no cat at his feet. When he returns to the living room, he sees a picture of feline bliss—the cat on the chair he just relinquished. Byrne attributes this behavior to first-order intentionality. The cat wants the chair and has learned the sequence of steps that have to occur before it can achieve its heart's desire: (1) It walks over to the door and meows. (2) The owner gets up and comes to the door. (3) The cat goes to the chair, hops on it, and goes to sleep. (Let's assume that the owner does not proceed to Step 4 and dislodge it.)

In all likelihood the chair-deprived victim is smitten by what he sees as his clever kitty tricking him and will tell the anecdote to anyone he can cajole into listening to yet another episode in the rich life of Snookums the Wonder Cat. The assumption of deliberate deceptiveness is one we make automatically when we witness this kind of behavior in an animal, because if *we* did a similar thing we would certainly know that we were being deceptive, in other words that our intention was to deceive in order to gain something at the expense of a dupe.

Dennett's (and Byrne's) second-order intentionality refers to the kind of knowingly deceptive behavior every one of us is all too familiar with. It is reserved for those cases in which an agent wants a dupe to believe something that the agent knows is not the case. Regarding the cat, its intention would be second order if it thought the nonverbal equivalent of the following: By pretending I want to go outside—which I do by acting accordingly—I'll make the large biped occupying the chair believe that this is the case. He'll therefore get up and move away from the chair to let me out. Whereupon I'll double back and take possession of the chair. Unless we have underestimated the mental acumen of the average house cat, this way of understanding the world is beyond its ken, whereas the ability to learn from experience what it needs to do to achieve a desired result—be fed, petted, let out or in—is well within it. In the words of Byrne: "Yes, the agent intended a free lunch, but it did not intend deception as such. Unless the agent knows that the *mechanism* of its free lunch was that it *made the dupe believe something untrue*, it could not even be said to understand its act of deception, let alone intend it. Nevertheless, it has carried out a deceptive act."

So how could the cat have learned the clever "trick"? Possibly from a time when its primary goal was the chair but when, finding the chair occupied, it settled on its secondary goal, which was to go outside. By a windfall, as far as the cat was concerned, its meowing at the door had the effect of liberating the chair. (This theory still assumes that the cat is smart enough to combine the fact that its owner is now at the door with a mental image of the chair, which must be unoccupied since, as the cat well knows, he cannot be in two places at once.) Ergo, Snookums learned that if she wants the chair, then, for reasons unknown to her—but does she care as long as the job gets done?—all she needs to do is go to the door and meow. What seems like intentionally deceptive behavior to us may simply be an appreciation of cause and effect that has been committed to memory.

The deceptive behavior of hunting predators can be seen in the same light. Lions when hunting alone stalk their prey downwind; when they hunt together, they hide downwind while one or two of them move into position to be smelled by the prey and thereby drive the prey into the ambush. Again, this obviously deceptive maneuver can be explained in terms of the lions having discovered that this approach works rather than having formulated the far more complicated idea that they are creating in the mind of the wildebeest or gazelle the impression of greater safety in a direction where there is in fact an ambush.

Byrne rolls zero-order and first-order intentionality into the single concept "unintentional" and contrasts it with second-order deception, which is "intentional." He thereby gets rid of the semantic confusion introduced when we talk about, say, deceptive insects yet think of deception as a willful act. Insects mimicking other species and behaving accordingly—and possibly cats tricking us into giving up the nicest chair in the house—are unintentionally (or nondeliberately, or unknowingly) deceptive; people working hard to make us believe something that isn't so are intentionally deceptive.

(By the way, it is not entirely impossible for *us* to be unintentionally deceptive. We may send the wrong signals to someone, or someone may misinterpret the signals we send. Our romantic life is particularly prone to this kind of muddle. Things we say, or how we say them, can easily be misread by someone enthralled. We may have no intention to deceive and may be flabbergasted to find what sort of conclusion someone jumped to. And we can also unknowingly deceive by, for instance, giving someone wrong directions that we think are right.)

What we have not yet addressed is the question whether animals can intentionally deceive other animals. In other words, can animal A formulate in its mind an idea of what goes on in the mind of animal B and realize that it may be able to manipulate B by making B think something that A knows is untrue in order to produce a desired result? Amazingly, not until the 1980s did scientific articles get published arguing that, yes, not only does deception exist among primates but some of the observed deception is clearly intentional. Byrne, who was one of the pioneers in this field, found that his colleagues had been reluctant to write about deceptive behavior they had observed among primates in the wild or in captivity. The fear of being accused of softheaded, naive thinking in assigning "uniquely human" abilities to animals was to blame.

Byrne's own interest began while he was studying the foraging of baboons. He observed a young baboon, Paul, using deception to get food from a larger, adult female baboon, Mel. Paul came across Mel, who was just finishing the laborious process of digging up a corm. The time of year was dry and cold, and this nutritious food was difficult to unearth even by adults. Paul was alone with Mel, with no other baboon in sight. After looking around, Paul suddenly screamed. Whereupon his mother, who was higher-ranking than Mel, ran into view grunting aggressively. The intimidated Mel ran off, Paul's mother chasing after her. With Mom and Mel out of the way, Paul ate the corm. Within the next several weeks, Byrne and a colleague saw Paul use this tactic three times, always when his mother was nearby but in no position to see that his scream had not been provoked by an attack.

Asking colleagues worldwide to supply him with accounts of deception they had observed among primates, Byrne gathered an impressive dossier on what he called "tactical deception" used by apes and monkeys on members of their groups and on people they were in contact with. His concept included both unintentional and intentional deception, and he ran the reported observations through a skeptical filter eliminating all those that might be explained in some way not involving deception. He found that chimpanzees and baboons outshone the other primates in the number of times they used deceptive tactics. Many of these tactics could be classified as unintentional deception like that of the cat liberating the easy chair. Even Paul the baboon, Byrne suggests, may have learned his "trick" through a fortuitous set of circumstances. Suppose he had as an infant come too close to a feeding adult of a rank lower than his mother's who threatened him, causing him to scream in fear and his mother to run to his aid, which made the adult drop the food, which Paul then ate. He might have learned the combination (1) food held by a baboon who was lower-ranking than his mother, (2) his mother out of visual contact, (3) his screaming, (4) his mother running to his aid, and (5) the food becoming available—without knowing the why of all this. My own suspicion is that Paul *was* intentionally deceptive and learned to be so the moment he realized that he could scream convincingly enough to make his mother believe he was frightened when in fact he was not. But Byrne was looking for evidence of intentional deception that could not be demolished by the argument that an animal had simply learned a sequence of steps producing a desired result.

What might constitute such evidence? For one, an indication that some primates are able to recognize deception used against them and respond by showing righteous indignation. One researcher studying infant behavior in Jane Goodall's chimpanzees at Gombe reported an amazing instance of such a response. On one occasion a female infant chimpanzee began to groom him. Physical contact between the animals and people is discouraged because the chimpanzees can catch any human disease. The researcher did not want to push away the chimpanzee because this might be seen as a hostile act by her mother. He instead tricked the youngster by acting as if he had seen an object of interest in the distance. He stared keenly into the bushes, and the ruse worked—the chimpanzee went off to investigate. When she found nothing, she returned and hit him over the head with her hand, and she ignored him for the rest of the day.

Another way to tell whether an animal understands deception is through its use of counterdeception. A researcher conducting experiments on spatial knowledge in chimpanzees recorded a remarkable sequence of events. One chimpanzee, Belle, was shown food hidden in the middle of a large, open enclosure while the other members of her group were kept out of sight. She was then allowed to join the group and all the chimpanzees were let out into the enclosure. Belle led the group to the well-hidden site and all shared the food. This experiment was repeated several times with the same result until a stronger chimpanzee, Rock, began refusing to let the others have any of the food. Belle countered by not uncovering the food if Rock was close and sitting on it until he left. He soon caught on, however, and when she sat in one place for more than a few seconds he came over, shoved her aside, searched the location, and found the food. Belle next stopped going close to the food, but again Rock caught on, and he expanded his search through the grass near where she had sat. With time, Belle sat farther and farther away, waiting until Rock looked in the opposite direction before she moved toward the food. His answer was to pretend to look away until Belle started to move. On some occasions he refined that ruse even more. He started to wander off, only to wheel around suddenly just as Belle was about to uncover the food. Rock's behavior showed complete awareness that Belle was trying to deceive him by staying away from the food and that countermeasures were called for to trick her into revealing its location.

Rock's attitude seems to have been "all is fair in food." The males of another species of primates apparently believe that all is fair in love. And, no, we're not talking about *Homo sapiens*, with its abundance of members of both sexes who subscribe to that motto. Field researchers in Africa have observed male vervet monkeys attracting females by uttering the vervet word for "food"—as opposed to that for "snake," "leopard," or "eagle," other vervet words the researchers have decoded. Unfortunately, the female rushing up to the male may discover that the advertised food is a twig or inedible leaf. (The words the females use upon making this discovery have apparently not yet been decoded.)

Homo sapiens, as we've seen, uses deception willfully, and has invested a googolplex of man-hours in practicing it and devising ways to detect and foil it. We are one branch of the primate line. Molecular taxonomy suggests that humans belong to the same lineage the apes belong to (or, properly speaking, that we *are* apes). Researchers like Richard Byrne argue that by studying chimpanzees and gorillas, our closest ape relatives, we can learn much about the evolutionary origins of intelligence. According to the most recent evidence, the chimpanzee lineage separated from that of humans only about six million years ago. By comparison, the gorilla line diverged from the human about eight million years ago and the orangutan diverged about fourteen million years ago. Given our recent common ancestry, it is hardly surprising that our chimpanzee cousins share a great many of our abilities, including the one to recognize deception for what it is, to use it for profit, and to take umbrage when it is used against them.

What can we conclude from all this trickery in the animal kingdom? Obviously that Mother Nature has designated deception, whether intentional or unintentional, a great and good thing in the struggle to survive in hostile surroundings. From the worm feeding on the vine, to the leopard stalking the goat, to the ape competing for food with another ape, to the general staging strategic deceptions, the number of creatures who have used it for their own benefit is vast. Barring a miraculous evolution to some world very different from the one we know—where the lion lying down with the lamb will be among the less startling of the changes—deception is here to stay.

Epilogue

Any book on deception invites obvious questions: Is everything in it true, or has a lie crept in somewhere and now sits on the printed page muddying the water, creating confusion, and furthering in its own small way the ruin of the Republic? Any bending of the facts for the sake of a juicier anecdote? Any unattributed quotes or conclusions not plucked from the writer's own garden but taken to market as if? Any claim or reported event that is false not because "mistakes were made" but because someone stood to gain by broadcasting a lie?

The answers are, respectively: possibly, no, no, and possibly. The nos have to do with my own role in this project. I take it to be a given that dishonesty in scholarship is an abomination. To be of use, any type of research has to be a search for truth, and its findings have to be truthfully represented. Fraudulent scholarship is not unheard of, but the reader subjected to it is justifiably outraged when it is exposed. In writing this book, I have at all times striven for honesty. If an anecdote was tempting fodder but not as interesting as it would have been with a slight exaggeration, I made do without the anecdote; if a point I was trying to make was potentially undermined by conflicting information, I either didn't make the point or included the conflicting information; I've been scrupulous in attributing to its sources all material I've used.

The possiblys are more complicated but only because I cannot attest to the moral character of the writers of the hundreds of books and articles I consulted in my research. Many of them were, or are, scholars, and I have no reason to doubt that devotion to truth motivated them. But only telepathy and, in many cases, communication with the dead as well would allow me to say with certainty that not one of them, and not one of the other writers from whose works I drew—journalists, essayists, psychologists, and so forth—ever lied. Nor can I vouch that no honest mistake, theirs or mine, is to be found on any of the preceding pages.

I wish it weren't so, but although I've tried my level best, this book should no more than any other be treated as a repository of the truth, the whole truth, and nothing but.

Notes

THE BIBLE: A CASEBOOK

3 "But of the tree": Genesis 2:17. All quotations are from the King James Version of the Bible.

4 These sources are known: A detailed breakdown of which sources are by scholarly consensus responsible for which books and episodes of Genesis is, for example, in Marks, p. 2.

5 Milton has the animal's body invaded: Milton's is far from the first literary treatment putting Satan in the picture. The twelfth-century mystery play *Mystère d'Adam* offered a full dramatic representation of Satan's temptation of Adam and Eve in Eden. See Russell, pp. 255–59.

7 shaped by unknown hands: All four gospels show evidence of a process of redaction of oral material about Jesus. Several theories exist on what gospel was written first and what editor used material from whom. One is that Matthew and Luke used material found in Mark and in a lost source known as "Q" (from the German *Quelle*, "source"). There is disagreement on whether or not the writer of John knew the synoptic gospels. See Kee, p. 609. The Gospel According to St. John departs from the other gospels in going to inordinate lengths to prove that Jesus is the anointed one. "Nay, but he deceiveth the people," the members of a crowd are heard to murmur at the Feast of the Tabernacle (John 7:12), and John expends an enormous amount of ink to disprove the claim by describing miracle after miracle in far greater detail than the other gospels do.

8 the serpent "in a sense speaks truly": Marks, p. 6.

10 a con artist often too clever by far: For a compelling view of the trickster, see Hyde.

11 Traditional Near Eastern associations with the snake: Hendel, p. 747.

11 "a primal horror of humankind": Alter, p. 13.

16 a pragmatic solution to a threat to Abraham's life: The wife-sister lie reappears once more. This time the patriarch using it is Abraham's son, Isaac, and the selfsame Abimelech, king of the Philistines, is once again the one lied to (Genesis 26:1–11). God tells Isaac to go to Gerar. He obeys and he and his wife, Rebekah, live there. Version Three promptly pops up: "And the men of the place asked *him* of his wife; and he said, She *is* my sister; for he feared to say, She *is* my wife; lest, *said he*, the men of the place should kill me for Rebekah; because she *was* fair to look upon" (Genesis 26:7). This time the lie is discovered when Abimelech looks out of a window and sees Isaac "sporting" with Rebekah. Quick on the uptake, Abimelech calls Isaac and says, "Behold, of a surety she *is* thy wife: and how saidst thou, She *is* my sister?" Isaac's answer is the familiar "Lest I die for her." The king apparently has no recollection of an earlier conversation with Isaac's father along those same lines. "What *is* this thou hast done unto us?" he asks; "one of the people might lightly have lien with thy wife, and thou shouldest have brought guiltiness upon us." The king's astute solution is to prohibit under penalty of death that anyone touch Isaac or his wife. Scholars have conjectured that this is the oldest version of the story and have shown that the story is connected with Hurrian (or Horite) laws whereby sistership was a transferable relationship—a woman given in marriage by her brother became legally her husband's sister. See Marks, p. 13.

20 "Therefore God dealt well with the midwives": St. Augustine, claiming that the Old Testament provides no precedents to justify lying, argued that God rewarded the midwives not for their deception but for their mercy, and perhaps pardoned the former because of the latter. See Zagorin, pp. 21–23. Following the saint's argument, the many instances of deception furthering the cause of the Israelites described in the Old Testament were all pardoned by God because they served a higher purpose. Possibly, but God's wholehearted approval of the most elaborate and murderous ruses (such as that resulting in Jehu killing all the prophets, servants, and priests of Baal in 2 Kings 10:18–30 or that setting up the Hivites for slaughter by the sons of Jacob in Genesis 34:1–31) suggests a more straightforward interpretation: deception in the service of God or to avenge wrongs done to his people is laudable.

DECEPTION AT FIRST LIGHT

29 "The net, the spell of Shamash": Assyro-Babylonian mythology. See *The Larousse Encyclopedia*, p. 65.

30 "devious-deviser": Hesiod, p. 155.

31 "Anger rose up": Hesiod, p. 27.

31 "lies, and wheedling words": Hesiod, p. 27.

32 which Kronos swallowed at once: Rhea's ruse had followed an even earlier one: Kronos had used deception to emasculate his own father, Ouranos, who (*plus ça change*) had kept children from being born out of his

wife and mother Gaia by pushing them back into her womb. Gaia, who was both the earth and the creator of the universe, fashioned an enormous sickle and gave it to her son, "devious-devising Kronos" (again, the epithet is Hesiod's). She hid her son in an ambush and when Ouranos, the sky, came to cover her at night, Kronos emerged from his hiding place and castrated his father.

33 a "crafty trickster" who needed to be bound: Aeschylus, p. 156.

34 remnants of the Titan's workmanship: Pausanias, vol. 1, p. 411.

35 Glooscap (or Gluskap): McLeish, pp. 221–22.

35 The Polynesian god Maui stole fire from the keeper: *The Larousse Encyclopedia*, p. 453.

35 Raven . . . stole daylight from the chief of heaven's house: Hyde, pp. 46–47.

35 stole water from a spring: Hyde, p. 189.

35 Loki . . . helped the other gods by tricking a rock giant: McLeish, p. 359.

36 "Do like the rest and show Balder honour": Frazer, p. 608.

38 *Homeric Hymn to Hermes*: Probably written down around 420 B.C., but the material it treats is much older. I'm paraphrasing from the translation of Hyde, pp. 317–31.

39 "You yourself know I'm not guilty": Hyde, p. 326.

41 Krishna the Butter Thief: For a wise and engaging work on the young Krishna, see Hawley.

42 The poet Sur Das: Sur Das is traditionally assumed to have been an oral poet who lived in the early or middle sixteenth century A.D.

42 "Then he laughs and laughs": Hawley, p. 113.

43 "desire and longings that wear out the body": these addle Pandora's head in Hesiod's *The Works and Days*. Hesiod, p. 25. "*O felix culpa, quae talem ac tantum meruit habere Redemptorem*" ("O happy fault, which has deserved to have such and so mighty a Redeemer"). *The Missal*, "Exsultet on Holy Saturday." The phrase has been attributed to St. Augustine or St. Ambrose.

43 "the mythic embodiment of ambiguity": Hyde, p. 7.

45 The West African spider, coerced by the lion: Arnott, pp. 25–31.

45 Iktome told an innocent young woman: Leeming, pp. 53–54.

46 Ormazd, the god of light and truth: *The Larousse Encyclopedia*, pp. 315–19.

47 *Malleus Maleficarum*: Written and published in 1486 by two Dominican Inquisitors at the instigation of Pope Innocent VIII, this monument to inhumanity, ignorance, and nonthinking became the standard handbook on the detection and persecution of witches among Roman Catholics and Protestants alike. It went through twenty-eight editions between 1486 and 1600. The cruelties it proposed against anyone accused of witchcraft—torture, imprisonment under the most wretched conditions, cleverly planned delays of scheduled hearings to raise hopes and dash them, and false promises of release or a mild sentence, all in order to secure the confession of guilt that was needed before the accused could properly be sentenced and burned alive—make reading it a wrenching experience. Anyone in the least disposed to believing in the devil will find evidence of

his work not in the superstitious twaddle of the authors but in the existence of a "learned" book dedicated to inflicting an appalling amount of harm under the guise of Christian defense against wickedness. Skeptics did exist. Reginald Scot published in 1583 *The Discoverie of Witchcraft*, a model of clear and compassionate thinking about the true nature of alleged witches and the appalling cruelty and ignorant fanaticism of those who hunted them. Scot accused the authors of the *Malleus* of publishing "stinking lies" in the form of fables, impossibilities, and absurdities. Scot, p. 273. That the popular imagination was fired up by a morbid interest in witchcraft in ecclesiastical circles was the complaint of another critic. No less a figure than Alonso Salazar de Frias, the Grand Inquisitor of Spain, wrote to the Supreme Court of Spain in 1610 that he had found no evidence that any of the alleged acts of witchcraft brought to his attention had in fact occurred and that epidemics of witches reported in the provinces had been caused by the credulity and suggestibility of the populace. Places suddenly teeming with witches had never had any until some zealous friar had come to town and preached about witchcraft. Williams, pp. 252–53.

47 "a marvellous cunning workman": Luther, pp. 287–90.

47 false opinions against Christ: Luther, pp. 590–91.

49 The infamous Foundation Myth: Plato, p. 182.

50 nonsyncretic religions have assimilated elements of other religions: An obvious example: Christianity owes the days of Christ's nativity and the feast of St. John the Baptist to the pagan winter solstice and Midsummer Day. The early Church took over these days of celebration, which go back to prehistoric times, by giving them a Christian meaning.

WHY LIARS LIE

58 "The Use of Speech was to make us understand": Swift, *Gulliver's Travels*, p. 207.

58 *animal rationale*: Swift made the distinction in his September 29, 1725, letter to Alexander Pope.

62 Erasmus . . . argued that the outright condemnation of all falsehood is futile: Erasmus, *Responsio ad Albertum Pium*, cols. 1194–96.

62 "a plague grown to huge proportions": Augustine, "Against Lying," ch. 18, para. 37.

62 officious, jocose, and mischievous lies: Aquinas, *Summa Theologica*, 2.2, ques. 110, art. 4.

63 "the greatest violation of man's duty to himself": Kant, *Ethical Philosophy*, pp. 90–91.

63 "To be truthful (honest) in all declarations": Kant, *Critique of Practical Reason*, p. 347.

63 benevolent motives are easily mixed with less altruistic ones: Bok, p. 212.

68 "It was a noble, a generous, a magnanimous lie": Twain, *Adventures of Tom Sawyer*, p. 298.

69 such sinful untruths as "How nice to see you": Martin, p. 96.

69 "I have a problem and need your advice": Abigail Van Buren, "Dear Abby," in *San Francisco Chronicle*, January 30, 1997, B12.

71 the "lying sessions" of African Americans: Hurston. Zora Neale Hurston researched these tall tales and their tellers in the 1920s.

72 "the lies he told his wife": Boylan, p. 29.

73 "the most self-satisfied class of people": Erasmus, *Praise of Folly*, p. 150.

74 "a Society of Men among us": Swift, *Gulliver's Travels*, p. 215.

74 If ads for Listerine now announced: Allen, p. 130. *Only Yesterday* is an informative and entertaining social history of the 1920s.

74 The "Vitamin O" scam: Park, pp. 46–49. Park discusses this and other fraud masquerading as science in his *Voodoo Science*, a book that should be required reading.

75 since the infancy of photography: Doctored images have, of course, been used for purposes more sinister than relieving people of disposable income. Stalin's propaganda machinery used to make a habit of cutting Communist Party functionaries and other personae non gratae out of pictures after they had been liquidated. Rewriting pictorial history was the name of the game, and anything went, from replacing ex-comrades who had run afoul of Stalin's paranoia with pillars, wood paneling, or a section of the Moscow–Volga canal to adding people to a crowd in order to make a minor rally seem to have been enthusiastically attended. On another page, the U.S. Postal Service's retouching of photographs used for postage stamps, although less sinister, still falls into the category of history rewritten for the sake of an agenda. A notorious example is the 1999 stamp of Jackson Pollock, based on a photograph in a 1941 *Life* magazine article. In the stamp, the cig between the lips of the artist caught in the act of creation, and the curls of smoke surrounding him—which are interestingly contrapuntal to the paint he is dripping onto the canvas on the floor—have been airbrushed out. Quite a few people may have applauded the revision, seeing it the result of the well-founded fear that the original photo glamorizes smoking and furnishes an unpaid ad for the tobacco companies. Others, myself included, see it as an example of patronizing censorship. What it certainly is is the deliberate falsification of a fact, also known as a lie. For a gallery of altered photos in Stalin's Russia, see King.

76 "If, like the truth, falsehood had only one face": Montaigne, p. 31.

78 Father Garnet, the alleged mastermind of the Gunpowder Plot: For Father Garnet's role in the plot and a lucid discussion of equivocation, see Fraser.

79 religious dissenters—Protestants in Catholic countries: For an informative discussion, see Zagorin.

80 "to conceal the truth prudently by means of an evasion": Aquinas, "The Evil of Lying," p. 218.

80 "promise that he will be merciful": *Malleus Maleficarum*, p. 231.

80 burn her "after a certain period": *Malleus Maleficarum*, p. 226.

82 " 'Gracious Heaven!' cried Adeline": Opie, *Adeline Mowbray*, pp. 107–8.

83 "What constitutes lying?": Opie, *Illustrations of Lying*, p. 7.

84 "If you allow yourself to violate truth": Opie, *Illustrations of Lying*, p. 10.

How to Weave, and Sell, a Tangled Web

86 "No one who is not conscious of having a sound memory": Montaigne, p. 30.

90 "possible according to the law of probability or necessity": Aristotle, p. 53.

90 "what has happened is manifestly possible": Aristotle, p. 53.

91 "no reason why some events that have actually happened": Aristotle, p. 54.

91 "probable impossibilities to improbable possibilities": Aristotle, p. 63.

93 "lazy fellows, who neither want to hew nor cut": Müller-Fraureuth, p. 34.

93 "With lies many feed themselves": Müller-Fraureuth, note 113.

94 "there are vain and vagabond men": Homer, p. 213.

94 "that man who under constraint of poverty": Homer, p. 214.

96 "an infinite and endless liar": Shakespeare, *All's Well*, act 3, scene 6, lines 10–11.

96 "but return with an invention": Shakespeare, *All's Well*, act 3, scene 6, lines 97–99.

96 "What shall I say I have done?": Shakespeare, *All's Well*, act 4, scene 1, lines 26–27.

98 Robert Leuci, a New York police officer: Daley, p. 101.

101 "Fenimore Cooper's Literary Offenses": Twain, "Fenimore Cooper," pp. 65–80.

101 "If Cooper had been an observer": Twain, "Fenimore Cooper," pp. 70–71.

102 "a person of quite extraordinary intellect": Twain, "Fenimore Cooper," p. 72.

102 "the eternal laws of Nature have to vacate": Twain, "Fenimore Cooper," pp. 69–70.

103 "If Cooper had any real knowledge": Twain, "Fenimore Cooper," p. 69.

103 "the man who talks corrupt": Twain, "Fenimore Cooper," p. 77.

103 Henri-Désiré Landru is on trial at Versailles: Alberts. The details of the case are found in Alberts' novel *Landru*, in the form of reproduced reports on the trial written by the Paris correspondent of the *Berliner Tageblatt*, a Berlin daily.

105 the consistency is admirable even if the pose is laughable: *L'affaire Landru* has an interesting coda. On tour in 1926, the world-famous clown Grock, for forty years an international star of circus and variety shows, thought he recognized Landru at a banquet in Buenos Aires—this recognition based on a photo he had seen of Landru before his execution. In his memoirs he describes the banquet, given by the Buenos Aires chief of police in Grock's honor. Sitting next to the chief, Grock points out to him the remarkable resemblance between the man opposite them and "you must know whom I mean." The chief does indeed: "Yes, yes, of course, you mean Landru. Well, he is Landru."

Later the chief tells Grock a fascinating story: Landru is living in Argentina on a pension from the French government. The murders were invented by the government to divert attention from certain political events of the day by feeding the public a sensational trial. Another man, made up to look like Landru, had been executed. The chief advises Grock to keep silent about his discovery, advice Grock claims in his 1956 memoirs to have heeded for thirty years.

Snap go the bounds of credibility. Not that governments have not been shown eminently capable of erecting huge screens of gaudy distractions to hide their doings and to lie, forge, cheat, and even murder. But let's compare the two possibilities: In the first, the Buenos Aires chief of police takes advantage of the resemblance of one of his friends to the notorious Landru—a resemblance that had no doubt been noted before—to pull the leg of a famous clown. In the second, a public spectacle was staged by the participants in a massive conspiracy involving government officials, police, prosecutors, a dozen witnesses, jailers, and the executioner. No matter how much we may distrust governments, the first possibility greatly outweighs the second in terms of probability. Add the fact that in the decades that followed not one of the alleged co-conspirators ever stepped forward to point a finger—which would mean that every last one of them took the secret to the grave—and common sense greatly favors a single waggish chief of police.

That Grock believed the man's fantastic story in 1926, when he heard it, and in 1956, when he recorded the event in his memoirs, is nevertheless understandable. Although he was, judging by his memoirs, stupendously oblivious to things unconnected with his engagements and comic routines, he had not spent his life on Mars. From the vantage point of 1956, he could look back upon the monstrous deceptions of the Nazi regime with its genius for propaganda and demagoguery. In 1926, that French debacle, the Dreyfus affair, was still fresh in people's minds. No overwhelming cynicism was required to believe that a government that had engaged in a succession of massive cover-ups involving lies, forgeries, planted documents, and an arrogant disdain for justice—all this in order to avoid embarrassing the army—would be capable of staging a diversion to hide some other embarrassment. Not much more than a decade separate the annulment of Dreyfus' verdict in 1906, fought tooth and claw by right-wing factions, from Landru's arrest in 1919. The government of 1919 was very different from that of 1906. (In fact, Georges Clemenceau, now Premier, had been Dreyfus' greatest champion in the press and in court.) But once an institution's credibility is undermined, distrust tends to move in to stay. Grock, like any skeptical citizen of the world, found it easy to believe that a government beset by problems—the grim economic situation after World War I comes to mind—might try to keep the rabble busy by throwing them a sensationalist bone, in this case the lurid one of an invented butcher of lonely women. That he was most likely wrong where Landru was concerned is less interesting than how ready he was to believe in conspiracy in high places and in lies fed to the populace. Three-quarters of a century later, the majority of U.S. citizens believed that their government was involved in conspiracies. Grock, pp. 151–55.

107 *Never Be Lied To Again*: Lieberman.

108 Whatever clues liars do provide: Paul Ekman points out the difficulties in detecting liars in his thorough study on the subject. Ekman, chs. 4, 5, and 6.

109 "Ha! I like not that": Shakespeare, *Othello*, act 3, scene 3, lines 33–40.

109 "Did Michael Cassio, when you wooed my lady": Shakespeare, *Othello*, act 3, scene 3, lines 96–109.

110 " 'Think, my lord?' ": Shakespeare, *Othello*, act 3, scene 3, lines 110–29.

111 "As I confess it is my nature's plague": Shakespeare, *Othello*, act 3, scene 3, lines 151–59.

111 "By heaven, I'll know thy thoughts": Shakespeare, *Othello*, act 3, scene 3, lines 167–74.

111 "Now I shall have reason": Shakespeare, *Othello*, act 3, scene 3, lines 197–201.

111 "Of her own clime, complexion, and degree": Shakespeare, *Othello*, act 3, scene 3, lines 235–38.

112 "This honest creature doubtless": Shakespeare, *Othello*, act 3, scene 3, lines 247–48.

112 "Trifles light as air": Shakespeare, *Othello*, act 3, scene 3, lines 326–28.

112 "Is't come to this?": Shakespeare, *Othello*, act 3, scene 3, lines 369–80.

113 "O wretched fool": Shakespeare, *Othello*, act 3, scene 3, lines 380–83.

113 "If imputation, and strong circumstances": Shakespeare, *Othello*, act 3, scene 3, lines 411–13.

113 Does Desdemona not have a handkerchief: Shakespeare, *Othello*, act 3, scene 3, lines 439–46.

113 "Now do I see 'tis true": Shakespeare, *Othello*, act 3, scene 3, lines 449–51.

114 " 'Tis done at your request; but let her live": Shakespeare, *Othello*, act 3, scene 3, line 478.

114 "Damn her, lewd minx!": Shakespeare, *Othello*, act 3, scene 3, lines 478–81.

115 "If Cassio do remain": Shakespeare, *Othello*, act 5, scene 1, lines 18–20.

115 "Strangle her in her bed": Shakespeare, *Othello*, act 4, scene 1, lines 202–3.

115 "Good, good, the justice of it pleases": Shakespeare, *Othello*, act 4, scene 1, line 204.

116 "She's like a liar gone to burning hell": Shakespeare, *Othello*, act 5, scene 2, lines 138–64.

117 "You told a lie, an odious, damnèd lie": Shakespeare, *Othello*, act 5, scene 2, lines 187–88.

THE HIGH COST OF LYING

118 "Every time you lie, deceive, or cheat": Poi Dog Pondering, "I've Got My Body," on *Volo Volo*, Columbia compact disc CK 46960.

118 "I hate, detest, and can't bear a lie": Conrad, p. 56.

118 *Generation of Vipers*: Wylie, pp. 19–20. In the eleven years following its publication in 1942, the book sold 180,000 copies. The publishers, Stanley Rinehart and John Farrar, had hoped to sell 4,000. Apparently the

book's teeth-gnashing indictment of America and its institutions struck a chord.

119 "Admitting that perpetual distrust attends": Opie, *Illustrations of Lying*, p. 182.

122 "But not a common thing": The entry is for Sunday, November 10, 1839.

122 "the virtues of the English gentleman": Trevor-Roper, p. 17.

123 the armed services' ceremonial swords: Recruitment ads have been known to exploit this kinship. In the late 1990s, the most impressive recruiting commercial for the U.S. Marines (shown during football playoff games) bludgeoned the viewer with the link to a chivalric tradition. After defeating his foes on a giant chessboard, a knight in shining armor morphed into a marine in dress uniform. In this spectacular example of misrepresentation for the sake of manipulation, the foes struck by the knight's sword vanished into thin air—a distinct improvement over the moaning wounded, dismembered corpses, and other horrors to which a knight was, and a marine is, exposed in battle. If these recruitment pitches work, the Marine Corps must be composed of the most amazing assembly of romantics.

123 some of "the best and the brightest": The conflict between loyalty and truthfulness is brilliantly explored in David Halberstam's *The Best and the Brightest*.

126 "If a person persists in violating his conscience": Baylis, p. 190.

136 "villain enough to have invented & persevered": For a section of the letter and some details about the argument, see Coleridge.

137 "Every violation of truth": Emerson, *Essays*, "Prudence" (First Series, 1841).

141 "In our time, political speech": Orwell, pp. 363, 366.

142 "absolutely essential to our hopes": See Lutz, p. 9. Lutz's read-it-and-weep book *Doublespeak* exposes the widespread use of deliberately misleading language by government, business, and advertisers.

142 Distrust grows with every new discovery: Former Representative Wes Cooley (R., Oregon) is an egregious example of bogus claims. Cooley had a history of shenanigans by the time he listed the bogus qualification "Army, Special Forces, Korea" in the 1994 state voter guide. (Two years' probation, 100 hours of community service, and a fine was the plea agreement, with one of two counts of "lying on official documents" dropped.) See *San Francisco Chronicle*, March 19, 1997, A2. For a look at the slimy underbelly of Wall Street, see Ted C. Fishman's hair-raising essay "Up in Smoke" in *Harper's Magazine*, December 1998, pp. 37–46.

143 "professional writers, most with advanced degrees": "Research Assistance," Catalog 27, p. 1.

143 "THE POPISH PLOT": "Research Assistance," Catalog 27, p. 129, S-42b: 9904.

146 "Their families and friends know": Ekman, p. 56.

146 "*Natural liars* know about their ability": Ekman, pp. 56–57.

LIARS, LIARS, LIARS!

151 "A fantasist and liar": Grafton, pp. 41–42.

151 "I have a decent lad as my tailor": Montaigne, p. 31. Fortunately for this "decent lad," his customer was not Absolute Monarch of France or he might have found his feet put to the fire for his nasty habit: in the same paragraph in which Montaigne uses him as an example of men enslaved by their knack of lying, he offers: "If we recognized the horror and gravity of an untruth, we should more justifiably punish it with fire than any other crime."

151 Pathological lying . . . is lying that is compulsive: See Ford, p. 133.

151 lying is identified as not only a characteristic behavior but the predominant one: Ford and co-workers identify the five specific personality disorders in which lying frequently occurs. Ford, "Lies and Liars."

152 the male-to-female ratio is about four to one: Cadoret.

152 bored by "human life itself": Cleckley, p. 428.

152 "a sort of quasi-life": Cleckley, p. 430.

154 An "addictive and unrelenting narcissism": Beldoch, p. 108.

155 parents who, often, were themselves narcissistically deprived: An insightful discussion of narcissistic disturbance is Alice Miller's *The Drama of the Gifted Child*.

155 A deficiency in serotonin: Ford, p. 142.

156 a significantly higher rate of frontal-lobe dysfunction: Ford. p. 110.

156 a lack of "quality control" for the pseudologue's verbal production: Ford, pp. 135–36.

156 efforts to preserve or create a sense of self: Ford, p. 136.

156 a self-deceptive cover-up of grandiosity: Miller, p. 45.

156 unresolved in the oedipal period of development: Ford, p. 113.

156 persistent and extreme lying in a child: Hare.

157 "The striving for the right to have secrets": Tausk, p. 519.

157 Lying . . . plays a role in the growth of self-regulation: Ford, p. 73.

158 It was as though Hans had told his father: Freud, "Analysis of a Phobia," p. 129.

158 "a number of lies told by well-brought-up children": Freud, "Two Lies," p. 305.

159 "When, later on, she learned to translate ice": Freud, "Two Lies," p. 308.

159 "The sense of guilt that was attached to her excessive fondness": Freud, "Two Lies," pp. 308–9.

160 It thus became "pathogenic": Forrester, pp. 85–86.

160 "It would be a serious mistake": Freud, "Two Lies," p. 309.

160 "People suffering from the kind of grandiosity": Jacoby, pp. 160–61.

DEEP DOWN, I KNEW . . .

162 "It makes sense to ask: 'Do I really love her . . . ' ": Wittgenstein, p. 154e.

162 "It is as if you were running in a race": Champlin, "Self-Deception: A Reflexive Dilemma," p. 283.

162 "On the way I felt hungry": *Alcoholics Anonymous*, p. 36.

163 To convince themselves that they were only normal drinkers: The "proofs" and others are listed in *Alcoholics Anonymous*, p. 31.

165 "What I'm doing is not right, but God will wink His eye": Süskind, pp. 132–33.

166 "did not confess to himself": Eliot, p. 111.

168 "You find yourself seated on a hard chair": What he calls "the familiar philosophical cell" and the situation are introduced by T. S. Champlin in "Self-Deception: A Reflexive Dilemma," pp. 281–83.

169 "You are guilty of self-deception": Champlin, "Self-Deception: A Problem About Autobiography," p. 92.

169 The ability to deceive ourselves: See Palmer.

170 "strains from hard-bound brains": Pope, *Epistle to Dr. Arbuthnot*, lines 176–214.

171 who could be viewed in rags and chains: Michel Foucault offers a captivating exploration of the evolution of the concept of insanity and the treatment of the insane in France during the Age of Reason. In England, the Hospital of St. Mary of Bethlehem (Bedlam in the popular vocabulary) similarly had throngs of visitors for whom viewing the antics of the inmates was much like a visit to the zoo.

172 "Know thyself" is one of the mottoes: Plato, *Protagoras*, 343 b.

172 In a more modern translation: See Robert Fagles' 1982 translation. The earlier quotes are from the 1904 Cambridge edition of *The Tragedies of Sophocles*, translated by Sir Richard C. Jebb.

174 "what we call a *mind*": Hume, p. 200.

174 "fell dead-born from the press": Hume, p. vii.

175 "*Denial* is the ego's way to protect the self": I've culled the mechanisms from a standard college textbook. See Ruch, p. 424.

176 "*Distortion*, which grossly reshapes external reality": These and other ego-defense mechanisms are discussed by Ford, pp. 38–43.

177 Objections can and have been raised: Jeffrey Moussaieff Masson has compellingly attacked the underpinnings of Freudian analysis in several books. See, for instance, his *Against Therapy*.

177 "the essential condition for any kind of self-knowledge": Jung, p. 8.

178 "The effect of projection is to isolate": Jung, pp. 9–10.

178 "whether one is not meddling too much": Jung, pp. 17–19. Jungian analysts tend to not let sleeping dogs lie. According to them, the interplay between conscious and subconscious is conducted through symbols. The conscious uses word logic and the subconscious dream logic, and never the twain shall meet except if we learn to translate the symbols encoded by the latter into the language of the former. ("The truth about your feelings regarding your mother? You can't handle the truth! But you may want to think about the witch that keeps appearing in your dreams.") The Jungian word-association test—the therapist says a word and the subject responds as quickly as possible with a word that comes to his or her mind—is one of the therapist's ways to coax out a patient's "complexes." Hesitation, gesticulation or laughter in response to a word, or repetition of the word, suggests that it addressed a problematic experience, an unconscious complex.

179 "individuals deploy strategies for the achievement of personal whole-ness": Rue, p. 144.

179 an adaptive mechanism by which nondepressed people: L. B. Alloy and L. Y. Abramson, "Judgment of Contingency in Depressed and Nonde-pressed Students: Sadder But Wiser?" *Journal of Experimental Psychology. General* 108:441–85, 1979. The article and other studies on self-deception are cited by Ford, pp. 251–62.

179 "the mentally healthy person appears": S. E. Taylor and J. D. Brown, "Il-lusion and Well-Being: A Social Psychological Perspective on Mental Health," *Psychological Bulletin* (1988) 103:204. Quoted by Ford, p. 253.

180 Even though this myth, like all the others, is a lie: Rue, p. 306.

182 "My conception of you was quite untrue": Augustine, *Confessions*, p. 88.

182 "I wanted to be just as certain of these things": Augustine, *Confessions*, p. 116.

182 "I had known it all along, but I had always pretended": Augustine, *Con-fessions*, p. 169.

182 "I had to make up my mind for myself": Newman, p. 122.

183 "all-sufficient light amid his darkness": Newman, p. 101.

183 "a lifetime of self-delusion": Don Lattin, "The Plant That Moves Their Souls," *San Francisco Chronicle*, March 26, 2000, Zone 3, p. 6.

184 "I was an ardent practicing Catholic": Malcolm Gladwell, "John Rock's Error," *The New Yorker*, March 13, 2000, pp. 52–63.

THE APEX TRUTH METER®

192 In 1915, one of Münsterberg's students: Overviews of the history of the polygraph can be found in Barland and in Reid, pp. 1–3.

193 Thus ended the quest to use scientific lie detection: Fisher, pp. 400–1.

193 By 1984 the results of stipulated lie detection tests: Kleinmuntz, p. 770.

194 The bill authorized 10,000 plus "National Security" screening examina-tions: All numbers are from a report to Senators Goldwater and Nunn, dated December 1985, on the DoD's Training Program for Polygraph Examiners.

195 No instrument that was not "type-approved": California Assembly, Committee on Labor, Employment, and Consumer Affairs, Hearing on Licensing of Polygraph Examiners (San Francisco, 1977), pp. 150–59.

195 Worse, the B&W could, after thirty-three years of use: Guertin.

195 the B&W was advertised: The brochure is appended to the report on the California Assembly's Hearing on Licensing of Polygraph Examiners, pp. 205–8.

196 "a sufficiently reliable method to be the sole determinant": Raskin, p. 97.

196 In a comparison of several well-designed and well-controlled studies: Lykken, "The Case Against Polygraph Testing," p. 124.

196 Their findings: lie detection is unscientific: Kleinmuntz.

197 Still, people have been successfully trained: Gudjonsson.

197 "So, I would not say that the polygraph was the initiating piece": *San Francisco Chronicle*, November 19, 1996, A1, 17.

197 Biting one's tongue or pressing one's toes against the floor: Gudjonsson, p. 129.

198 They had told him to relax—lie detectors didn't work: Ames's claim was mentioned by Robert L. Park in a *New York Times* editorial attacking the practice of polygraph testing and in particular that ordered by Energy Secretary Bill Richardson for Los Alamos National Laboratory in the wake of the alleged passing on of secret information to the Chinese government by one of the laboratory's nuclear weapons scientists. "Liars Never Break a Sweat," Monday, July 12, 1999, Editorial Desk.

199 He persisted in maintaining his innocence: Cimerman.

199 One of them told him that he would have interpreted the charts as "truthful": Lykken, "The Lie Detector and the Law."

199 Fay claimed that after fifteen to twenty minutes: Lykken, *A Tremor in the Blood*, p. 240.

200 "no consensus that polygraph evidence is reliable": Linda Greenhouse, "Justices Find No Inherent Right to Use Lie-Test Evidence in Trial," *The New York Times*, April 1, 1998, A19.

200 Government officials alleged that it was a failed polygraph test: James Risen and Jeff Gerth, "China Spy Suspect Reportedly Tried to Hide Evidence," *The New York Times*, Friday, April 30, 1999, Foreign Desk.

200 Wen Ho Lee, the alleged spy: The case against Lee was dismissed in September 2000 after he pleaded guilty to a single charge of mishandling nuclear secrets. "Nuclear Scientist Set Free in Secrets Case," *The New York Times on the Web*, September 14, 2000.

200 Then, in April 2000, an FBI agent testified: "Scientist Had Passed Polygraph," *San Francisco Chronicle*, August 19, 2000, A1, 4.

200 In the state-of-the-art polygraph: Julie N. Lynem, "San Mateo County to Use Computerized Lie Detectors," *San Francisco Chronicle*, August 17, 1999, A13, 17.

202 Ergo, the truth about the nonembezzlement: For a detailed description of polygraph questioning see, for instance, Reid.

203 ironically, some researchers found the Guilty Knowledge Technique: Ekman, pp. 185–86.

203 "It's as much of a myth as the tooth fairy": Quoted by Susan McCarthy in "The Truth About the Polygraph," Salon.com, 03/02/2000. Park protested the order in an editorial in *The New York Times*. See "Liars Never Break a Sweat," Monday, July 12, 1999, Editorial Desk.

203 *In vino veritas*: Two centuries before Plato the Greek poet Alcaeus' insight was that "wine is a peephole on a man."

203 In the 1961 movie *The Guns of Navarone*: The Alistair MacLean novel by the same name on which the movie is based does not have the drugging episode.

204 In others, therapists were successfully sued: See Yapko.

204 When in 2000 Paul Fray accused Hillary Clinton: "Ex-Clinton Aide: She Said It and She Knows It," FOXNews.com, July 18, 2000.

207 Ekman claims he can teach people: Ekman, pp. 129–30.

207 Bedouins until quite recently made conflicting witnesses: Kleinmuntz, p. 766.

208 Post–World War II Germany: Barland, pp. 77–78.

209 What this frequent encounter with the polygraph: Some names in those headlines: Anita Hill, Caspar Weinberger, O. J. Simpson, Monica Lewinsky.

209 "If they are innocent": Matthew Rose, "British Anglers Carp About Rules That Imply Their Tales Are Fishy," *The Wall Street Journal*, April 30, 1996, B1.

THE ORDEAL

212 "He who seeks to conceal the truth by a lie": Bartlett, p. 88. Bartlett's *Trial by Fire and Water: The Medieval Judicial Ordeal* is an excellent study of all aspects and implications of the medieval ordeal.

213 The eleventh-century church at Canterbury: Southern, p. 263.

213 Anselm suggested the following procedure: Goitein, pp. 56–57.

214 A look at St. Anselm's theological writings: Anselm, pp. 273–79.

214 "an illustration of the fact that great academic reputations": Southern, p. 84.

214 But a detailed history of Laon that includes a thumbnail sketch of Anselm of Laon's life: Devisme.

214 the crowd occasionally lynched on the spot accused heretics: At Soissons in 1114, for instance, condemned heretics were lynched by a crowd while the bishop's court was still discussing the sentence. See Bartlett, p. 23.

215 In the ordeal by boiling water: Other types of ordeals ranged from the small-claims court equivalent of the "trial of the cross" to combat with clubs and shields (and fists, thumbs, and teeth). In the former, two people disagreeing over, say, who owned a piece of property stood at a cross with their arms stretched out to their sides à la crucifixion. The one whose hands sank first was judged to be in the wrong. In the latter ordeal, the vanquished fighter was judged to be the guilty party or the proxy of the guilty party (those incapable of fighting could get a champion to do it for them).

215 "I call to witness the Sun": *Bulfinch's Mythology*, p. 39.

216 ". . . Rough talk flew thick and fast": Sophocles, p. 54.

216 Cunigunda, wife of the emperor Henry II: Bartlett, p. 17.

217 "She put her white hand into the water": Terry, p. 204.

217 "a detestable and wicked custom": Bartlett, pp. 105–6.

217 In Anjou in the 1070s: Bartlett, p. 50.

218 "If you are innocent of this charge": Bartlett, p. 21.

219 "I make a decree, That in every dominion of my kingdom": The parallel conclusion to the story of the Three Holy Children uses an even larger sledgehammer and in the King James Version is hilarious to the modern ear in how it presents Nebuchadnezzar's post-fiery furnace assessment: "Therefore I make a decree, That every people, nation, and language, which speak any thing amiss against the God of Shadrach, Meshach, and Abednego, shall be cut in pieces, and their houses shall be made a dunghill; because there is no other God that can deliver after this sort" (Daniel 3:29).

219 "If a thief is proved guilty of seven thefts": Bartlett, p. 68.

220 "Let all believe in the ordeal": Bartlett, p. 12.

220 "If a woman's husband accuses her of adultery": Compare this with the Old Testament's even more chilling procedure under these circum-

stances: God tells Moses what is to be done if a jealous husband suspects his wife of unfaithfulness but has no proof. He is to take her to the priest, who will pronounce over her a ritual curse promising horrific consequences if she is guilty. Then the priest is to force her to drink "bitter water that causeth the curse." If she is innocent, nothing will happen, but if she is guilty, menstruation will set in and "her belly shall swell and her thigh shall rot" (Numbers 5:13–30). It would seem that any woman with a jealous husband was well advised to stay on the good side of the local priest since he was the one who concocted the "bitter water."

220 "carnal dealings with cattle of any sort": Bartlett, p. 19, n. 17.

220 "O God, the just judge": Bartlett, p. 1, n. 1.

221 Teeth bared, eyes upturned: The illustration is in the MS Lambach Cml. LXXIII, the twelfth-century *Rituale Lambacense*, fo. 72^r (trial by fire).

222 According to one ecclesiastical critic: The critic in question was Hugh of Saint-Victor, a mystic St. Thomas Aquinas called one of his teachers. See Leitmaier, p. 67.

222 In 943, the tale goes: Bartlett, p. 15 and n. 5.

224 If an accused witch will not confess: *Malleus Maleficarum*, p. 231.

225 "The judicial process advocated in the *Malleus*": Anglo, p. 28.

225 Volunteering to pass through fire: Bartlett, p. 22 and n. 32.

225 "ordeal by hot iron or water is illicit": Aquinas, *Summa Theologica*, 2.2.95.8.

225 On September 15, 1692, near Fairfield, Connecticut: Smith-Booth, p. 70.

GENERALS, GREEKS, AND OTHER LIARS

229 "In wartime, truth is so precious": Winston S. Churchill, *The Second World War*, vol. V (1952), p. 338. Quoted in Howard, p. 107.

231 "The C.O.S. Committee went into the whole question": Montagu, pp. 52–53.

232 The fortuitous interception of Nye's letter: See Howard, p. 92. Another sign of the success of Operation Mincemeat, pointed out by Montagu in *The Man Who Never Was*, was that the enemy's forces and minefields were concentrated on the western and northern side of Sicily to defend against an anticipated diversionary assault during the invasion of Sardinia or a genuine assault after that invasion.

233 "The genuineness of the captured documents is above suspicion" ["*Die Echtheit der erbeuteten Dokumente steht außer Zweifel*"]: Montagu, p. 128, plates 4 and 5.

235 "We decided to assume that an officer who carried": Montagu, pp. 69–70.

236 Thus Operation Purple Whales was a series of red herrings: The information on the various operations and agents is in Howard, passim.

238 He consents to do so and to "hide nothing of the truth": All quotes are from Mandelbaum.

239 " '. . . by the High Ones' ": Mandelbaum, p. 34, lines 199–204.

240 " 'You everlasting fires' ": Mandelbaum, p. 34, lines 216–23.

240 " 'I tell the truth and so repay you fully' ": Mandelbaum, p. 35, line 227.

240 " 'Such was the art of perjured Sinon' ": Mandelbaum, p. 36, lines 276–78.

241 Virgil drew on accounts of the Trojan War: See Arthur S. Way's Introduction to Quintus Smyrnaeus, *The Fall of Troy*, p. vi.

241 "Some brave man, unknown of any in Troy": Quintus Smyrnaeus, Book XII, p. 505.

242 To "the wise and prudent man": Quintus Smyrnaeus, Book XIV, p. 575.

243 the Chinese strategist who wrote under that name: Various opinions concerning authorship are sketched by Samuel B. Griffith in his Introduction to Sun Tzu's *The Art of War*. According to some scholars, one Sun Pin, a military strategist living in the fourth century B.C. and writing around 341 B.C., was the author. The conjecture is that Sun Pin for the sake of prestige used the name of Sun Tzu, allegedly a famous general who lived a century and a half earlier.

243 "All warfare is based on deception": Sun Tzu, p. 66.

243 "The enemy must not know where I intend to give battle": Sun Tzu, p. 98.

243 China's Taiping Rebellion (1851–64): See Samuel B. Griffith's essay on Sun Tzu and Mao Zedong, in Sun Tzu, *The Art of War*, pp. 45–46.

244 "In our dynasty Chief of Staff Ts'ao once pardoned": Sun Tzu, *The Art of War*, p. 146.

245 An Egyptian text from the fifteenth century B.C.: See Smith, p. 127b.

246 "many deception-related skills": *Battlefield Deception*, p. 1-0.

246 "create the illusion of strength where weakness exists": *Battlefield Deception*, p. 1-2.

247 The story is rich in marvels and incidents: The *Mahābhārata* contains many episodes unconnected with the main theme and large sections concerned with teachings on ethics, polity, or philosophy—the most celebrated of those being the *Bhagavad-Gita*. The narrative in which the main theme unfolds occupies about 4,000 of the total of 88,000 verses that appear in the epic's shortest recension.

248 "Hence you must put aside fair means": The episode of "the contrivance" by means of which the Pāṇḍavas are victorious is described in the *Mahābhārata*, pp. 157–59.

250 "If I had not adopted such deceitful ways": *Mahābhārata*, p. 175.

251 "after he had uttered that lie": *Mahābhārata*, p. 158.

THE BRIAR PATCH REVISITED

255 Thus, in an instance of ethnic cleansing: The man was an ethnic Albanian among a group of fellow villagers executed by paramilitary Serbs. Reported by Peter Finn, *Washington Post*. See "A Witness to Chilling Brutality," *San Francisco Examiner*, April 18, 1999, A1,4.

255 Morris found himself surrounded by an angry mob: See Cooper, pp. 43–44. W. B. Carnochan, a descendant of Morris, has told me that the story is considered apocryphal by his family.

255 "retained a cynically aristocratic view": Cooper, p. 43.

258 Stories about him circulated in the fourteenth and fifteenth centuries: The title of the 1515 Strasbourg edition was *Ein kurtzweilig Lesen von Dil Ulenspiegel*.

259 Till claims that his insides were as much in need of cleansing as his outside: Oppenheimer, pp. 172–74.

262 "I've decided not to spring on Pseudolus": Plautus, p. 147.

262 Thucydides records the desertion of tens of thousands: Thucydides, Book Seven, paras. 27 and 75 (pp. 494 and 528 in the Penguin edition).

263 They chose to carry their own gear rather than entrust it: Thucydides, Book Seven, para. 75 (p. 528 in the Penguin edition).

264 He had an ear for the dialect: See the Introduction by Hemenway to Harris, *Uncle Remus*.

265 "John-Massa" anecdotes were collected after the Civil War: See, for instance, Anderson or Hurston.

265 Ole Massa in one tale tells John that he is God: Hurston, pp. 75–78.

265 Ole Massa runs away so fast it takes an express train: Hurston, pp. 88–90.

265 "the only weapon of self defense that I could use": Osofsky, p. 66.

266 Women disguised themselves as men: Osofsky, p. 28.

266 "Oh yes," Brown lied, "I have been in Ohio": Osofsky, p. 214.

266 "This incident shows how it is that slavery makes its victims lying": Osofsky, p. 200.

266 "Deceit in a slave is only a slight reflex": Osofsky, p. 60.

267 Some told their slaves about the awful fate: Osofsky, p. 18.

267 In response, Chinese immigrants bought false identity papers: For an account of one Chinese immigrant family's secret life see Kimberly Chun, "Secrets & Lies," *San Francisco Chronicle*, October 23, 1998, PN 1, 5.

268 "For a clever man, nothing is easier": Huxley, *The Devils of Loudun*, p. 44.

268 Your state will not approve a proposed hate-crime law? . . . Your school's security is too lax?: These attempts to change the world were made in 1998 by, respectively, a lesbian living in South Carolina and a teacher in West Virginia. *San Francisco Chronicle*, July 16, 1998, A2.

269 Much of this "fayninge and counterfeyting": All of these instances were reported by Charles Wriothesley in his Tudor chronicles. See Jones.

270 "To succeed in anything one had to be sly": Moynahan, p. 221.

270 "Inequality before the law relieves us of the obligation": Libera, p. 249.

270 In 1997, a sixty-three-year-old woman gave birth: Rick Weiss, "Baby Born to Mom, 63—Likely World Record," *Washington Post*. In *San Francisco Chronicle*, April 24, 1997, A1, 17.

271 In a 1999 nationwide survey of United States physicians: "Doctors OK with Lying to Insurance Companies," *Los Angeles Times*. In *San Francisco Chronicle*, October 25, 1999, A3.

EVEN EDUCATED FLIES DO IT

273 *Thecla togarna*: The drawing is in Edmunds, p. 177, and was redrawn by Edmunds from a painting in W. Wickler, *Mimicry in Plants and Animals* (London: Weidenfeld & Nicolson, 1968), fig. 15.

274 While language is enormously important: In his *How the Mind Works*, Steven Pinker writes: "While the brains of monkeys and apes are subtly asymmetrical, the human brain, especially in the areas devoted to language, is so lopsided that the two hemispheres can be distinguished by shape in [a] jar." New York: W. W. Norton, 1997, p. 184.

274 "I have an artificial minnow": Quoted by Gould, p. 35.

274 Nature's own compleat angler is the anglerfish: Gould, pp. 35–36.

275 Brazil has the matamata: The matamata and the alligator snapper are discussed by Cloudsley-Thompson in his highly informative and charmingly written book *Tooth and Claw*, p. 41.

275 "Insects often resemble for the sake of protection": Darwin, pp. 283–84.

276 A fake head painted on the tip of its rear wing: Edmunds, p. 177.

277 "resemblances in external appearance": Cloudsley-Thompson, p. 140.

278 The preponderance of the unpalatable "model": Cloudsley-Thompson, pp. 140–41.

278 The caterpillar of one large tropical American sphinx moth: Cloudsley-Thompson, p. 157. See also the color illustration on plate 7b in Edmunds.

279 Mertensian mimicry, named after R. Mertens: Cloudsley-Thompson, pp. 152–54.

280 It conceals itself in vegetation but raises its rear end: Cloudsley-Thompson, p. 41. Regarding the bird tricked into perdition by the anus-distending mongoose, the reader may agree with a friend of mine who, when I told him of this stratagem, opined that "anyone who can't tell an asshole from a fig is too stupid to live."

280 The rare American zone-tailed hawk: Cloudsley-Thompson, pp. 154–55.

280 But the female of one species, *Photuris*: Cloudsley-Thompson, pp. 154–55.

281 "When the male wasp lands on the female dummy": Dawkins, p. 261.

281 Darwin used the example of the hen who ruffles her feathers: Darwin, p. 256.

282 The Brazilian toad *Physalaemus nattereri*: Edmunds, see photo on p. 170.

283 Some beetles, bugs, grasshoppers, and other insects: Edmunds, pp. 172–73.

283 Other birds . . . will creep along on the ground: One such make-believe mammal is the dunlin (*Calidris alpina*). See Edmunds, p. 174.

283 "The chief difficulty in resembling a leaf": Cloudsley-Thompson, p. 43.

284 *Sphex argentatus . . . Bembix sayi . . . Sphex flammitrichus*: Cloudsley-Thompson, pp. 240–42.

284 the deceptive behavior of certain tropical spiders: Cloudsley-Thompson, p. 143.

286 even "animals low in the scale of nature": Darwin, p. 318.

286 Byrne uses these concepts to differentiate: Byrne, pp. 120–21.

287 "Yes, the agent intended a free lunch": Byrne, p. 120.

289 He observed a young baboon, Paul: Byrne, pp. 124–25.

290 On one occasion a female infant chimpanzee began to groom him: Byrne, p. 131.

290 One chimpanzee, Belle, was shown food: The observation was made by E. E. Menzel in 1974. It is described by Byrne, p. 132.

291 Field researchers in Africa have observed male vervet monkeys: Keay Davidson, "Animals Chatting Amongst Themselves?" *San Francisco Examiner*, April 13, 1997, C5.

291 the chimpanzee lineage separated from that of humans: For a lucid discussion of how evolutionary history can be reconstructed, see Byrne, pp. 9–30.

Bibliography

Aeschylus. *Prometheus Bound.* E. H. Plumptre, trans. In *Nine Greek Dramas by Aeschylus, Sophocles, Euripides and Aristophanes.* Charles W. Eliot, ed. New York: P. F. Collier & Son, 1909. 156–94.

Alberts, Jürgen. *Landru.* Stuttgart: Klett-Cotta, 1987.

Alcoholics Anonymous. 3rd ed. New York: Alcoholics Anonymous World Services, 1976.

Allen, Frederick Lewis. *Only Yesterday: An Informal History of the 1920's.* New York: John Wiley & Sons, 1997.

Alter, Robert. *Genesis: Translation and Commentary.* New York: W. W. Norton, 1996.

Anderson, John Q. "Old John and the Master." *Southern Folklore Quarterly* 25 (1961): 195–96.

Anglo, Sydney. "The Malleus Maleficarum." In *The Damned Art: Essays in the Literature of Witchcraft.* Sydney Anglo, ed. London: Routledge & Kegan Paul, 1977.

Anselm, St. *Cur Deus Homo.* Chapter XVIII(a) in *St. Anselm.* Sidney Norton Deane, trans. and intro. Chicago: Open Court, 1939.

Aquinas, Thomas. "The Evil of Lying," in *Summa of Theology.* In *The Pocket Aquinas.* Vernon J. Bourke, ed. New York: Washington Square Press, 1968. 218.

———. *Summa Theologica.* Literally translated by Fathers of the English Dominican Province. London: Burns, Oates & Washbourne, 1922.

Aristotle. *Poetics.* In *Critical Theory Since Plato.* Hazard Adams, ed. New York: Harcourt Brace Jovanovich, 1971. 48–66. Reprinted from S. H. Butcher, trans. *Aristotle's Theory of Poetry and Fine Art,* 4th ed. New York: Dover Publications, 1955.

Arnott, Kathleen. *African Myths and Legends*. New York: Henry Z. Walck, 1963.

Augustine, St. "Against Lying." *Treatises on Various Subjects*. Roy J. Deferrari, ed. *The Fathers of the Church*, vol. 16. Washington: Catholic University of America Press, 1952.

——. *Confessions*. R. S. Pine-Coffin, trans. and intro. Harmondsworth, Middlesex, England, and New York: Penguin Books, 1981.

Barland, Gordon H. "The Polygraph Test in the USA and Elsewhere." *The Polygraph Test: Lies, Truth and Science*. Anthony Gale, ed. London: Sage Publications, 1988. 73–95.

Bartlett, Robert. *Trial by Fire and Water: The Medieval Judicial Ordeal*. Oxford: Clarendon Press, 1990.

Battlefield Deception. Field Manual No. 90-2. Headquarters, Department of the Army, Washington, D.C., October 1988.

Baylis, Charles A. "Conscience." *The Encyclopedia of Philosophy*. New York: Macmillan and The Free Press, 1967, vol. 2.

Beldoch, Michael. "The Therapeutic as Narcissist," in *Psychological Man*. Robert Boyers, ed. New York: Harper & Row, 1975. 105–23.

Bok, Sissela. *Lying: Moral Choice in Public and Private Life*. New York: Vintage Books, 1989.

Boylan, Roger. *Killoyle*. Normal, Ill.: Dalkey Archive Press, 1997.

Bulfinch's Mythology. New York and Avenel, N.J.: Gramercy Books, 1979.

Bulgakov, Mikhail. *The Master and Margarita*. Mirra Ginsburg, trans. New York: Grove Press, 1967.

Byrne, Richard. *The Thinking Ape: Evolutionary Origins of Intelligence*. Oxford: Oxford University Press, 1995.

Cadoret, Remi J. "Epidemiology of Antisocial Personality." In *Unmasking the Psychopath: Antisocial Personality and Related Syndromes*. W. H. Reid, D. Dorr, J. I. Walker, et al., eds. New York: W. W. Norton, 1986. 28–44.

Champlin, T. S. "Self-Deception: A Problem About Autobiography, II." In *The Aristotelian Society*, supplementary vol. 53 (1979): 77–94.

——. "Self-Deception: A Reflexive Dilemma." *Philosophy: The Journal of the Royal Institute of Philosophy* (1977): 281–99.

Cimerman, Adrian. "The Fay Case." *Criminal Defense* (May–June 1981):8:3, 7–10.

Cleckley, Hervey. *The Mask of Sanity*. 4th ed. St. Louis: Mosby, 1964.

Cloudsley-Thompson, J. L. *Tooth and Claw: Defensive Strategies in the Animal World*. London: J. M. Dent & Sons, 1980.

Coleridge, Samuel Taylor. Letter to William Wordsworth, May 4, 1812. Excerpt in *The Oxford Book of Friendship*. D. J. Enright and David Rawlinson, eds. Oxford: Oxford University Press, 1991. 300–1.

Conrad, Joseph. *Heart of Darkness*. In *Tales of Land and Sea*. William McFee, intro. Garden City, New York: Hanover House, 1953.

Cooper, Duff. *Talleyrand*. New York: Fromm International, 1986.

Daley, Robert. *Prince of the City*. New York: Berkley Books, 1981.

Darwin, Charles. *The Origin of Species by Means of Natural Selection, or, The Preservation of Favored Races in the Struggle for Life*. New York: Random House, 1993.

Dawkins, Richard. *Climbing Mount Improbable.* New York: W. W. Norton, 1996.

Devisme, J.-F.-L. *Histoire de la Ville de Laon.* Laon, 1822.

Dictionary of Deities and Demons in the Bible. Karel van der Toorn, Bob Becking, and Pieter W. van der Horst, eds. 2nd ed. Leiden: Brill, 1998.

Edmunds, Malcolm. *Defence in Animals: A Survey of Anti-predator Defences.* Harlow, Essex, England: Longman, 1974.

Ekman, Paul. *Telling Lies: Clues to Deceit in the Marketplace, Politics, and Marriage.* New York: W. W. Norton, 1992.

The Elder Edda. See Terry, Patricia, trans.

Eliot, George. *Middlemarch.* J. W. Harvey, intro. Harmondsworth, Middlesex, England: Penguin Books, 1979.

Erasmus. *Responsio ad Albertum Pium.* In *Opera Omnia,* vol. 9. Leiden, 1706; reprinted Hildesheim, Germany, 1962.

———. *Praise of Folly and Letter to Martin Dorp 1515.* Betty Radice, trans. A. H. T. Levi, intro. Harmondsworth, Middlesex, England: Penguin Books, 1971.

Eulenspiegel, Till. See Oppenheimer.

Fisher, Jim. *The Lindbergh Case.* New Brunswick, N.J.: Rutgers University Press, 1994.

Ford, Charles V. *Lies! Lies! Lies!!!: The Psychology of Deceit.* Washington, D.C.: American Psychiatric Press, 1996.

———, Brian H. King, and Marc H. Hollender. "Lies and Liars: Psychiatric Aspects of Prevarication." *American Journal of Psychiatry* 145 (May 1988): 554–62.

Forrester, John. *Truth Games: Lies, Money, and Psychoanalysis.* Cambridge, Mass.: Harvard University Press, 1997.

Foucault, Michel. *Madness and Civilization: A History of Insanity in the Age of Reason.* Richard Howard, trans. New York: Vintage Books, 1973.

Fraser, Antonia. *Faith and Treason: The Story of the Gunpowder Plot.* New York: Nan A. Talese, Doubleday, 1996.

Frazer, James George. *The Golden Bough: A Study in Magic and Religion.* 1 vol., abridged ed. New York: Macmillan, 1948.

Freud, Sigmund. "Analysis of a Phobia in a Five-Year-Old Boy." In vol. 10 of *The Standard Edition of the Complete Psychological Works of Sigmund Freud.* James Strachey, ed. London: The Hogarth Press and the Institute of Psychoanalysis (1953–74). 102–29.

———. "Two Lies Told by Children." In vol. 12 of *The Standard Edition of the Complete Psychological Works of Sigmund Freud.* James Strachey, ed. London: The Hogarth Press and the Institute of Psychoanalysis (1953–74). 305–9.

Gale, Anthony, ed. *The Polygraph Test: Lies, Truth and Science.* London: Sage Publications, 1988.

Goitein, H. *Primitive Ordeal and Modern Law.* London: Allen and Unwin, 1923.

Gould, Stephen Jay. *The Panda's Thumb: More Reflections in Natural History.* New York: W. W. Norton, 1980.

Grafton, Anthony. *Forgers and Critics: Creativity and Duplicity in Western Scholarship.* Princeton, N.J.: Princeton University Press, 1990.

Grock. *Grock: King of Clowns.* Basil Creighton, trans. London: Methuen, 1957.

Gudjonsson, Gisli H. "How to Defeat the Polygraph Test." In *The Polygraph Test: Lies, Truth and Science.* Anthony Gale, ed. London: Sage Publications, 1988, 126–36.

Guertin, Wilson H., and Paul L. Wilhelm. "A Statistical Analysis of the Electrodermal Response Employed in Lie Detection." *Journal of General Psychology* 51 (1954): 153–59.

Halberstam, David. *The Best and the Brightest.* New York: Random House, 1969.

Hare, R. D., A. E. Forth, and S. D. Hart. "The Psychopath as Prototype for Pathological Lying and Deception." In *Credibility Assessment.* John C. Yuille, ed. Dordrecht, Netherlands: Kluwer Academic Publications, 1989. 25–49.

Harris, Joel Chandler. *Uncle Remus, His Songs and His Sayings.* Robert Hemenway, intro. New York: Penguin Books, 1982.

Hawley, John Stratton. *Krishna, the Butter Thief.* Princeton, N.J.: Princeton University Press, 1983.

Hendel, R. S. See *Dictionary of Deities.* 744–47.

Hesiod. *The Works and Days, Theogony, The Shield of Herakles.* Richmond Lattimore, trans. Ann Arbor: University of Michigan Press, 1991.

Homer. *The Odyssee. The Odyssee of Homer.* Richmond Lattimore, trans. New York: Harper & Row, 1975.

The Homeric Hymn to Hermes. Lewis Hyde, trans. In his *Trickster Makes This World: Mischief, Myth, and Art*, Appendix I. New York: Farrar, Straus and Giroux, 1998. 317–31.

Howard, Michael. *Strategic Deception in the Second World War.* New York: W. W. Norton, 1995.

Hume, David. *A Treatise of Human Nature.* A. D. Lindsay, intro. 2 vols. London: J. M. Dent & Sons, and New York: E. P. Dutton, 1968.

Hurston, Zora Neale. *Mules and Men.* Bloomington: Indiana University Press, 1978.

Huxley, Aldous. *Antic Hay.* Normal, Ill.: Dalkey Archive Press, 1997.

———. *The Devils of Loudun.* New York: Carroll & Graf, 1996.

Hyde, Lewis. *Trickster Makes This World: Mischief, Myth, and Art.* New York: Farrar, Straus and Giroux, 1998.

The Interpreter's One-Volume Commentary on the Bible. Charles M. Laymon, ed. Nashville, Tenn.: Abingdon Press, 1971.

Jacoby, Mario. *Individuation and Narcissism: The Psychology of Self in Jung and Kohut.* Myron Gubitz and Françoise O'Kane (in collaboration with the author), trans. London: Routledge, 1991.

Jones, Michael. "Theatrical History in the *Croxton Play of the Sacrament.*" *ELH* 66 (1999): 223–60.

Jung, C. G. *Psyche and Symbol: Selections of Writings of C. G. Jung.* From *The Collected Works of C. G. Jung*, vols. 8, 9, 11, 13, 18, Bollingen Series XX. R. F. C. Hull, trans. Violet S. deLaszlo, ed. Princeton, N.J.: Princeton University Press, 1991.

Kant, Immanuel. *Critique of Practical Reason and Other Writings in Moral Philosophy.* Lewis White Beck, ed. and trans. Chicago: University of Chicago Press, 1949.

———. *Ethical Philosophy. Metaphysical Principles of Virtue.* James W. Ellington, trans. Indianapolis, Ind., and Cambridge, Mass.: Hackett Publishing Co., 1983.

Kee, Howard Clark. "The Gospel According to Matthew." In *The Interpreter's One-Volume Commentary on the Bible.* Charles M. Laymon, ed. Nashville, Tenn.: Abingdon Press, 1971. 609–43.

King, David. *The Commissar Vanishes: The Falsification of Photographs and Art in Stalin's Russia.* New York: Metropolitan Books, 1997.

Kleinmuntz, Benjamin, and Julian J. Szucko. "Lie Detection in Ancient and Modern Times: A Call for Contemporary Scientific Study." *American Psychologist* 39 (1984): 766–76.

The Larousse Encyclopedia of Mythology. Richard Aldrington and Delano Ames, trans. London: Chancellor Press, 1996.

Leeming, David, and Jake Page. *The Mythology of Native North America.* Norman: University of Oklahoma Press, 1998.

Leitmaier, Charlotte. *Die Kirche und die Gottesurteile* [*The Church and the Ordeals*]. Vienna, Herold: 1952.

Libera, Antoni. *Madame.* Agnieszka Kolakowska, trans. New York: Farrar, Straus and Giroux, 2000.

Lieberman, David J. *Never Be Lied To Again: How to Get the Truth in 5 Minutes or Less in Any Conversation or Situation.* New York: St. Martin's Press, 1998.

Luther, Martin. *A Commentary on St. Paul's Epistle to the Galatians.* Philadelphia, 1875.

Lutz, William. *Doublespeak: From "Revenue Enhancement" to "Terminal Living": How Government, Business, Advertisers, and Others Use Language to Deceive You.* New York: Harper & Row, 1989.

Lykken, David T. "The Case Against Polygraph Testing." In *The Polygraph Test: Lies, Truth and Science.* Anthony Gale, ed. London: Sage Publications, 1988. 111–25.

———. "The Lie Detector and the Law." *Criminal Defense* (May–June 1981): 8: 3, 19–27.

———. *A Tremor in the Blood: Uses and Abuses of the Lie Detector.* New York: McGraw-Hill, 1981.

The Mahābhārata: An English Version Based on Selected Verses. Chakravarthi V. Narasimhan, trans. New York: Columbia University Press, 1998.

The Malleus Maleficarum of Heinrich Kramer and James Sprenger. The Rev. Montague Summers, ed. New York: Dover Publications, 1971. Originally published by John Rodker, London, 1928.

Mandelbaum, Allen, trans. *The Aeneid of Virgil.* New York: Bantam Books, 1981.

Marks, John H. "The Book of Genesis." In *The Interpreter's One-Volume Commentary on the Bible.* Charles M. Laymon, ed. Nashville, Tenn.: Abingdon Press, 1971. 1–32.

Martin, Judith. *Miss Manners Rescues Civilization.* New York: Crown, 1996.

Masson, Jeffrey Moussaieff. *Against Therapy: Emotional Tyranny and the Myth of Psychological Healing.* New York: Atheneum, 1988.

McLeish, Kenneth. *Myth: Myths and Legends of the World Explored.* New York: Facts on File, 1996.

Miller, Alice. *The Drama of the Gifted Child: The Search for the True Self.* Ruth
    Ward, trans. New York: Basic Books, 1990.

Montagu, Ewen. *The Man Who Never Was.* Philadelphia: J. B. Lippincott,
    1954.

Montaigne, Michel de. *Essays.* J. M. Cohen, trans. and intro. Harmondsworth,
    Middlesex, England: Penguin Books, 1978.

Moynahan, Brian. *The Russian Century: A History of the Last Hundred Years.*
    New York: Random House, 1994.

Müller-Fraureuth, Carl. *Die deutschen Lügendichtungen bis auf Münchhausen*
    [*German Lying Fiction Up to Münchhausen*]. Hildesheim, Germany:
    Georg Olms, 1965. Reprinted from the 1881 edition.

Newman, John Henry (Cardinal). *Apologia pro Vita Sua.* London: J. M. Dent
    & Sons, and New York: E. P. Dutton, 1927.

Opie, Amelia. *Adeline Mowbray, or the Mother and Daughter.* London: Long-
    man, 1805. Vol. 3.

———. *Illustrations of Lying, in All Its Branches.* Hartford, Conn.: Silas Andrus,
    1827.

Oppenheimer, Paul, trans. *A Pleasant Vintage of Till Eulenspiegel.* Middletown,
    Conn.: Wesleyan University Press, 1972.

Orwell, George. "Politics and the English Language." In *The Orwell Reader:
    Fiction, Essays, and Reportage by George Orwell*, Richard H. Rovere, intro.
    New York: Harcourt, Brace, 1959. 355–66.

Osofsky, Gilbert, ed. *Puttin' On Ole Massa: The Slave Narratives of Henry Bibb,
    William Wells Brown, and Solomon Northup.* New York: Harper & Row,
    1969.

The Oxford Book of Friendship. D. J. Enright and David Rawlinson, eds. Ox-
    ford: Oxford University Press, 1991.

The Oxford Companion to the Bible. Bruce M. Metzger and Michael D. Coogan,
    eds. Oxford: Oxford University Press, 1993.

The Oxford English Dictionary, The Compact Edition. 3 vols. Oxford: Oxford
    University Press, 1980.

Palmer, Anthony. "Self-Deception: A Problem About Autobiography, I." In
    The Aristotelian Society, supplementary vol. 53 (1979): 61–76.

Park, Robert L. *Voodoo Science: The Road from Foolishness to Fraud.* Oxford: Ox-
    ford University Press, 2000.

Pausanias. *Guide to Greece.* Peter Levi, trans. and intro. 2 vols. London: Pen-
    guin Books, 1971.

Plato. *The Republic.* Desmond Lee, trans. and intro. 2nd ed. (revised). Har-
    mondsworth, Middlesex, England: Penguin Books, 1980.

Plautus. *Pseudolus.* In *The Menaechmus Twins and Other Plays.* Lionel Casson,
    trans. and ed. New York: W. W. Norton, 1971.

Quintus Smyrnaeus, *The Fall of Troy.* Arthur S. Way, trans. and intro. London:
    William Heinemann, and New York: Macmillan, 1913.

Raskin, David C. "Does Science Support Polygraph Testing?" In *The Poly-
    graph Test: Lies, Truth and Science.* Anthony Gale, ed. London: Sage Pub-
    lications, 1988. 96–110.

Reid, John E., and Fred E. Inbau. *Truth and Deception: The Polygraph ("Lie-
    Detection") Technique.* Baltimore: Williams & Wilkins, 1966.

Ruch, Floyd L., and Philip G. Zimbardo. *Psychology and Life*, 8th ed. Glenville, Ill.: Scott, Foresman, 1971.

Rue, Loyal. *By the Grace of Guile: The Role of Deception in Natural History and Human Affairs*. Oxford: Oxford University Press, 1994.

Russell, Jeffrey Burton. *Lucifer: The Devil in the Middle Ages*. Ithaca, N.Y.: Cornell University Press, 1984.

Scot, Reginald. *The Discoverie of Witchcraft by Reginald Scot: with an introduction by the Rev. Montague Summers*. Mineola, N.Y.: Dover Publications, 1972. Unabridged and unaltered republication of the work originally published in Great Britain by John Rodker in 1930.

Shakespeare, William. *All's Well That Ends Well*. In *The Complete Oxford Shakespeare*, 3 vols. Vol. 2: *Comedies*. Stanley Wells, Gary Taylor, John Jowett, and William Montgomery, eds. Oxford: Oxford University Press, 1987.

———. *Othello*. In *The Complete Oxford Shakespeare*, 3 vols. Vol. 3: *Tragedies*. Stanley Wells, Gary Taylor, John Jowett, and William Montgomery, eds. Oxford: Oxford University Press, 1987.

Smith, Robert Houston. "The Book of Joshua." In *The Interpreter's One-Volume Commentary on the Bible*. Charles M. Laymon, ed. Nashville: Abingdon Press, 1971. 122–34.

Smith-Booth, Salley. *The Witches of Early America*. New York: Hastings House, 1975.

Sophocles. *Antigone. Sophocles: The Three Theban Plays*. Robert Fagles, trans. New York: The Viking Press, 1982.

Southern, R. W. *Saint Anselm and His Biographer: A Study of Monastic Life and Thought 1059–c. 1130*. Cambridge: Cambridge University Press, 1963.

Sun Tzu. *The Art of War*. Samuel B. Griffith, trans. Oxford: Oxford University Press, 1963.

Süskind, Patrick. *Perfume*. John E. Woods, trans. New York: Washington Square Press, 1991.

Swift, Jonathan. *A Tale of a Tub*. In *The Writings of Jonathan Swift*. Robert A. Greenberg and William Bowman Piper, eds. New York: W. W. Norton, 1973.

———. *Gulliver's Travels*. In *The Writings of Jonathan Swift*. Robert A. Greenberg and William Bowman Piper, eds. New York: W. W. Norton, 1973.

Tausk, V. "On the Origin of the 'Influencing Machine' in Schizophrenia." *Psychoanalytical Quarterly* (1933) 2: 519–56.

Terry, Patricia, trans. "The Third Lay of Gudrun." *Poems of the Vikings: The Elder Edda*. Indianapolis: Bobbs-Merrill, 1969.

Thucydides. *The Peloponnesian War*. Rex Warner, trans. Harmondsworth, Middlesex, England: Penguin Books, 1980.

Trevor-Roper, Hugh. *The Hermit of Peking: The Hidden Life of Sir Edmund Backhouse*. New York: Fromm International, 1986.

Twain, Mark. "Fenimore Cooper's Literary Offenses." In *Mark Twain on Writing and Publishing*. New York: Book-of-the-Month Club, 1994. 65–80.

———. *The Adventures of Tom Sawyer*. New York: Grosset & Dunlap, 1946.

Uncle Remus. See Harris.

Virgil. *The Aeneid*. See Mandelbaum.

Williams, Charles. *Witchcraft*. Cleveland and New York: Meridian Books, 1968.

Wittgenstein, Ludwig. *Philosophical Investigations*, 2nd ed. G. E. M. Anscombe, trans. Oxford: Basil Blackwell, 1958.

Wylie, Philip. *Generation of Vipers*. Normal, Ill.: Dalkey Archive Press, 1996.

Yapko, Michael D. "Repressed Memories." In "Year in Review 1994: Health and Disease: Special Report," *Encyclopaedia Britannica, 2000*.

Young, Jean I. *The Prose Edda of Snorri Sturluson*. Berkeley: University of California Press, 1966.

Zagorin, Perez. *Ways of Lying: Dissimulation, Persecution, and Conformity in Early Modern Europe*. Cambridge, Mass.: Harvard University Press, 1990.

Acknowledgments

Now and then a book may be written without the influence or help of those in contact with the writer. This book is not such a one. I'm indebted to a great many people for it and for the shape it took. John O'Brien, of the *Review of Contemporary Fiction*, suggested I turn an intended fifty-page satire on lying into a treatise on deception (and owes me four years of my life as a result). Thomas Thornton gave me astute feedback the moment I had finished a chapter or section. Both are much-valued friends. David Lougee was indefatigable in placing useful articles in my mailbox. He played the practical joke of the ages on me with respect to the book, and I strongly advise him to keep looking over his shoulder. Jenny Offill suggested the book to her editor. I cannot thank her enough, and I forgive her for having written the novel I'd give my eyeteeth to call my own. To the late Ned Polsky I owe the renewed awareness—after a decade of writing fiction—that scholarly writing can entertain as well as inform.

Mary McDevitt gave me several useful leads, Michael Jones provided an anecdote exactly when I needed it—both are colleagues at Stanford University's School of Engineering without whom work there would be considerably duller, and the same is true of Midge Eisele. Boyd Murphy's enthusiasm for my writing is in its third decade and I deeply appreciate his cheerful encouragement and friendship. W. B. Carnochan has been unstinting in his support throughout the years, and Barbara Gelpi, too, has helped, in addition to contributing to the sense of well-being one gets from being among like-minded folk. Dr. Peter Barglow gave me helpful information on the truth serum. The staff at the Stanford Libraries was unfailingly ready to assist me with my many book-related needs. Our cat K.C. slept through most of it in an easy chair ten feet from my desk. I cannot overstate the therapeutic benefits of a snoring cat.

Ethan Nosowsky of Farrar, Straus and Giroux is every writer's dream editor. The book profited immensely from his intelligence, sensitivity, and guidance. Naturally, what faults it still has should be blamed entirely on him.

Index